BESTIARY

HELEN DUNMORE

Bestiary

BLOODAXE BOOKS

ISBN: 1 85224 401 1

First published 1997 by
Bloodaxe Books Ltd,
P.O. Box 1SN,
Newcastle upon Tyne NE99 1SN.

Bloodaxe Books Ltd acknowledges
the financial assistance of Northern Arts.

Cover printing by J. Thomson Colour Printers Ltd, Glasgow.

Printed in Great Britain by
Cromwell Press Ltd, Broughton Gifford, Melksham, Wiltshire.

for
STEPHEN MOLLETT
and
STEPHANIE NORGATE

Acknowledgements

Acknowledgement are due to the editors of the following publications in which some of these poems first appeared: *Nineties Poetry, Orbis, Poetry London Newsletter, Poetry Review, Poetry Wales, The Printer's Devil, Smoke, Southfields, The Spectator* and *Waterstones Guide to Poetry Books*.

'Need' is a version of a passage from Langland's *Piers Plowman*. It was commissioned for the 1996 Poetry International at the Royal Festival Hall, London, and an extract was broadcast on *Bestwords* (BBC Radio 3).

Contents

        ...I was at home
And should have been most happy, – but I saw
Too far into the sea, where every maw
The greater on the less feeds evermore. –
But I saw too distinct into the core
Of an eternal fierce destruction,
And so from happiness I far was gone.
Still am I sick of it, and tho', to-day,
I've gather'd young spring-leaves, and flowers gay
Of periwinkle and wild strawberry,
Still do I that most fierce destruction see, –
The Shark at savage prey, – the Hawk at pounce, –
The gentle Robin, like a Pard or Ounce,
Ravening a worm...

JOHN KEATS
Epistle to John Hamilton Reynolds

Candle poem

(after Mahmoud Darwish)

A candle for the ship's breakfast
eaten while moving southward
through mild grey water
with the work all done,
a candle for the house seen from outside,
the voices and shadows
of the moment before coming home,

a candle for the noise of aeroplanes
going elsewhere, passing over,
for delayed departures, embarrassed silences
between people who love one another,
a candle for sandwiches in service stations
at four am, and the taste of coffee
from plastic cups, thickened with sugar
to keep us going,

a candle for the crowd around a coffin
and the terrible depth it has to fall
into the grave dug for everyone,
the deaths for decades to come,
our deaths; a candle for going home
and feeling hungry after saying
we would never be able to eat the ham,
the fruit cake, those carefully-buttered buns.

At the Emporium

He is the one you can count on
for yesterday's bread, rolling tobacco
and the staccato
tick of the blinds
on leathery Wednesday afternoons.
He has hand-chalked boards with the prices
of Anchor butter and British wine.
He doesn't hold with half-day closing.

He's the king of long afternoons
lounging vested in his doorway.
He watches the children dwindle
and dawdle, licking icepops
that drip on the steps.
His would be the last face that saw them
before an abduction. Come in,
he is always open.

Next door

is the same as ours, but different.
Back to front stairs, and a bass that thuds
like the music of demolition
year after year, but the house
is still standing.

When we have parties they tense into silence,
though they are good at fighting.
After the last screech and slam, their children
play war on their scab of a lawn.

We are mirrors of one another,
never showing what's real.
If I turn like this, quickly,
and look over the fence, what will I see?

He lived next door all his life

One year he painted his front door yellow.
It was the splash of a carrier bag
in the dun terrace,
but for the rest he was inconspicuous.

He went out one way and came back the other,
often carrying laundry and once compost
for the tree he thought might do in the back yard.
Some time later there was its skeleton
taking up most of the bin.

He passed the remark 'It's a pity'
when it rained on a Saturday,
and of a neighbour's child said 'terror'.
He picked his words like scones from a plate,

dropping no crumbs. When his front door shut
he was more gone than last Christmas.
But for the girls stored in his cellar
to learn what it meant
to have no pity, to be terror,
he was there.

Under the leaves

How rangy they are, and lean, these leaves
tasting and licking.
These leaves are leaping
the intersections of Crewe Junction
on the back of the September wind
shushing along the sidings.

This is a place of rust, where murder
spurts and dies down, where spikes
of stilettos lodge in the points.
Not pretty, not. What we saw
when we opened the binbag was not
a resurrection of leaves.

This is a country of policemen, slowly tramping
a line that doesn't waver but vanishes
in teatime mist. Here the search
is begun, called off, resumed.
The tack of rain falling on plastic
will lead them home.

The surgeon husband

Here at my worktop, foil-wrapping a silver salmon
– yes, a whole salmon – I'm thinking
of the many bodies of women
that my husband daily opens.

Here he lunges at me in wellingtons.
He is up to his armpits, a fisherman
tugging against the strength of the current.

I imagine the light for him, clean,
and a green robing of willow
and the fish hammering upstream.

I too tug at the flaps of the salmon
where its belly was, trying to straighten
the silver seams before they are sewn.
We are one in our dreams.

The epidural is patchy, his assistant's
handwriting is slipping. At eleven fifteen
they barb their patient to sleep, jot 'knife to skin',
and the nurse smiles over her mask at the surgeon.

But I am quietly dusting out the fish-kettle,
and I have the salmon clean as a baby
grinning at me from the table.

Fishing beyond sunset

The boy in the boat, the tip of the pole,
slow swing of the boat as the wash goes round
from other boats with lights on, heading home
to islands, from islands: anyway they come.

Thirty-four bass, small bass, not worth keeping.
See them in the water, the hang
of twice-caught fish playing dumb,
then the shake-off of air. The kickdown

always surprises you, makes your feet grip
on the planks of the boat. There is the line
disappearing into the sunset
or so it seems, but it is plumbed

by your finger, which sees nothing
but a breeze of line running through water.
Behind you a sheet of fire
does something to pole, to boat, to boy.

Painting of the sun

In his painting of every garden,
field, vineyard, village,
heat-stupefied railway station,
there is the sun.

Yellow as a smile
it sits on the horizon,
keeping the moon down
and the night from blowing
its smoke of stars across heaven.

He believes in heaven,
he believes in the sun
with its fangs of heat teething
on human skin.

In fact there are two suns, his
and a second, a small, wild
pupil whirling
among the cypress shadow.

Why has the sun two eyes?
Why is the world as it is
and not otherwise?

In every painting
there is the sun
spoked, spiked
on its frame of light.

Hare in the snow

Hare in the snow cresting
the run of winter, stretching
in liquid leaps over the hill,

then the wind turns, and
hare stands so still

he is a freeze of himself, fooling
the shadows into believing
he is one of them.

Need

(a version from Piers Plowman: *'The Pardon sent from Truth')*

I know that no one dare judge another's need,
for need is our neighbour, blood to our bone:
the prisoner in Long Lartin, the poor of shantytown
bearing children, burdened by bad landlords,
struggling to scrape together what goes straight out
on rent, on never enough food for the children
who cry like crickets from hunger, night-long.

They slave while they're sick with hunger,
wake in the damp of winter, crouch between wall and cradle
to rock the crying baby, their raw fingers
chapped with outworking, seaming denim
for half nothing, pitiful labour paid by the hour
which takes them nowhere, only to one more
half-hour's heat on the meter, scraping and struggling,
working for nothing.

The misery of women in run-down hostels
the misery of the men crammed in with them
racked by the nothing that is all they have,
too proud to beg, to show they are slowly starving
withering away, their poverty hidden like AIDS,
a shame that must never be shown to their neighbours
a shame that has made strangers of neighbours
and hunger the only guest at all their meals.

The world has kicked into me the future
of children born into poverty's welcome
to parents who have nothing but surplus labour,
empty hands, thoughts nobody wants.
Chips are their Sunday roast, dog-ends rolled up in Rizlas
damp down the parents' hunger as they look on
while the kids eat baked beans and bacon.
By the State's cold calculation
they could get by on carrots and bakers' leavings.
Only love can help them.

These will not beg, but there are beggars
who shoot up everything they're given
who have nothing at all wrong with them
who could perfectly well do a day's work
who deserve no pity, no money, nothing.
Even if they collapse on the streets, coughing
from the come-back of ancient diseases
think nothing of it. Don't be ashamed to walk past
with your wallet stuffed with credit cards
as the Bible says.

But yet. Look again. What about these beggars
who look perfectly all right, able to do a day's work,
ought to be cleared off the streets – all that? And yet
some of them come from another world, or another time.
Care in the community is the cold calculation
that takes care of them. Stop. Look again.
They live by the phases of the moon
by an inner fire that will not leave them alone.
They are penniless as time and tide, wander with nothing
like the holy apostles, Peter and Paul.
They have no time for preaching or miracles
but they can speak in tongues if you listen,
and catch the wind of truth in the sails
of what seems like play.

God who can do anything
might have made them businessmen,
but instead he made them his own children
and sent them out with empty bank accounts
holey jeans and a blanket to wrap around them.
These secret disciples break all the rules but his,
the one rule that tells us to love, and give.

Think. You will even put up with poets
for the sake of their patrons, if these are rich men,
publishers who fancy culture, and keep a newspaper.
Think of the Lord of heaven who has sent his children
to be called madmen, and please him
if you can, by throwing some cash at them.

And think again. When you are begging
for God's pardon, when the daylight after death
shines on your sins, think of them,
God's secret children, born pardoned,
and what you did for them.

The thorn

There was no berry on the bramble
only the thorn,
there was no rose, not one petal,
only the bare thorn
the night he was born.

There was no voice to guide them,
only the wind's whistling,
there was no light in the stable,
only the starshine
and a candle guttering
the night he was born.

From nothing and nowhere
this couple came,
at every border
their papers were wrong
but they reached the city
and begged for a room.

There was no berry on the bramble,
no rose, not one petal,
only the thorn,
and a cold wind whispering
the night he was born.

Veterans in Rome

It was all black and white in Rome that winter,
snow on the square, a huddle of doorstepping
priests who were up for a gossip.
He's good for another year
they promised themselves, while nuns from Gabarone
snapped the roof where there'd be white smoke.

They were here at the sexy heart of things
where the latest news grew cold quicker than coffee
at marble tables in chilly
pavement cafes. Intimate, steamy
sessions between cardinal and cardinal
weighed gains and losses, made speculations.

There were continents of consciences to play for.
In his native language the Holy Father
spoke more stiffly every hour,
but days passed and he was still there
saying Mass in a batsqueak,

packed and ready to go
into the whisper that would take him everywhere,
the white-out on Vatican Radio.

Sometimes in the rough garden of city spaces

Sometimes in the rough garden of city spaces
where I believe a mugger will not approach me
because so far no mugger has approached me
I stop to take breath.
The city exists by acts of faith
that we and our children are safe,

that the pounding wheels of cars will miss them,
that the traffic will stop when the lights turn,
that parks will stay green, that money is not everything,
that the lime trees that line our streets are lopped and cropped
with the best of intentions,
that the orange glow of the streetlamps is moonlight
to that couple there, locked in each other, lost
in the city's night-time suspension.

I should like to be buried in a summer forest

I should like to be buried in a summer forest
where people go in July,
only a bus ride from the city,

I should like them to walk over me
not noticing anything but sunlight
and patches of wild strawberries –

Here! Look under the leaves!
I should like the child who is slowest
to end up picking the most,

and the big kids will show the little
the only way to grasp a nettle
and pick it so it doesn't sting.

I should like home-time to come
so late the bus has its lights on
and a cloud of moths hangs in their beam,

and when they are all gone
I should like to be buried in a summer forest
where the dark steps
blindfold, on cat foot-pads,
with the dawn almost touching it.

The scattering

First, the echo
at night, when I said
'I'll hold you'

and your voice like a bird's in the grey morning
came back 'Hold you',
and your feet in my palm
were barely hardened by walking,

and then the scattering,
the start of grammar
and distance.
You say, 'Hold me.'
You'll say, 'Don't hold me.'

All the things you are not yet

(for Tess)

Tonight there's a crowd in my head:
all the things you are not yet.
You are words without paper, pages
sighing in summer forests, gardens
where builders stub out their rubble
and plastic oozes its sweat.
All the things you are, you are not yet.

Not yet the lonely window in midwinter
with the whine of tea on an empty stomach,
not yet the heating you can't afford and must wait for,
tamping a coin in on each hour.
Not the gorgeous shush of restaurant doors
and their interiors, always so much smaller.
Not the smell of the newsprint, the blur
on your fingertips – your fame. Not yet

the love you will have for Winter Pearmains
and Chanel No.5 – and then your being unable
to buy both washing-machine and computer
when your baby's due to be born,
and my voice saying, 'I'll get you one'
and you frowning, frowning
at walls and surfaces which are not mine –
all this, not yet. Give me your hand,

that small one without a mark of work on it,
the one that's strange to the washing-up bowl
and doesn't know Fairy Liquid from whiskey.
Not yet the moment of your arrival in taxis
at daring destinations, or your being alone at stations
with the skirts of your fashionable clothes flapping
and no money for the telephone.

Not yet the moment when I can give you nothing
so well-folded it fits in an envelope –
a dull letter you won't reread.

Not yet the moment of your assimilation
in that river flowing westward: river of clothes,
of dreams, an accent unlike my own
saying to someone I don't know: *darling*...

Ferns on a hospital window

From behind the curtain an open window
fans the room with ferns of ice.
In this institution
health takes us by surprise.
We are tuned to a different station.

All night threads of cold make stars
like cells dividing on glass.
Behind me, monotonously,
Charlotte roars. In tinfoil, shaking,
they bring in another baby.

Long ago the ferns died into coal.
They give out their breath in sighs
fanned into flame, in pandemonium
hissing through pipes to this room
where a baby burns in my arms.

Train dirt

Polish, polish those pearls
of soot under your nails.
Nibbling the fringes of sleep
your baby gets ready to feast
on the nipple she never finds quick enough
in the black city jacket. New
tastes have gone into her milk.
At the tang of the aïoli you ordered –
thinking only of yourself –
she'll arch and pull off,
scan you with eyes as dark
as the gaps between stars.

Diving girl

She's next to nowhere, feeling no cold
in her white sluther of bubbles.
She comes to a point like a seal
in his deep dive, she is sleek.
As her nostrils close
she's at home. See how salt water slides
as she opens her eyes

There is the word *naked*
but she's not spelled by it.
Look at her skin's steel glint
and the knife of her fins.
With the basking shark
with the minke whale
and the grey seal
she comes up to breathe
ten miles offshore.

Those deaths

The wind walks on the roofs
along Back Road West
in its knockabout boots.

The sea gulps, the wind blows away.
You say your worst dream
is if you were crying, and I
thought it was the wind.

A pretty shape

I never stop listening to you sing
long enough to know what I think.
All I do is let it go on.

The bubble of song bounces towards me
over the wet surfaces of the kitchen
and you with your arms folded
in that tiny immemorial way you've observed,
your soft, small arms folded
over your chest where your breath
flows and unflows easily,
don't need to look at me.
The bubble of your song bounces towards me
its surface tension strong
as it shudders, recovers.
You let the song go where it wants.

When you've fallen asleep, or I think you've fallen
I withdraw, still singing
or perhaps still listening to you sing,
but you feel me going. Why am I going
always going, instead of listening to you sing?
Your hand knows better than mine
and with authority
of touch I cannot match
wraps me round you again.

Viking cat in the dark

Viking cat in the dark
is paw-licked velvet, sinew of shadow,
a thread of smoke bitterly burning,
a quiver of black like a riddle.

The huts lie low
a hoard half-hidden
a clutch of eggs
in the dune's hollow

and horned helmets
are nightmares to wake from
shapes cut from dreams
– but the cat leaps.

Like rain falling faster
the shadows whisper
and rain spatters
like death's downpour:

'Fight for me, dawn-slayer,
wake with me, sleep-sower,
keeper of dreams,
the dream we came for.'

There is no noise.
Only the quick
paws of the cat in the dark
like feet on the stairs,

but the cold grey hands of the sea clap
on the beached long-ships,
and a shape pours itself flat
to the chink of sword music.

Viking cat in the dark
is paw-licked velvet, sinew of shadow.
A thread of smoke, bitterly burning
quivers her body like a riddle.

Baby sleep

's
not like any other
day sleep   night sleep
long drive sleep
too cold   too hot sleep
What's that window doing shut?   sleep
get a bit of peace sleep
hungry   thirsty
need to pee
sleep,

baby sleep's
all over the shop sleep
new nappy and babygro poppers
done up to the neck sleep
fat fingers
starfishing
damp feathers
on neck curling
baby lotion and talc sleep
sleep in Mum and Dad's bed sleep
cry in sleep and then sleep sleep
sleep while the big peop
le wash and dress sleep
baby sleep

Toad breathing

Just as you kneel to catch it
the toad leaps
from the tub of autumn geraniums
and spotted leaves.

Your hands are too slow for it.
How it rocks
after contracting
away from your touch.

It will die under the bookcase.
Don't go after it.
It believes in the radiator's cold
and in curled lino.

All winter let's not switch the heating on
in case it stays there.
All I hear is a contraction
which might be the toad breathing.

Heavy

(in memory of Gertrude Maud Quinn)

How long would I keep my hands small enough
to slip between the spines of the gooseberry bush
and seize the green fruit?

I never asked my grandmother.
though she was there on the path, not liking to come close
for she was heavy, her ankles bags of water
overflowing her shoes,
her legs no use.

That was a skin into which I'd melt like cream
while my small, firm tongue
made play with her name.

Frostbite

When you grow tired of the flame
wumping to life in the central heating boiler,
and the duvet sweats like obstinate flesh
in the middle of winter,

don't finger the lightswitch. Leave the coil
of electricity sleeping. Go down
tread after tread by the draught
of heat coming upward. The voice

of the house is warning. *Get out*
it breathes, *Leave us alone*
to our shuffling of dust-mites, our sorting
of smell and shadow into home.

First the bolt, then the chain, then the Chubb.
You're outside, but even in a nightdress
that comes to the thighs, you can't rub the warmth off.

The phone's ring

Months after their boy had left home
and the wonderful woman he called his wife
had remembered to stop buying Marmite

he woke in the dead of the night
in the scum of a night's breathing
and knew from the sound of the phone

that it was *him*. And she slept on,
she who had broken her wrist
charging to get to the phone first

with the soft wreathed look on her face
that always put Jim in his place.
I want to talk to my son.

Who was it said that? What with the snoring
and the phone's ring, it could have been anyone.

Writing block

When the rowing-boat comes in over grey stones
and clear water, no need for a touch
on the oars,

when the bird on the summer bough drowses,
his song bubbling to nothing
between the leaves,

when memory runs clear as water
over its words, no need for a touch
on pen or printer,

when thick leaves shelter
what will be stripped in winter
and forced to sing.

Basketball player on Pentecost Monday

With his hands he teaches wind to move –
not this shuffle of leaves
from rows of pollarded trees
but the salt-laden, incoming
breath of the Indies.

He's six foot seven,
liquid in dull grey track suit,
his trainers undone.
There's a small keen boy
at his heels, yapping
for ball-time, air-time.
It's playtime in the gardens
with children sagely going round
on patient horses they strike with small
privileged hands.

Behind him, gravelly sand,
a guitarist picking
the bones of a tune
mournful as Sunday,
the empty horses
of carousels turning.

Tell the basketball player how tight
time is, how he's reached perfection
at the same time as the man with his rake
puts the gravel straight on something.
Tell him this is the moment
the arrow of his life flew out of
to return into his breastbone.
Or say nothing.

Tiger lookout

Refrigerator days.
Ours is the size of a walk-in larder,
casing everything.

One word
which has gone out of fashion
is *putrefaction.*

When Simmonds fell from his tiger lookout
it was not the growl
nor the stripes
that said *tiger.*

It was the tiger's breath.
All that old, bad meat
furring its teeth.

For a moment Simmonds was critical,
sniffing the exhalation of corpses,
the walk-in larder where he was going.

Tiger Moth caterpillar

Two spines curve in
as the sisters face on a gate
in their matching cardigans.

They are looking into something –
a stolen Swan Vesta box
plump with green privet,

and there's one match left
with which to poke it –
their marvellous possession.

Inner thighs chafe on a crust of lichen.
Riding the gate is the best game
these two have ever come on.

The more bloody a ballad
they more they love it. Cigars,
betrayal, the flames of hell

and the slaughter of innocence
are what speaks, makes the gate creak.
Girls, give us a song

in your tidy cardigans. Your hair's
deceptively sleek, you are
tangled, complicit, in on it.

Hungry Thames

Hungry Thames, I walk over the bridge
half-scared you'll whittle me down

where the brown water is eager
and tipped with foam.

You sigh and suck. You lick at the steps
you would like to come up.

Hungry Thames, we feed you on concrete,
orange-peel, polystyrene cups,

we hold our kids by a handful of clothing
to let them look at your dimples,

your smiling waters. We should hold them tighter,
these are whirlpools, this is hunger

lashing its tail in the mud, deep down
where the river gets what it wants.

The wasp

Now winter comes and I am half-asleep
crawling the hollow of an apple, my sound
a battery toy in a child's cupped hand,

or I climb to a ledge and lie, dulled
by its half-warmth. Half-wasp, I'm still
helpless not to sting your exploring finger

helpless in the pulse of my body.
The paddle of your hand churns
as you find something to kill me.

I keep on stinging. I cannot learn
through my crispness, the coat of warning
that says what I am.

The woodlouse at the hem of St Francis' habit

The woodlouse at the hem of St Francis's habit
lay on its back, waiting for the saint to stroke it
and spin a prayer around its name.

Little woodlouse, God's armoured car
true inspiration of the Roman testudo
you and I are brothers, the same.

To the side of the picture St Clare
looked at St Francis with her face ajar
and the light coming out of it
onto woodlice and spiders.

If a million woodlice honouring Francis
bore him on their backs, a burden
fit for their armour,
then Clare would be carried alongside
by the hundred million feet of centipedes –

she would not want more,
but in the light of being a woman
she would want the same.

The Gethsemane garden competition

Out of moss and twigs, daisies and fallen cherry blossom,
the chipped bit of a handbag mirror, cottonwool lambs,
I made my Gethsemane garden.

I soldered the circuitry of Easter
on a tin tray, getting everything into proportion
I knew better than to dwarf my green hill with daffodils,
or mould the dank mouth of the tomb
too small to fit in a lamb.

My tray was alive and breathing.
There was dawn in that garden,
the surprise of birds.
I could talk myself down
where ducks paddled soft black mud
in the reeds round the pond.

On growing a black tulip

I was in the kingdom of pointed raspberries,
edible thistles, a green rose.
Everything was true yet false
like the yellow of whiteheart cherries.

As the tulips yawned it was simple.
The colour they call black is purple.
The veins in it are loaded, lifting
winter into a lamp of spring.

My dream was a hedge of tulips,
black tulips, glossy as swans
sailing the river of their leaves.
Next, golden delphiniums.

A tortoise wrapped in newspaper

You could have any one you liked for five shillings –
or I misremember, make grander
the handwritten sign and the shopkeeper's gesture,
and it was really a shilling an inch
and a pennypinching
choice in the size range *small to medium*.

Would it be that one there
with the steep-domed shell and bold marking,
or the one with the livelier air
treading down brothers and friends?

A tortoise wrapped in newspaper stirs
with slow claws. It is reptilian
irrevocably. You have bought time
and must take it home.

And who was it said to feed the shell with cottonwool
soaked in olive oil, to make it shine,
and that other advice, to paint a flash
of red or yellow, or drill a hole
for tethering. Tortoises roam.

Lifting its shell on long hydraulic legs
it sped to the woods, but that was no go
when through the dampness of alien dock leaf
shone its stripe of yellow,
and the sideways sawing of its mouth
met nothing edible.

A tortoise wrapped in newspaper
cannot get out, but keeps swimming.
I remember how it made the headlines
crawl in my hands.

Little Ellie and the timeshare salesman

The man who gave little Ellie his forever
love was a timeshare salesman.
He let her look round the place
when the carpet was freshly steam-cleaned
and the teabag box was full to the brim,
but he left little Ellie for an instant
and she spied the used teabag jam-jar
sodden and rusty as iron.

Oh Ellie, whispered little Ellie,
there have been many here before you.
But she was smiling at the door
when he gave her his hand, wet from the ballcock
he'd quickly fixed in the cistern.
In a serenade of gurgles and yawns
the plumbing talked itself down
and perfect Ellie was his dream.

How could he replace or kill her
with her genius for noticing nothing
but the nice day, the short walk to the pool
the view of the beach from the bathroom window?
Sweet Ellie never crossed the time-share salesman,
but tended her one week like a garden.
She did not keep a diary where the others
might be noted or brooded over.

Kindly she watches him run on the wheel
of his weeks till he gets back to nineteen
where she is always happy to wait for him.
Dusty geraniums come back to life
in the days where Ellie waters them,
and the time-share salesman slackens his smiles
at the sight of Ellie's daring paëlla:
in week nineteen she is his forever.

Signals

Not the business-brown letters you open too quickly and lose
     before I read them,
not the Access bills I don't need to worry about because you've
     already paid them,

not the excessive number of well-spoken double-glazing saleswomen
whose voices on the telephone sound remarkably the same,

not that retread you shouldn't have bought slow-puncturing on
     your way home
and the battery suddenly gone in your mobile phone,

not the bright idea of buying her the same perfume
(though it echoes back strangely from another skin),

not these easy things. But the silence that hums
as we sit together watching *News at Ten*,

and your look of distaste when I weep at an item
about the fight for survival of four-months'-premature twins.

Weekend on the Somme

'What is of interest to history may not be relevant to Personnel'
COMMONWEALTH WAR GRAVES COMMISSION

As you dig round history you know
it'll put up with anything. Chop at the roots,
leave it upturned to sun, then plant
in a dry hole, and slosh water on.

All day you tramp the graveyard in boots
you bought when you were last home,
not the cheapest but the next cheapest,
the shape of the average foot.

There are permanent jobs in this garden,
tending the green grass.
You will not get one.
You should get up off your arse

and do your duty
week after week after week
in this close-shaven graveyard
smooth as men's cheeks.

As the TGV to London
whacks its way through the Somme
on a moneyed sneeze, a sizzle of rails,
are we of interest to history? How come

I'm watching you pack soil round the roots
so they won't die in air pockets?
Tread down. Break in those boots
on skulls and eye sockets.

Bouncing boy

(for Paul)

All the squares of trampoline are taken
by children leaping like chessmen
who won't play the game. Up, flying.
from tiny freeholds, hitting the sky's
elastic surprise, then down.

There's a space for you always.
Two kids eating ice-cream
with careful darts of the tongue
watch as you start to climb
the icy November sky, hand over hand.

You hear the clap of the sea
and your bright blue trampoline applauding
with the dull fervour of rubber
each time you go down,

and the kids eating ice-cream
with wind in their teeth say nothing
as the time mounts and your turn
grows impossibly long.

Ghost at noon

On the white path at noon when the sun
burns through olive and eucalyptus
and the pale stones rattle
as if someone's walking,

when the goat jumps and the sea shivers
like a dog turning its belly upward
to a hand that teases it,

and the sky is cloudless but suddenly
dark drops spatter the dust
and there, where no one is walking,
a line of wet footprints.

Crickets crackle in the dry maquis,
their sound unbroken.
No one is walking.
If you touch your finger to the dust, quickly,
you'll catch the pressure just gone.

Greek beads

Small, silvery, slipping
from finger to finger,
beads for street corners,

beads for white noon
when shadows curl by the walls
and the dog in the square lolls
with his tongue unfurled,

beads for navy-blue evenings
when the smell of oranges
drifts to the fountain,

beads for waiting on the landing-stage,
for the heat that shimmers
from village to village,

for the boy guarding the goats
and the old woman hoeing in black,
beads for leaving to find work
and for the dream of coming back,

beads for remembering
and for forgetting,
wrapped round the wrists of babies
and the dying,

beads for the life we live in,
small, silvery, slipping
from finger to finger.

Tea at Brandt's

Music plays gently. Yesterday's morning paper
flutters at the end of its long emigration
from being news. This is the present,

but when? Coconut cake, a stained napkin,
a tea-glass bisected by long spoon.
Any minute now it's going to rain.

What kind of animal is the past?
A wooden screen makes two rooms of one.
On the other side, where I saw her last,

my baby girl. I'll wipe her nose with the napkin,
take her to the Ladies and change her,
blow the bubble of words towards her
that says, *This is the present, there is no other.*

We are men, not beasts

We are men, not beasts
though we fall in the dark
on the rattlesnake's path
and flinch with fire of fear
running over our flesh
and beat it to death,

we are men, not beasts
and we walk upright
with the moss-feathered dark
like a shawl on our shoulders
and we carry fire
steeply, inside a cage of fingers,

we are men, not beasts,
and what we cannot help wanting
we banish – the barn yawn, the cow breath,
the stickiness we come from.

ON MY WAY

IAN WILLIAMS

ON MY WAY

Contents

This book is dedicated to:

my Dad Alan Williams
23rd June 1935 to 13th May 2021
Amiable, honest and kind.

my ex-wife for pushing me beyond breaking point,
without which I would never have left behind my
kids to chase my dream.

my girlfriend Erika, a truly special person and
the best thing to happen to me in many years.

And finally...

A special thanks to those who recognise
my hilarious,magnetic personality and boyish good looks,
complimented by a modesty envied by every
saffron-robed monk I ever met.

Chapter 1
Permulaan

It was an animated act of self-pleasure. A spontaneous one-man performance of light-hearted banter, smug with synthetic determination, that found me stood holding aloft a dog-eared sheet of paper, proclaiming each item of its hand-written contents in turn, to all of nobody. "Camera, rucksack, clothes, phone, money, money belt, wallet, bluetooth keyboard, snorkel, GoPro, toiletries, ticket printouts, passport." I opened my fingers like a releasing claw and mic-dropped the crossed-off list down onto the bed. "And breathe," I instructed, continuing to speak out loud. It was the signal to leave but the fear of missing something obvious, and possibly crucial, held me there like the headlights that freeze a rabbit to the spot. The longer the rucksack sat alone outside on the communal landing, the greater the risk it might be snatched by an opportunist druggie, seizing their chance to rinse their way though the next few desperate hours, but still I hesitated. Now was not the time to be zoning out, half-heartedly scanning the room in hope that something I might have missed, would jump out and reveal itself. Then, from nowhere, intrigue clapped its hands and freewill booted me up the ass towards the hallway. I tapped in the alarm code and pulled shut the door on the life I once considered normal.

My hope was a two-hour drive, three plane journeys and a train ride would create enough cultural distance to convince my broken head to heal my injured heart, the symptom of my imminent second divorce. To cleanse my wounds submerged in seclusion, with pure spring sunrise bathing, as tangerine skies dilute into a new day, or to sit and deflect the flow with my shoulders, below a tension-melting relentless torrent of white water, while a silent symphony of flickering brilliance sparkling from behind a windswept lush Asian fauna, would provide the treatment I required.

I'd pre-booked a couple of nights in a budget hotel in Brickfields, a suburb of Kuala Lumpur, as it was near to KL Sentral, the main hub for pretty much all transport links according to the internet. Leanne, my beautiful moon-faced eldest daughter, had agreed to run me to Heathrow. I would have booked a coach but the flight time meant I had to be at the airport by the early hours of the morning, resulting in setting off the night before, to sleep rough for a few broken hours, between shiny tiles, bright lights and loud speaker announcements. In the end, it was my firstborn's boyfriend, Connor, who kindly took on the role of driver. It avoided having to disturb my grandkids, Lainey and Callan. You tend not to get the best out of kids if they're woken up in the middle of night, unless you have a pot belly, red suit with white trim and a bulging sack.

Connor was an amenable, tall, quite handsome young man, gullible and gangly, with a short cropped, dark, wet look comb over and a close shave to the back of his neck. The plan was for me to drive the twenty minutes to Leanne's house, pick him up and take him with me down the M1. Once at the airport, he would shoot back up and leave the van on my Dad's drive till my return.

Seeing a light from inside put me at ease as I pulled up at Leanne's house. Connor was waiting in the kitchen drinking tea.

"Ey up pal. Leanne asleep?" I asked quietly, but he didn't know I was there until he turned around.

"Eyy uuup. Are you all ready?" he asked in his usual amiable manner.

"I hope so. Bit late if I'm not now, eh?"

I liked Connor. If I hadn't, I may have made that comment to wind him up on purpose, but I hadn't. I was aware of how simple that task was from recent history, but my view is: why tread carefully just because someone has littered my path with their eggshells? "Come on then. Let's do it," I ordered. I didn't mind Leanne wasn't there to see me off, glad in fact our father-daughter bond allowed her to be able not to feel the need to hang around, waiting for me to arrive. However, I had been slightly apprehensive about the prospect of spending two hours confined alone with a young guy eager to impress, yet blissfully unaware he was floating in a spectrum of intellect some might deem dangerous. Somewhere between being bright enough to think you know about a subject and to have an opinion but just not quite enough to know when some things you believe to be true, because your mate told you, defy logic. How many times would I have to stop myself contradicting him

6

on a two-hour rally of bullshit stories? It actually went a lot better than I had anticipated; in fact, there was an element of bonding by the time he dropped me at the airport car park.

"Thanks, Connor. I really appreciate it. Are you going to get a quick drink before you head back?"

He followed me out of the van. "No, it's okay. I'm going to get straight back," he replied while opening the back doors to help me out with my luggage. I gave him a hug and left.

Now it was crunch time. I'd booked the flights through a website with an unknown company. The price seemed too cheap so I'd put on my gloves, picked up my spade and done a bit of digging to find comparable flights. Worryingly, they were over a hundred quid more than I had paid, so I dug some more. The thing is, if you dig deep enough, or rather look intently enough into something with a suspicious eye, you will always find something to back up your theories. So with stories of non-existent flights jetting around my head, the glass doors opened and heat blew down on the prospect of heading straight back home having paid £435 for a handful of A4 sheets full of lies.

If genuine, my ticket was with Southern China Airlines but, according to my paperwork, the first leg to Amsterdam was contracted out to KLM.

"How many bags do you have, sir?" the check-in staff asked as I passed over my printout.

"Just the one."

"Passport, please". All doubts were about to be settled any second now. "Oh sir! There is a problem."

"Yes?"

"Please could you tuck in your loose straps? They may get caught on the belt, thank you. Your boarding pass, sir".

The half hour flight to Amsterdam was an opportunity to make the most of complementary drinks. A dress rehearsal with free bar, if you will, in preparation for the double drop Diazepam flight: 11 hours 15 minutes to Guangzhou. Like a bouncer on his birthday, the holiday spirit extended the boundaries of my patience today. Not even a jolt in the back at five-minute intervals could induce a confrontation with whoever was sat directly behind me. Three action films, an hour of Sudoku and two pisses later, I was suitably knackered to attempt sleeping, hopefully without dribbling on my neighbour's shoulder. After a number of false starts, head-butting thin air with a grunt, I eventually dropped off for what felt like five minutes.

"Any item for disposal, disposal? Disposal, sir?" It might have felt strange to dream about a camp air steward with a false tan and even more of a false smile, asking for the rubbish from a meal I didn't eat, but after a quick one-eyed scan, I realised it wasn't a dream. Elbows up, I pushed my head back into my hands and gave out a noise like I was trying to push out a constipated log as quietly as possible.

"How was your food?" I asked the guy next to me.

"Surprisingly good," he replied. He was a tall, older gent, well-spoken with a kind, harmless tone to his southern English voice, with a bald head and school teacher clothes.

"I can't believe I missed it. I must have been bang out!"

"You certainly looked is if you needed it."

"I must have done. I don't usually sleep well on planes!"

"Me neither. I don't like flying."

"Same here. Well, I'm a lot better than I used to be. I've learned not to let it bother me. I used to be terrible."

"Are you one of those Dutch courage fellows?"

"Well again, I used to be, but I will take tranquilizers if I can get hold of them. Only ever on planes though. It's like time travel, isn't it?"

"Well my wife might have agreed with you. She was a terrible flyer."

Shit – his wife's dead. What do I say? Just be yourself man! I looked directly into his eyes and with one raised eyebrow said, "Plane crash?"

"Sorry?" he replied, as if not to have heard me, although he definitely did, with a face as straight as a Roman road. I could feel his eyes draining the colour from my cheeks, and he knew it. They say comedy is all about the timing and, just as I reached for the spade to dig myself an even bigger hole, he laughed, then so did I, accompanied by a relieved shake of the head. "My name is Alan, and you are?" he smiled, holding his hand across his chest for a typically British greeting.

8

"Alan! That's my Dad's name. Ian. Pleased to meet you, Alan."

"Likewise, young man."

"So how did she die?"

"She's not dead, not technically. She has had dementia for a while now. She needs full time care."

"Oh sorry to hear that."

"So, Ian, what is it that finds you in China?"

"I have a connecting flight to Kuala Lumpur," I explained.

"Ah, doing a little travelling?"

"Something like that, and you?"

"My son is a lecturer at the University."

"In Guangzhou?"

"Yes, well nearby."

"Have you been here before?"

"Too many times, young man."

"China is on my bucket list. I bet the food is amazing."

"Guangzhou is the birthplace of Dim Sum you know?"

"We love a bit of Sui Mia and Har Gaw in our house. Oh, that reminds me, if I fall asleep again, would you mind telling the steward to leave some food for me?"

"It would be my pleasure, Ian."

I did eventually get some food and it was excellent. Sticky rice with chicken in black bean sauce lends itself to being warmed up far better than potatoes with English omelette and I can honestly say, even after taking into account the four complementary beers, it was the best airplane food ever. Another positive to come out of a flight as long as an elephant's memory was that the prospect of a four-hour flight to Kuala Lumpur now seemed like a doddle.

My needle was deep into the red after such an epic itinerary, but it was almost over. All that was stopping my head from hitting the pillow was the distance between ear and cotton-soft case, apart from the small task of getting to the digs. I made the half-hour journey on the Aerotrain, automated people mover, or APM if you like abbreviations, from KLIA, Kuala Lumpur International Airport, as the frequency of my yawns began breaking the minute barrier. 'My Hotel', as it is known literally, was a five-minute walk from the station. So close, in fact, that it took longer to check in than it did to drag my throbbing feet along the pavement. I dropped my bags, my trousers and my eyelids – in that order.

Excitement woke me after a couple of hours. "Oh my god! I'm here!" The prospect of a whole month to do all the things I love hit me like a double espresso. Travel, explore, eat, drink and take photos, starting with a shot of the Petronas Twin Towers that night at dusk. I don't show my camera the love it deserves as regularly as I should – it's often neglected to the point I keep forgetting how to use it – so in preparation for this trip, I'd brushed up on some of its functions. One of which was going to help me to create some special images in a couple of hours' time, hopefully.

All roads lead to KL Sentral and I took the one that leads back to the Light Rapid Transit, or LRT for short, for a train to the spot I was about to stand my tripod and watch the sun go down on my first day, six and a half thousand miles from home, in the shadow of one of the most recognisable buildings ever knocked up.

There's an old saying round our end: "I've forgotten more than you know." Well, when it comes to my camera, it's probably true for me because, after learning a new trick with my DSLR, I usually don't get a chance to do it again till it's gone from my head. Like balancing aperture and shutter speed to draw in light at dusk, achieving a warm glow from very little light. Like I said, I'd refreshed myself on the functions of my Nikon and, with a bit of luck, was about to reap the benefit.

Stood under the shade of an ornamental footbridge, beside a backlit ceramic watercourse, I set up my camera on its tripod and waited, killing time by studying in detail the design profile of what once was the most iconic building in the world.

Vaguely reminiscent of traditional British egg and dart coving, the cross section of each tower follows a repeating pattern of a dome and triangle, touching on a classic repetitive Islamic theme but with a neo-classical subtlety. Reflected by its mirror-like metallic cladding, sunlight creates a stylised grid of light, pronouncing its superior form amongst other lesser structures close by. Splined shafts of intermittent brilliance direct a path up through a pair of

roofs, like up-turned goblets, whose stems joust through an innocent baby blue haze, piercing heaven's back yard.

The trick here was to open the shutter long enough to draw in enough fading light, to create a surreal glow. The issue with this process is keeping the camera still during the long exposure to avoid unwanted blurring. Yet another clever app on my phone allowed me to solve the problem by releasing the shutter remotely using a Bluetooth connection, leaving the camera untouched and wobble free. I stood in appreciation of immaculately kempt lawns, fountains, topiary shrubs and stainless-steel railings as the sun began to fade on day one. My equipment seemed to create an increased respect from the public. People passing by would smile at the sight of what they presumed to be a professional photographer at work, patiently waiting for that perfect moment. If only they knew the real me. The man who found himself in the local rag after eventually fulfilling a bucket-list wish to experience the feeling of injecting heroin, overdosing and finding himself in hospital at the side of a policeman, under arrest for being in possession of ten Es. As time passes, things change and, in contrast to the fading light conditions required for my photographic experiment, life for me was much brighter than the day I got my fingers burned by the golden death dragon.

A lack of holistic knowledge of my camera's functions meant I was by no means sure the image would turn out the way I hoped but, in the end, I did get the shot and another slightly darker, and five others, all decent. The biggest problem was deciding which one I liked best as I packed up and headed back.

I love buffets and I love curry, so sooner or later I was always going to be frequenting the place a few doors down from my hotel that ticked both those boxes. The Sentral Chapatti House looked a bit of a dump – in fact it was a bit of a dump – but the food was great and extremely easy on the pocket. There was a framework of steel beams running across its frontage outside at ceiling height that formed the underside of the overhead train line running parallel, between the buildings either side of the road. Just out of reach, a chaotic spaghetti of dangling cables looped their way along the foot path. Partially blocking the entrance stood a metal stanchion supporting the track above, zigzagged with numerous diagonal iron braces, where the convoluted scent of spices permeated out into the street creating a symphony of culinary chords, conveyed by the nostrils into songs of exotic indulgence. Above the window, an oxidized air-con unit continued to clean a tiny circular patch of pavement directly beneath it, with its perpetual dripping and the rolled-up, galvanized shutter door shivering in fear each time the powerful and fearsome noise returned, rattling past overhead at speed. Above the door, the underside of the sign along with much of the frontage was dulled with a layer of soot from a large wood-burning tandoor just inside the doorway. Beyond the huge black clay pot and the till was the restaurant area, but to get there you had to run the gauntlet of bain-marie counters either side of the foyer where I first amused myself with a game of culinary lucky dip. Jugs of water, paper napkin dispensers and plastic tumblers sat in neat clusters at the centre of each table where the space opened out at the back.

"You want food?" asked an oversized Indian man, with a pockmarked face.

"Yes, please."

"Take this." He handed me a stainless-steel prison tray with built-in compartments. "This is meat here and vegetarian on this side. You take what you want," he explained.

I filled my tray with stew, pickles, a meaty curry with chunks of some sort of unknown vegetable and sat down. Once you've taken your food, the man comes back over and, after a quick scan, writes the price of your food down on a slip of paper and hands it to you. "How many chapatti do you want?" he asked.

"I don't know. How many do you think?"

"I think two."

Up to now I'd had my own communal table, until a lonesome multi-chinned teenager muffin-topped his ass onto a chair opposite me. Table manners were not his thing: eating was his thing. I glanced over occasionally as he devoured his mound like a prison scrote expecting to be taxed at any moment, oblivious to anything other than his calorie intake. My bill came to 15.2 Malaysian ringgit or £2.80 sterling. "They might see this face again if my guts don't drop out," I thought.

12

Being predominantly Muslim, there were no bars in the city, just a smattering of shisha lounges. The city wasn't completely dry though; you just needed to know where to look. In the tiny shop adjoining the foyer of my block for instance. I say 'block' because I was staying in a room on the fourth floor of an overflow building, an annex 50m away from the main hotel. As I arrived back in the lobby to get my head down for the night, I pressed for the lift and waited. Glass panelling on the left separated the lobby from that little retail outlet and, although partially obscured by shelves, I could see through to the clear-fronted fridges located on the back wall. The shop was run by another Indian guy, not surprising bearing in mind it was the Indian quarter. Although around 11 pm, there were customers. Two Indian guys were hanging around near the fridges, drinking the strong stuff. I chose to double-back for a couple of cans before bed. We exchanged nods as they made room for me to swing open the fridge door. 'Maybe there's no drinking on the street,' I thought as the shop keeper dropped my purchases into a tiny black plastic carry out bag. Beer is not cheap there, about the same amount as at home. The night watchman, still sat at the bottom of the stairs, didn't break eye contact from his phone as I passed back through the lobby to the lift on the back wall. I realised the shop had been squeezed into what was once a much larger lobby, as the lift door slid open. Half an hour after laying on my bed editing photos and drinking beer, it was about to be tomorrow.

A combination of advancing years and excitement woke me very early the next morning with thoughts of yet more spicy food. The novelty of curry for breakfast coaxed me out of bed and gave me my first focus of the day. Across the road in front of a fence around a clearing, there was a long shed with table and chairs on the footpath selling food. It looked more in keeping with a rural setting than an inner-city roadside, but a lack of customers rather than the aesthetic found me wondering in the direction of KL Sentral, the busier end of the street.

A place on a side road to the left didn't have the same difficulty in attracting custom. Raised up from the street by about 70cm, the bulk of the tables were inside on a white-tiled floor but it also had overflow tables down at the street level up against the kerb. I sat and stashed my camera bag under the table, with one foot through the strap. The man on the next table had one of the prison trays that seemed popular around here, with a large, thin pancake and three different sauces in each of the compartments. Pulling off bite-sized bits with his fingers, he'd eat the sauce, using the pancake as a scoop.

"Yes?" said the waiter from up on the top level, pen and pad in hand. There was a menu on the table but I didn't need it.

"This one here please and a chai," I ordered, pointing to the man's tray in front.

A badly disabled old man wearing white dhoti and kurta, the pyjama set with trousers that resemble ruffled curtains, was begging his way through the outer tables. His legs were thin and bent, with one foot turning in at right angles: I'd guess it was polio. He got moved on quickly by a staff member and I watched as he struggled to negotiate his way through parked motorcycles four deep in the cul-de-sac next to me.

Sweet milky tea is not something I normally have, but then again neither is corsay, the thin pancake that had just been placed on my table. The three accompaniments all had differing levels of spice. A cream-coloured, mild, thin dahl; a green curry sauce; the hottest of the three was white. Today was the only day to explore this vast metropolis, or at least that's what I thought at the time, so I formulated a plan starting with a taxi to Lake Gardens, a former mine back in the 1880s. "Bill, please."

Like Uber cars back home, Malaysia has its own version called Grab. One of the first things you should do as a backpacker here is download the app. "Four ringgit seventy four," said the waiter. I paid the 90p and walked back to the digs to wait for the ride.

With a name like Tun Abdul Razak Heritage Park, there's no surprise it's known to most simply as Lake Gardens. It's named after the second president, who is fondly remembered for setting up an organization called FELDA, the federal land development agency, in the 1950s. It was founded to handle the resettlement of the rural poor and to organise small holder farms growing cash crops. Long since Abdul's death in 1976 while in office from a long-standing battle with leukaemia, FELDA has become a huge corporate monster, massively involved in the palm oil trade, turning over billions of

14

dollars, and not without controversy. Stories of dodgy property investment deals with purchase prices at three times their true value and government loans for farm worker share deals, whose money quickly loses two thirds of its original share value as it plummets due to a combination of bad management and falling cooking oil prices are an unfortunate reality for the organisation: that's before mentioning the escalating deforestation issues.

As you follow the path around the two lakes in this vast 227-acre shallow valley, big enough to squeeze in well over 100 football pitches, slap bang in the centre of real-estate heaven, with nearby skyscrapers, lush vegetation, gigantic forest trees, events bandstand and the odd monitor lizard, it makes you appreciate the value of the need for well-being placed on it by the authorities, especially on a day like today – warm with blue skies and a light breeze.

It was still quite early in the morning when a couple of groundsmen, casually killing time raking beside a motorized trolley-trailer, partially loaded with leaves, under the shade of towering trunks on the banking to my left, watched me follow the path around the waters' edge; otherwise the place would have been exclusively mine as I spotted my first photo opportunity. It was a white ornamental hump-backed devil's bridge, partially engulfed at its far end by a screen of glossy vivid green leaves, framing clumps of pale mauve shower pouf blooms of giant rhododendron flowers on the opposite bank.

When you fail to find the deer park, a 10,000 square metre orchid garden with 800 species and the 6,000 butterflies said to be housed amongst fountains surrounded by swirling patterns of dwarf topiary hedges, it makes you realise how huge an area a 100 football pitches really is. Even the humble fern isn't spared the immoderate treatment. There's over a 100 species, somewhere between rowing boats and rare specimen fruit trees. The world's largest covered bird park, home to storks, hornbills, eagles, macaws and ostriches is just past the mini self-fly, kiddie helicopter rental. Ok I made that bit up but there are rides, a cafe and pergolas by the lake to enjoy a bit of al-fresco dinning. Oh and if there's time left in the day, hire a Segway and explore the sculpture park. After half a lap around the gently rippling centrepiece, I was almost about to leave until an indulgence in sexy, exotic landscape design whistled and called me over with a beckoning finger. First, I checked over my shoulder, then obeyed. It was a circular excavation, partially concealing a sunken garden with a radius as long as a horse's lead rope. Ten stone steps take you down to a flat opulent inner area, surrounded by a steep grass banking. A pattern of interconnected dwarf hedges, reminiscent of an ancient Inca pattern, accentuated by white stone gravel surround a raised ornamental central pond. The pond has a circle of diagonal faces in a zig-zag formation creating an eight pointed star effect and, in the centre, a fountain adds an additional splash of interest. An hour in, snapping and strolling, was all the time I could afford here today. The clock was ticking on tomorrow's flight.

I'd always intended to spend some time on one of the islands in or around Malaysia but not the one called Perhentian. The first I heard of it was yesterday. I was planning my next move and saw a post on Tripadvisor from a traveller saying, "Why are you going to Langkawi? Perhentian is better." That was enough for me to book a flight – not directly to Perhentian because you can't, but to the airport nearest to it. I needed to set an alarm to wake in the middle of the night to make it happen. I took a last couple of photos of the lake before veering off past a jogger and a nanny pushing a pram, up the hill towards the exit. It was going to turn out to be an epic day for hot throbbing heels. Up the hill to the National Mosque, then the central market at Pasa Seni and finally to the KL tower via Chinatown. Apart from some impressive ceramic-tiled domed fountains, the sunken Inca garden and a man-made waterfall, I'd missed the recommended attractions here. Who knows where the botanical gardens were at, but it was time to move on to the National Mosque of Malaysia for Friday prayers. You just knew it was going to be busy, but what I didn't know was that every person there seemed to have arrived on a motorcycle. God might move in mysterious ways but his followers use a more traditional method: Yamaha 135 LCs and, at just over a grand sterling for a brand new one, it's not surprising. I managed to overcome the sea of mopeds, a couple of street food vendors and three legions of blokes chatting, to be stopped at the bottom of the steps by a big, miserable bloke in a long white gown.

"Are you Muslim?" he asked.

"No."

"You cannot come in here, Muslim only. You must come another day."

16

Although he could have been a little less abrupt, I respected the rules and did as I was told. "Okay, that's fine. Thank you."

I doubled back to the tables outside one of the stalls selling cold drinks, sat down and took it in. My timing must have coincided with either side of prayers, allowing me an insight into what was obviously more than just a simple weekly religious gathering. A relentless energy of peaceful chatter, interspersed with the odd benign yet boisterous shout, charged the air and put me at ease.

"You want drink?" the woman from the stall asked.

"Yes, what is this one?" I asked as I pointed to a dark purple tank.

"This one grep. You want large of small?"

"How much is large?"

"Two ringgit,"

"Large please."

My feet ached slightly less as I turned my back on an empty glass ten minutes later.

From this point the route wasn't so suitable for pedestrians. I walked at the side of the dual carriageway, then across it, before realising a taxi might have been a better option. I looked behind me and raised my arm: right on cue there it was. "Where you want to go?" he asked. There's very rarely a welcoming chill in our English climate, but here Jack Frost was suddenly my best friend, as the car door opened. With no firm plan the default was back to base.

"Brickfields, please."

We passed a number of reasonably large buildings by the side of the road as he followed my instructions, telling me, "This is the old Petronas building before they built the towers." The twin towers were completed in 1999 but they didn't look 20 years old as we kept catching glimpses of glinting steel between the other less iconic structures en-route. He became held up at an intriguingly busy junction.

"What is this place?" I asked.

"This is Pasa Seni. The Central Market," he told me with a surprised tone.

It seemed worthwhile to invest an hour of my time here and it did look like we weren't going to be doing anything other than crawling in the traffic for a while.

"Let me out here, please."

"Okay boss, no problem."

He dropped me on the main road outside a roadside vendor of sugar cane drinks. Stacked up at the back of the counter, soft, fat, crooked six-foot canes quietly leaned back against the corner of the stall oblivious to the brutal treatment that would see them come out of the other side of large metal mangle a flaccid mess of matted fibres in a process to relieve them of their juicy nectar. This was practically the same dangerous looking extraction technique used by my Nannan when I was a child to ring out her clothes before going in the spinner of her twin tub washing machine.

Stalls either side of an area of hexagonal block paving, patterned with an oriental symmetry of contrasting coloured blocks, marked the start of the market. A stickle brick mountain of spiky red fruit similar to lychees huddled under bunches of bananas hanging in a row along the underside of the roof canopy of a fruit stall, amongst other similar shed-like structures, offering mechanical toys, clothes, bags and, of course, street food. The first stretch of stalls near the main road were uncovered but a little further in, under a robust yet ornamental canopy constructed from steel and glass, running the length of the rest of the path, continuing the oriental theme, with an ornate brown and red façade, decorated in gold leaf patterns, a small stainless steel trolley stall with a fabric canopy, selling sweet treats, had drawn a small crowd.

A man holding a thin metal plunger was removing shiny steel cylinders, filled with a firm pale green translucent jelly, one at a time from a stainless-steel plate around half a metre square. Later I found out I'd stumbled across a Muchi stall: a sticky confection made from glutinous rice flour and brown sugar of Japanese origin. The plate had a grid of holes each just under an inch in diameter, allowing steam from underneath to cook the contents of each tube, positioned over each corresponding vent. Once cooked the vendor uses tongs to pick up each tube in turn and with the plunger pushes the contents out of their respective casings on to a tray in front of his colleague. Running the sticky rolls in desiccated coconut achieves a triple effect, producing a mouth-watering garnish, contrasting texture and an eye catching speckled white contrast of colour against the pale jade roll. A woman in a black and white striped headscarf, completed the process by laying four rolls side by side in

18

each of their clear plastic containers, before closing the lid and handing them over in turn to each of the small crowd of eager customers.

I fell in line to watch his almost hypnotic percussive performance, mesmerized by a combination of speed, precision and rhythmic beats, obviously intended to drum up custom. His job was much about entertainment as it was about processing delicious looking sweet treats. I wasn't prepared to wait any longer than I had to for the taste test so, after an agitating wait and once presented with my prize, I walked slowly away, simultaneously opening the clear-hinged lid while weaving a tight path through my fellow shoppers, managing hand to mouth while still on the move. A texture somewhere between a firm blancmange and an agreeably squelchy jelly benefitted from the contrasting firmness of the crunchy less sweet coconut crumb, complementing the subtle hint of sweet rice starch. With my appetite somewhat comforted by a couple of these dreamy, sweet, soft pillow confections, I forced myself to tuck up the remaining morsels for a nap back under the lid until their similar fate on waking later.

My plan was to buy a Malaysian SIM card while here to save the cost of international roaming so I called in at a stall that I'd noticed on a corner nearby, opposite the bureau de change.

"Hi, I need a pay-as-you-go SIM card, please," I asked the young chubby lad wearing a white collar shirt.

"Which one do you want?"

"I don't know. Which one do you think I should buy? I am here for one month."

"Do you have ID?"

"Why do I need ID?" He pointed to a poster behind him on the wall with images of passports and driving licences. It seems activating a SIM here is a little more involved than back home. I gave him my passport and sat on a stool while he fiddled around for a while. "Maybe I will call back in a few minutes," I told the lad.

"It won't be long now," he explained, but it was.

After repeating the same reassuring comment three times, he rang a colleague. Sitting opposite a bureau de change for half an hour with a pocket full of pound notes and not changing any of them into ringgit turned out to be costly later down the line. What wasn't so costly was the brand new smartphone I picked up for 40 quid while waiting to receive an activated local SIM. I figured I could use it with the new SIM here, then give it to Bailey as a gift when I returned. After 20 minutes, his colleague returned to spend another ten minutes dealing with an issue too taxing for his colleague. "Okay, all done."

Illuminating the curtains of bedrooms around the globe, perpetually waking the world one country at a time, as with every other day, the sun was on its way to completing its daily rounds. Soon the fading light would leave little time in the day for much more sightseeing before tomorrow's flight. Conscious of that fact, after my unexpected technical delay, I bombed it to the landmark that used to get all the attention before the Petronas Twin Towers to take some photos of the KL Tower.

Chance took me through another retail area, a grid of alleyways and pedestrian lanes. Strings of red and gold decorative oriental lanterns hanging from above gave me a good indication of where I might be. A European-looking woman walked towards me from the opposite direction.

"Excuse me. Is this Chinatown?"

Not stopping for fear I wanted more than advice, she answered from over her shoulder, "Yes."

Inquisitive to know its extent, sheer scale and variety, intrigue pulled me down a seemingly endless path of stalls three deep. Jewellery, bags, trainers, tee-shirts, watches, this was a place I need to come back to. It took a trip on public transport and a decent walk afterwards before removing the SLR out of its bag in order to try and capture an image of the world's seventh highest communication tower that not even the most brain dead, free-climbing nutter has managed to scale. The most difficult thing for me with a shot like this was getting across the sense of scale. I attempted to use a couple of architectural landscape spheres outside a nearby hotel as foreground, but I wasn't sure if it did the trick. One thing I am sure of though: I would rather photograph it than attempt to climb it.

Chapter 2
Perhentian Island

It was 3.30 am as I pressed snooze through squinting eyes. I'd packed my case the night before so, after a few seconds of aimless wondering with my balls in my hand, I stumbled into the bathroom for a quick shower before check out.

Outside, my pre-booked Grab car was waiting.

"Good morning."

"Good morning, sir," the driver replied. He was a young, native looking man, in his mid-twenties driving a tidy little runabout.

"How long do you think it will take to arrive at the airport?" I asked.

"Maybe one hour," he replied.

Check-in was required three hours early so if I arrived at the airport on time, I had plenty to kill. Distracted by the novelty of being far from home, it took me until that point, two days into the trip, to realise that I could ring the kids using the call feature of my Messenger app. Luckily it came to me while sat in the airport's WiFi range so I rang while eating a breakfast of McDonald's sausage and egg McMuffin with coffee.

It was lunchtime back home as I eventually managed to get through.

"Hello?" came a boy's voice. It was Bailey AKA Monkey-Nuts.

"Hi, sweet-heart. How are you?" I asked, slightly guilty I'd not yet spoken since leaving a couple of days ago.

"Hi, Dad. Where are you?"

"I'm in the airport waiting for a flight to Perhentian Islands," I explained.

"Have you been snorkelling yet?" he asked.

"Not yet, sweetheart. I am on my way there now. That's the flight I am waiting for."

"Oh," he said.

I explained the time difference, which was I bit mind-boggling for him to get his head around.

21

"So it's still the night time?"

"Well it's very early in the morning here. Let me have a quick chat with your sister in case we get cut off. I love you and I will be in touch soon sweetheart," I explained.

"Love you, Dad," he replied.

Moments later Isabella came to the phone. "Hi, Dad!"

"Hello, my little princess! Are you okay?" I asked excitedly.

"Yeah. Is it the middle of the night there?"

"Not quite but it is very early."

"What are you doing?" she quizzed.

"I'm having a McDonald's breakfast and watching all the people rushing around with their trolleys in the airport," I explained.

Not knowing what to say next, she copied her brother. "Have you been snorkelling yet?"

"Not yet, sweetie. I'm just about to get a flight to the island where I am going to do the snorkelling."

"Where is it?" she asked.

"It's a place called Perhentian. It's a little island off the coast," I told her.

"Oh. Is it nice?"

"I hope so sweetie. I will tell you all about it later."

"Okay," she replied.

"I have to go now, princess, so make sure you are good and I will speak to you soon. Love you, love you, bye, bye, sweetheart, bye."

"Bye, Daddy, love you."

The first leg of my planned trip had already been changed. After the advice from that Tripadvisor post I found, I was on my way to the Perhentian Islands. I'd not booked a room yet, just the flight. In my experience, pre-booking accommodation mostly ends up costing more and committing you to something you end up regretting. This was backpacker heaven so the usual last-minute walk-in it was to be.

I imagined this scheduled airline route to be less popular than most with fewer passengers, more suited to propeller plane, so it was a relief to see a jet on the tarmac. The fear of relying on a mechanical device to constantly fight against an ever-present downward force in order to keep my organs from being burst like water balloons at a pool party as they slam into terra firma, was a fear I had mostly overcome little by little on each flight as I grew older, although I must admit, propeller planes do still give me anxious tinges. Maybe it's their association with white silk Biggles scarves flapping horizontally behind leather head gear back in the day when someone had to stand on step ladders and yank the prop to start the engine. Luckily I didn't notice a single twirled moustache on the hop, skip and jump across to Kota Bharu on the west coast, the capital city of the state with the same name. So short, in fact, was that hop, the cabin crew almost skipped and jumped down the aisle, sloshing fruit juice into flimsy plastic beakers and thrusting packs of complementary peanuts into the hands of bemused passengers at an amusing pace.

There was a lot less commercial activity outside the airport than I'd expected. Nothing much other than a roadside cafe on the corner over the main road was visible as I left the building. It looked like the obvious starting point to enquire how to get to the ferry at Kuala Besut so I headed across. I'd not noticed how much it benefitted from the monopoly on serving food and drinks until drew closer. Tables spilling out onto the path were mostly taken by what seemed to be taxi drivers. I walked inside, sat at a one of the last available plastic patio sets and waited to be served.

After a couple of minutes of being ignored, I caught the attention of the scarf-headed waitress. "Hello, chai?" I quizzed. She returned a blank expression. "Tea please," I continued but still no joy. Then, just as I began to point at someone else's drink on the table behind, a man sitting at the next table came to my assistance.

"You want drink?"

"Yes, maybe this," still pointing at the dark orange brew over my shoulder. Maybe it was tea. It was difficult to tell but, if so, tea had never been such a threat to freshly laundered white linen.

Soon an overflowing clear glass mug was placed in front of me. You could clearly see the variegation between two liquids: a lighter, creamy-white coloured underbelly and a strong, dark, burned-tangerine main fluid on top, like some weird layered all-inclusive holiday cocktail. I sipped a bit off the top without lifting it off the table. It was definitely tea, strong and bitter like turmeric's big sister, whose depth of colour warned of ruinous stains, destined to remain well after the complaints from the finger wagging laundry granny are forgotten. Stood out like a pervert hanging around the shallow end of the local swimming pool, a pre-inserted teaspoon looked wrong leaning back against the rim. I picked it up but, as I began to stir, there was a resistance not normally associated with the good ol' British cuppa: more similar to a wellie treading a muddy puddle. Apparently there's much more to condensed milk than eating it with a spoon straight from the can as a childhood treat. It can also be used to exercise your wrist while trying to dilute it in a mug full of steaming hot wood stain. Carpal tunnel isn't a beauty spot in the country where trains cut through a hillside, it's an RSI, Repetitive Stirring Injury, brought on by the effort needed to bring together two ingredients that do eventually make a lovely refreshing mug of chai, or whatever it is they call it round here.

The helpful guy started to chat to me in broken English. "Where you from? Where you go?" The usual local-to-traveller spiel. Once he realised why I was there, the guy offered to take me to Kuala Besut, the place I would find the boat to Perhentian. He was asking 60 ringgit but I refused at first because you always have to expect they are trying it on.

"I'm going to ring a Grab car," I explained.

"Why?" he pestered. "They are more expensive. I do it very cheap." After a little more convincing, I agreed to go with him. He finished his food, paid for my tea and we left.

This guy had the sort of face that had probably saved him many confrontations over the years but, having spent a little more time in his company, I realised he wasn't the thug my first impression gave me. "How long before we get there?" I asked.

"One hour," he said. I hadn't expected it to be such a long journey. The 60 ringgit price tag had turned out to be worthwhile. After idle chat about what was the best model of car and English football, we arrived at the port city.

Past customers sat side saddle amongst drifting charcoal smoke, on their parked-up mopeds at the counters of rustic, wooden, roadside food stalls, eating grilled cobs of sweetcorn, we turned into a side street past a car park with a clutch of mango trees in one corner. We must have been close but, rather than stopping on the side of the jetty as expected, the guy turned into some narrow dead end back street. He opened the door.

"Where is the jetty?"

"Wait. I will get my friend. He will help you." He got out and disappeared down an alley on foot, returning two minutes later with a teenage boy.

"What are we doing here?" I asked.

"He will help you."

"Why? I don't need any help," I explained.

"He will take you to the boat." This bloke thought I was daft enough to think I would believe that you cannot drive a car to the dock.

"I don't need help. Just take the car to the jetty. It's not that difficult."

It didn't take any more for him to realise he wasn't getting a share of the tip I was supposed to pay the lad for carrying my bags around the corner. Embarrassed, the lad quickly left at this point and, because I hadn't handed any money over yet for the taxi fare, the driver had no choice but to do as I said. He gave in, shut up and got back in the car. After reversing back down the lane and driving literally around the corner, the man pulled up and headed for the boat guy at the jetty. They chatted while looking over in my direction as I loaded myself up with bags. I marched across to a ramp leading down to a floating pontoon jetty on the other side of a metre-high concrete harbour wall for round two of 'let's rip off the tourists'.

There were a handful of large speedboats with twin engines, bench seats and canvas roofs to accommodate around 15 passengers. All but one was moored up empty. "Here!" a local guy shouted as I made my way towards him. His boat was half full of passengers but their bags took up most of the rest of the room. I climbed aboard, found a space for my luggage and took a seat. I knew I was going to be paying four times the amount of my fellow passengers but the 50 ringgit asking price could have been worse.

Although at first quite tiny, the two islands were visible from quite a way off. The profile of their jungle covered central peaks, home to species of reptiles, primates and birds never before seen by my eyes at least grew slowly on the horizon as we rattled, bumped and skipped across an unforgiving swell.

25

After 30 minutes mostly flat out, slowing only to jump the biggest crests, each time landing hard with a dull slap, we pulled up at the jetty of a cove, whose modestly-sized, hut-lined beach had been coming into view for the past few minutes. Along with one other person, I got off. The remaining people on board made me realise this was the first stop of a multi-drop trip but, before I could quiz the skipper in any detail, the boat was out of reach. He saw the anxiety on my face as they pushed off "Everything closed. This is the best place for you," he said as they drew away.

A snake of ivory foam followed the boat around the headland, disappearing behind a silhouetted outcrop of sharp, distant, chaotic rock. I'd been left cut off behind a turquoise infinity of latent perils and there was nothing more I could do about it today. Stood on a ten metre-wide concrete-roofed jetty with a 40-metre concrete walkway on submerged columns, running at right angles from its centre back to the beach, I look around. My eyebrows struggled to keep the sweat from my eyes in the energy zapping glare as I surveyed tufty grass-topped huts and corrugated tin-roofed buildings, around 15 in total, lining the top fringe of the beach. 'Taxi boat' read one of many hand-painted signs on the makeshift resort, advertising whatever a holidaymaker might need from diving to food, but the place was deadly quiet. There were no signs of life apart from one Indian looking guy hanging over the jetty railings watching a school of needlefish skimming the surface of the impressively clear blue depths.

"Why are you here? Everything is closed. The rainy season," he explained, as the sun burrowed its way into the back of my neck.

"I have come for the snorkelling," I explained. "Is everything closed?" I asked.

"Yes," he replied but, like so many times in the past as a tourist new to an area, being kept in the dark can be a way of controlling you in order to squeeze out more cash. Until you have learned enough about your surroundings, you have to rely on what you are told and, usually by that time, you have been rinsed and repeated at least once.

I spotted a bit of a chalet complex at the other end of the beach. It looked like my best chance of finding some accommodation so I set to it over across the powder beige sand, rucksack, hand luggage and camera bag in tow. Two huts

26

in, I noticed some sort of scale-covered, sabre-clawed, prehistoric monster, known to prey on cats and even the occasional small dog, shading motionless under the roof of a front porch. It was a monitor lizard, huge and dark, almost black, with sandy coloured spots in circular shapes, stripes under its belly and along its tail, thin head and elongated snout. My attempt not to act like a giddy dog, as it spots its owner after being left alone all day, failed as I approached far too quickly while fumbling with my camera bag. Maybe I scared him off but you don't grow to five feet long without being cautious. It wasn't about to risk being processed into half a dozen handbags, with the old 'I'm just taking your photo' trick so, on seeing me and my Nikon, it quickly employed stealth waddle mode. Employing a technique involving curving its torso from left to right alternately, while flailing its limbs like a camp child drowning in the deep end, looks quite cumbersome but it did the trick. It shot off noisily between the buildings, over discarded rusty corrugated tin panels and dead palm leaves, to the rear. If it hadn't been the size of a seven-year-old child in a crocodile suit with claws bigger than a tiger, the way it moved might have been more amusing, like a huge mechanical wind-up toy. I tried to follow but, before I could get anywhere near, it disappeared further into the undergrowth.

The distraction had taken my mind off the heat but I was soon reminded. Like a solar headlock, with forearm clasped tightly around my neck, I weakened the further across the beach I reached, almost choked out by a brutal heat that seemed to increase in intensity as it moved up to a more dominant position in the sky. Beads of sweat trickled down my chest and tummy into my waist band. Being the meat in a fully loaded rucksack sandwich, helped to turn my legs to jelly; then came the dizziness forcing me to rest. I sat on a picture postcard swing hanging from a tilted palm half-way across the beach. Imagine a scene in a TV holiday advert: a swing with high hessian ropes and rustic driftwood seat, that produces a long, slow, laid-back sway perfectly matched to its environment. It should have been an enjoyable experience under normal circumstances but the swaying motion turned out to be the straw that broke the camel's back, inducing a sickness culminating in a bought of retching that refused to stop until well after the vomit ran out. The feeling of cramp from repeated muscle spasms was still fresh in my mind as I wiped the tears from my eyes and rinsed out my mouth with the last of my water. It was time to drop my bags before they dropped me.

In the end, the clutch of huts that had looked promising from a distance were a waste of time and, as pretty much everywhere else up to now, it was deserted. Now the alarm bells really started to ring as I headed back for my bags. It was a long way to come for nothing. No smoke, no fires, no noise and no headache tablets. Other than a giant lizard, the only sign of life since watching the boat disappear was the Indian guy who was still on the jetty.

"Is this the little island?" I asked, brushing the sweat from my stinging eyes with the back of my hand.

"Yes. Here is Coral Bay," he explained.

"I think I need to be on the big island. Maybe it will be better for me there?" I quizzed.

"It's all closed, the rainy season." After a bit more of the same, he explained that I could stay at the hotel he worked at which was just on the end of the jetty, so I followed. This was a cove surrounded by forest hills. It seemed the hotel I was heading for that was perched on the far-left outcrop. It marked the end of Coral Bay and any chance of finding anything useful.

It was pretty obvious that in its day this building was amazing but the process of aging leaves nothing untouched. A once opulent, now geriatric, dark teak timber construction of colonial style, with stilted pattern concrete walkways, incorporating wood-grained log effect railings in a repeating pattern of cross brace, hand rail and post as it led to empty chalets in all directions.

Through buckled, pinned-back teak and bevelled glass bi-fold doors, I could see a short, stocky girl inside wearing jeans and a white T-shirt lounging sideways on a sofa chair, legs tucked up and slippers dangling from the strap between her toes, in the foyer watching TV with a couple of guys sat on sofas opposite. "She is the one you need to see about room," he explained as he led me up two full-width wooden steps to the inside. On hearing this, she got up with a plump, nubile, forced grin framed within a shoulder-length lustrous ebony mane and made her way to reception, turning to check I was following. With taut denim against fulsome swaying buttocks, she negotiated a further two steps up to an open plan reception facing back down over a handrail and stood behind the till on the counter to the right.

In preparation for the inevitable price hike, I kept 50 ringgit in mind, around a tenner, as a ball park figure for one night. "How much for a room please?" She pressed a few keys on the calculator and spun it around to face me. The display said 150. "Do you have anything cheaper or a smaller room? It is too expensive," I enquired.

"That is smaller room," she explained so I tried the oldest trick in the book.

"Ok thanks," I replied whilst turning and walking off. I hoped to be called back any moment but each retreating step led further to disappointment. I headed back to the jetty to work out my next move. The Indian guy followed me back along the path to the shade of the jetty roof. I explained it was too expensive and, surprise surprise, he remembered somewhere else.

"I know a man. He has hut on the beach there. 10 ringgit maybe. There!" He pointed back down to the beach I'd just crossed. We chatted while we made our way back down and along the beach. "What is your name?" he asked.

"Ian. What is yours?"

"My name Ali. Where you from?"

"England, and you?"

"I am Bangladeshi." There was a calm tone to his voice and a sincerity in his eyes that put me at ease, even after steering me in the direction of the overpriced accommodation. He was of average height, gangly, with naturally dark, yet unnaturally tanned skin, almost African, emphasizing the whites of his bloodshot eyes on a face more western than African. Thin nose and chisel jaw with a straight cropped comb over as black as a midnight cave.

We arrived to find the owner, as was everyone else, nowhere to be seen. Having had the benefit of a closer look, I realised why the hut was the price of a motorway service station coffee. Apart from being serenaded to sleep by the sound of swaying waves drifting through the window each evening, nothing else was appealing about this hut. No proper door locks or curtains, just a bare room with a partially collapsed mattress on a grotty handmade double bed, stood on a patchwork of dated, overlapping vinyl flooring oddments.

"There is other place you can stay. It is Long Beach there," he informed me, pointing inland.

"Okay, how much is it?"

29

"Maybe 30 or 40 ringgit. You need go where the huts here behind, up the hill and down with the path to the beach. It the right side, Roke Garden it name. The end, last one."

"Thank you, maybe I will see you again before I leave?"

"You will come for food because this the one you only can find," he continued.

"For food? Where?" I asked.

"Hotel here," he pointed.

"Oh right, thanks."

Back facing the sea, I set off from 'Crappy Bay' and trudged along a narrow winding path between tightly packed buildings squeezed in behind the beach. A block-paved path around a metre wide guided me from then on, up through virgin jungle. The path had seen better days, having been washed away in places by one too many monsoons. It wasn't wide enough for a car, but it was the nearest thing to a road I had seen since hitting dry land. Continuing up and over the crest of the hill, through a thinly populated scrubland of palms and vine, then back down the other side, buildings started to reappear as I approached Long Beach.

Now just sand and the odd pile of dumped refuse, the path led out between two single storey buildings onto an unsurprisingly long beach, around five times the size of the beach at Coral Bay, with dark rocky outcrops at either end. I'd like to think it would have benefitted from being shown a rake but it was low season. Looking back, my footprints marked my route across the sand, over leaves, branches and even an old washed-up motorcycle helmet, towards a chalet-smattered, rocky hillside to the far right, which I hoped was Roke Garden.

Reassuringly, there were other humans around here, one in a hammock and a couple stood in the distance. The beach began to run out as the hillside complex became clearer. Rocky cliffs and a series of flights of concrete steps slalomed their way down an abrupt incline, negotiating a path around a precarious ancient rock on its way down from a green plateau, ubiquitous with cabins and palms, past an open terrace at the halfway point, continuing down to a white hand-painted sign wedged in between boulders at the lowest fringe saying 'D'Rock Garden resort' in blue lettering. A stream leading into the sea had cut a deep swathe through the sand, right at the point the steps leading up to the complex started. A large blue plastic sewage pipe around 40 cm in diameter bridging the gap was the only way across the ravine without taking the long way around, so I shuffled tentatively along its slippery incline with aeroplane arms and full complement of luggage.

Across without incident and up as far as the terrace, I knew I was halfway. Populated with tables, a kitchen and, most importantly, a water dispenser, I stashed my bags behind stacks of chairs in an open room next to the kitchen and helped myself to three cups of water before continuing up the path to find someone to negotiate with. I headed for an area with clothes hanging on rows of lines, a sign of life, outside a building further up the hill but there was no one there either. Eventually, at the very top, three men were constructing chalets. The smallest of the three came forward.

"Hello, I need somewhere to stay and I have been told you have rooms for 30 ringgit," I explained.

"No 50," he demanded abruptly.

"Can I have a look?"

"Okay, follow me." He walked back down the hill along a path splitting off, connecting chalets in all directions. He rummaged around in the drawer of a desk full of loose keys, back down under the large roofed drying area around 20 metres square. He grabbed a couple of keys and continued down the hill. "Electricity off after 11 until 7, okay?" he explained as he opened the door of room three. "Okay?" he repeated as he handed me the key.

"Yep, that's fine."

It was a relief after hours of uncertainty to be climbing three open wooden steps into a porch leading to the door of the semi-detached, stilted wooden cabin that would be home for tonight. A separate bathroom with wash basin, toilet and shower was through a door near the exit and in the main room a double bed, 1960s chest of drawers, matching wardrobe, a double sofa bed and, less sliding – more screeching, aluminium patio doors leading to a balcony just big enough to fit a circular plastic patio table and a couple of bums on seats.

One of the advantages of staying in an empty resort is getting your pick of the

31

accommodation. The elevated position of cabin number three overlooking the bay provided a spectacular vantage point.

Between a canopy of gently swaying green gloss leaves, and dark Neolithic craggy cliff top foreground below, was an almost perfect interpretation of nature's unspoilt spirit. An invitation to sit and immerse the eye in one of nature's ubiquitous incarnations. A timeless image of constantly evolving white water ribbons, relentlessly chasing their way to shore, in perpetual patterns of rhythmic, snaking energy from the vastness beyond, sliding in to massage the shore with reassuring regularity and a soothing tone.

It was the much-needed rose-tinted glasses this cabin needed to take your eye off a very shabby room. I sat resting while my head wondered off with the visual gift for five minutes, before attempting to charge my electrical items but there was no power. Maybe I'd misunderstood the times he mentioned and the electricity was going to come on, not off, at 11. Even without power, things had vastly improved since a couple of hours ago; fears of finding myself stranded with no options had been laid to rest and no longer was I compelled to trudge around with every possession at all times. Just the issue of a rumbling tummy to deal with now.

As yet there were no roads, cash machine, mobile signal, streetlights, shops, police officers: not even a kiosk or man with a little trolley selling his wears, and my hunger was growing. I stashed my bank cards, my spare smartphone and passport inside the hollow top of one of the plastic patio table legs that I had removed for the purpose then replaced. I hid my camera, lenses and GoPro behind the low drawer of the wardrobe too. In the bathroom, I turned on the tap for a quick freshen-up to find it dispensing something completely unlike anything you might want to put in contact with your skin. All those unrealistic scenes in crap films where clattering pipes splutter out agitated black treacle through juddering taps, suddenly weren't so unrealistic as I watched it dispense what resembled the contents of a freshly- brewed cafètiere. I gave the wash a miss, took a photo to show my mates and headed back to Coral Bay.

Over the hill in search of food, something bright red flashed by angrily across the path a couple of metres in front, startling me with its vivid warning.

I followed it with my eyes, watching it seemingly disappear as it approached the trunk of a tree just off to the left. On first glance I presumed it was a giant butterfly or a bat but, as I drew closer, I noticed a dull green and black striped grasshopper around nine centimetres long clinging to the trunk. It had black hoops on its legs but not a trace of red was to be found anywhere. I needed to satisfy my curiosity as to whether or not it was responsible for the dazzling display so I drew closer in order to force it to bolt. It obliged and took flight, bright red wings and all, but rather than retreat, its flight path curved around heading straight at my head forcing me to duck as it passed and landed on the next nearest branch. The trick seemed to be to scare and confuse its aggressor into looking elsewhere, then quickly land motionless until the danger was clear. Today I found this not-so-little, amazing creature pretty easy to spot but in the right environment it would have probably been better camouflaged and much harder. Further proof, if needed, of nature's ability to use colour as a distraction with impressive efficiency.

The girl, who I presume is the daughter of the owner, was sat on the sofa again with her head buried in her phone along with Ali and one other guy as I stepped up into the foyer of Hotel Shari-La for the second time. Ali got up and came over to greet me with a smile.

"Hi, could I get some food please?" I asked.

"Yes, please take a seat," he said, pointing upwards towards the dining room on yet another level.

The building was constructed using stilts and multiple floor levels as it follows the natural curve of the rocky mounds it sits on. He bowed his head slightly and shuffled backwards as I passed him to climb a further three wide stairs bringing me one level above reception. I found myself a table in the corner of the restaurant, with its mahogany panelling, net curtains and red tablecloths. It told a story of an opulent past and the moth-bitten holes; scratches and discolouration were clues to the timeline of those good old days. All it needed was Uncle Fester to emerge from the kitchens with a silver platter and I was out of there. Instead it was Ali that approached with a single-sided laminated menu. He passed it to me and waited submissively close by. Chicken fried rice, chicken with noodles, chicken with boiled rice, chicken omelette and chicken salad.

"Do you not have any seafood," I quizzed.

"No we have big menu but rainy season sir."

"But the sea is right there," I complained while looking out through the window. Ali laughed nervously as I ordered the chicken fried rice.

I'd brought my mask and fins, remembering Ali had mentioned a good snorkelling spot near the hotel while chatting earlier so, while waiting for my order, I walked to the window to see what I could see. Between smatterings of vegetation and chalets, I could just make out the jetty down below but not much else. My food arrived quickly and was well presented. Topped with a fried egg, the rice had been shaped into a dome then upturned onto a plate resembling the contour of the bowl they must have used to mould it, but the portion size was child-like. I could have eaten double. It was delicious though and a mere 12 ringgit.

"Was the food okay, sir?" Ali asked on noticing me finish.

"Lovely, thank you. You mentioned a beach nearby for good snorkelling?"

"Yes, sir, Romantic Beach. It's through the chalets behind hotel. If you go here," he pointed to a second empty adjoining dining room up some further steps with French doors leading out into a maze of pathways.

I paid my bill and wandered through what was now a storeroom/dumping ground for old furniture and chairs. Dusty cracked windows gave clues to the length of time since it had been used for its original purpose.

Outside I followed a concrete path in the general direction Ali had mentioned, soon to be shadowed by him once again.

"Down here," he informed me as I reached a circular concrete pergola with a conical concrete roof, concrete wood-grain effect handrails and steps meandering down a steep bank. "This was my shop but now rainy season," he explained, stood under the circular roof.

"What do you sell?"

"Cigarette, sun cream, magazine, but now nothing until next season."

"Are you waiting here till next season?"

His head dropped. "Yes," he replied with a despondent expression.

"And your family? Are they in Bangladesh?"

"Yes."

34

"How many children do you have?"

"I have four children."

"You must miss them very much?"

"Yes."

"So you stay two seasons then see your family?"

"Yes I hope."

Between the trees, the sun's reflection glitter-balled off the gentle ocean ripples below, as I parted ways with Ali and headed down. I heard voices and even though it wasn't a language I recognised, the words 'Thank god it's not just me' rang through my head. There were four people, one local and three others, all up to their waists enjoying a warm dip. I approached the group to say hello and the local guy warmed to my prescence. With an excessive collection of string and bead beach-bum bangles around both wrists, a little goatee beard, long dark surf dude ringlets and big smile, he wasted no time in familiarising himself with my situation.

"Hi. Where are you stay?" When he heard I was paying 50 ringgit per night, he explained, "You can stay with us guys at my place 30 ringgit."

"Where is it?" I enquired.

"Just over there," he pointed towards the beach that I'd investigated earlier at the other side of the jetty. It did sound interesting but not interesting enough to relocate before benefitting from the hike that gained me a view I would struggle to tire of.

"Thanks but I don't want to move around just yet. I have heavy bags and I've only just carried them over to Long Beach."

"No problem. Where are you from?"

"England," I replied.

"My friends here are from Argentina," he explained, holding his outstretched hand in their direction.

I said, "Hi!" The two girls and one guy replied with varying levels of understanding, in between chatting amongst themselves in their native tongue. "Do you want to borrow my spare snorkelling gear?" I asked the guy. He smiled silently.

35

"He no good English," one of the girls told me.

I walked back to my spare gear, picked it up, took it over and handed it to the guy. As he took the mask and flippers, I pointed at my watch to make sure he didn't think I was giving them away. He understood that.

Entering the water with fins proved to be more of a task than I remembered, mainly due to the odd rock hiding under the surface, so I took them off and waded in until it was deep enough to swim. Out at waist height, you could see the concrete jetty where I'd arrived from behind the rocks. There was a concrete stilted walkway with concrete handrails, a tin roof and two sets of concrete steps leading down to the water at both ends of the main platform where one of the locals had come out of the woodwork to cast his bait. It was within a two minute swim but I figured the opposite direction towards a quieter spot may lead to better encounters. I dipped in my mask and instantly spotted fish but nothing special. Smaller fish have a tendency to congregate around objects they can use to conceal themselves so I headed for a patch of space hopper-sized brain coral a little further out and it paid off. Even if I had a good memory, I would struggle to recall half of the species I found myself surrounded by. Flat heads, stripy, bright or with trailing tails, the array of marine fish made me wish I had some sort of food to bring them in closer. The biggest and most noticeable was around 40 cm long, with a stereotypical shape and impressive shimmering pallet of lime green, orange, purple and electric blue.

I headed back to the shallows and, just as I reached the point I could touch down my feet, a small sandy-coloured fish sat motionless on the sea bed, hoping it had not been spotted. With an almost perfect colour match to its surroundings, it was pretty well camouflaged apart from slightly darker spots that gave it away close up. I moved in to see how long it could hold its nerve. Weirdly similar to my encounter with the flying grasshopper earlier in the day, in an almost identical ploy, it was the fish's turn to create a distraction. I was subjected to a dazzling display of bright yellow flashes coming from the vivid underside of its outstretched fins. While I was still stunned at what had just happened, he took his opportunity to shoot off, hoping not to be noticed amongst the confusion, and it worked. In my head I felt like I'd been out there ten minutes, but the cramp building up in my leg muscles made me realise it had been a bit longer. The guy and the Argentineans had gone when I returned to the beach. I picked up the spare snorkel, left by the path and looked forward to a good night's sleep as I walked back over the jungle path.

Up to now the weather had been mostly dry and hot but at some point during the night I was woken by the sound of a torrent of noise. Of all the roofs in all the world, why did a million tap-dancing pixies have to choose my roof for their world record attempt? Or was it just simply a shitload of rain? Probably the latter. I tried to get back off to sleep but I noticed a dripping noise coming from inside. I got up and turned on the light, but it didn't work. As my eyes became more accustomed to the dark, I could see the roof was leaking. Rain was forming a puddle on the floor in front of the sofa bed. It didn't seem to be doing any harm so I returned to my pit but it must have intensified later in the night, causing the leak to splash up from the floor onto nearby items. The next morning the sofa bed had become wet along with the items I'd left on there. It was mostly clothes but also my Bluetooth speaker. I dried it off as much as I could and put it to one side in the hope it wasn't ruined. Environments such as these have a knack of making big problems out of little issues, like drying your clothes in almost 90% humidity, which can take up to two days or more. Fabric feels constantly damp even without rain soaking your clothes from a poorly maintained roof and, just to make matters worse, there was still no electricity. Time to turn and walk away.

Half-way along the path between Long Beach and Coral Bay, I noticed a path at right-angles off into the jungle. That in itself wasn't a big deal but the fact it was constructed out of block paving, albeit mostly washed away at its starting point, and that there was a modern aluminium sign on a pole reminding people to respect the environment, intrigued me. There was no indication where it led and no one seemed to understand when I asked them. I made it a mission to investigate further but not yet. I was on my way back to Shari-La in the rain for breakfast. There had been no let up since my rude awakening in the middle of the night.

The hotel had WiFi but it was very poor. It wasn't up to Messenger calls but, sat up on higher ground in the dining room, I had managed to get a couple of messages out the day before after several attempts. I tried and failed again while waiting for my chicken. A skinny white cat sauntered by. I beckoned it with a series of sharp squeaks from pursed lips and a rub of my fingers in its direction. It stopped, turned round, hissed and continued on its way. This time I went for the noodles but the fried rice was better and, as I twisted my fork into another childlike portion, the fickle feline rubbed up against my chair. I thought how hard life must be for the humans in the rainy season let alone the cats. I turned to the cat and explained how its rude behaviour might upset people: "Tissssssssse!" I think it got the message. "See you later, Ali!" I shouted as I walked out to a break in the clouds. This was my chance to satisfy my curiosity surrounding the mystery path.

Not a hint of human existence other than a disused path and a relatively new road sign, it was too intriguing not to investigate. It was an easy route to start with. The virtually non-existent path didn't prove to be an issue. Like on the other hillside, it was obviously rain that caused the damage. Whoever was responsible for commissioning the work misjudged the velocity of the monsoon deluges running down from the jungle hillside. Over the first crest on higher ground, the block paving was mostly fully intact for ten minutes, following a rollercoaster landscape of forest, overgrown brush and the occasional fallen palm. Although I couldn't see it, or anything else other than the green screen of vegetation either side of the path, I felt I was following the coast. Further on, the path started to show increasing signs of erosion again. There was a good chance that, if the jungle hadn't enveloped the path in an exchange of route for root, so to speak, up ahead, previous torrents running down from the hills may have caused their own problems. Temporary rapids caused by flash floods, with the power to carve out deep ravines and wash down boulders big enough to uproot trees like pins down a bowling alley, may await around the next corner.

Although there were remnants of the same block paved path as I continued deep into No Man's Land, it was severely damaged. Water had tunnelled under the kerb stones in many places, completely washing away the sand base the full width of the path in some areas and many of the blocks had been taken by the once raging swell. Wading up to 40 cm was necessary in places, where mini-weir pools created by regular deluges running over solid kerbs had dug out underwater trenches. At some points there was no sign of a path whatsoever and at others the only thing remaining were the concrete kerbs, cast to keep the blocks in place. Tightrope walking a path just wider than the width of my foot along a bridge that was once a kerb was the easiest option at this moment in time. As the block paving reappeared further on, a covering of green slime proved to be treacherous. Suddenly both feet slipped away from under me in what could have been a spoof black and white movie scene, landing me square on my arse, luckily without so much as a niggling reminder. I'd got lucky so now as sunset was beginning to be a consideration so was my footing. I moved over to the left side of the path to use the bit of grip the undergrowth provided, even though unbeknown dangers were lurking.

I wasn't sure what time it went dark but, bearing in mind the electricity was supposed to come on at seven, sunset must not be long after. I set off just after 4 pm and my feeling was I'd been walking for maybe a little over an hour so it didn't take too much working out that I may have been in trouble without my head torch that, luckily, I had brought along.

Once again the path had all but gone: just a clearing between the forestation was the only sign a path had ever been there, and it was about to get slightly damp as I approached a torrent of water crossing the path up ahead. A waterfall with large boulders and skeletons of fallen palms resembling giant fish bones floating around in the pools either side of the white water beckoned. I stood staring up at the potential adventure, acutely aware of the pending dusk. "Fuck it!" I wrapped my camera in a carrier bag and tucked it under my T-shirt. I needed two hands for this job.

Climbing up started easy. Boulders the size of settees, stretching up the hill as far as the view between the trees allowed, were spaced out at an optimum distance for humans to ascend. A tree caught my eye as I reached 20 m upstream. It was a species I'd seen many times in other countries such as Thailand, with wavy fan roots projecting out from all sides above ground level creating the impression of triangular sails connected around the base. It wasn't its size that made it stand out, rather its position on the water's edge. One fin was redirecting the flow of water back over a boulder as if it was its job to do so. Further up the hill a yellow plastic tape, with the words 'Police line do not cross' repeated along its length, was stretched across the water. The fact some tape had become submerged was a sign it had been around for a while but most of it was still in its original position in an attempt to cordon off the path of anyone foolish enough to continue up the hill. I stepped over the tape and continued. I would love to have something more exciting to tell you about what happened next but the truth is five or six metres on I saw no change in the terrain so I turned back.

Moving on, the path started to improve once more then, over the next peak, a roofed walkway covered the path for five metres or so: a definite sign there was light at the end of the tunnel, then another roofed walkway and a modern, pretty new looking public toilet, not at all in keeping with its surroundings. I was definitely getting close to something. A metal handrail had been provided to aid the descent, as the path took a steep drop down, but its primary role seemed to be an ant highway so I managed without it. The forest thinned out to the left at the bottom of the hill. It gave way to my first sight of the big island, quite close by.

Perhentian, meaning 'stopping point' in Malaysian, is made up of two islands. Besar, meaning greater, and the one I was marooned on, Kecil, meaning lesser, more commonly known by tourists as the big island and little island. There are other tiny islands dotted around but none catering for tourists.

The sight of taxi boats, huts, chalets and a jetty across the water spurred me on. There had to be other inhabitants nearby. Around the next bend, a two-metre-high painted cement and chicken wire sculpture of two giant turtles swimming through reeds had been erected near to the coast. Past a skip that used to be a boat, I walked towards a stainless-steel Arabic building, moderately large for its location, with architectural feature dome and overall religious style, gave more than a suggestion of a mosque up ahead. On the other side of a small, rustic, wooden foot bridge with hand-polished rails, across ebony slats worn to a curve by grandparents who chased each other across as kids, the path merged into a wider gravelled area marking the beginning of a community I might have never known about if not for the

40

mysterious path. It provided dry dock storage for small boats mostly, some fishing, some taxi, some knackered.

They say knowledge is power and, although physically I felt far from powerful at this moment in time, I'd undoubtedly gained some well-earned knowledge today. I approached a sign showing the price of journeys to points around the island, shouting out to be photographed, along with a map showing locations no one mentioned at the other end of the path.

To my amazement, I had wondered into a fishing village with a shop, police station, school, a concrete jetty and people.

After passing a couple of locals, each time saying, "Hi!" with a smile, I turned onto a path running towards the heart of the village, passing a short man with a bald head around 50 years old. As an after thought, I turned back around and asked if he knew of anywhere I could stay.

"You? Stay?, How many?" he quizzed.

"It's just me."

Stood beside a pair of impressive stainless-steel school gates you might expect to find on the entrance to a gypsy travellers' site, he pulled out his mobile phone and made a call. After a two-minute conversation, he turned and explained, "Someone is coming."

He had two missing teeth together on the top, just off centre, and a habit of filling that gap with his tongue while squinting and pulling back his cheeks, screwing up his face between sentences like a constipated bulldog and, as much as I found it hilarious, it wasn't meant to be amusing.

"Wait here they are coming. It up there, that one blue," pointing up to the hillside to the back of the village.

Luckily for him, I was alone, as the smirk I was hiding might not have been so easy to conceal. While waiting, I had to move to one side of the path to allow a boy riding a motorbike and side cage to come past carrying a wrinkly granddad sat on sacks in his cargo basket. A couple of bare-chested men, sat chatting with beverages and cigarettes on the wall across, stared as a gentle masculine voice coming from the shiny steel mosque began to sing over a loudspeaker.

A young, short, chubby girl appeared from further down the path with headscarf, trousers and flip flops. I could tell by her determined mannerisms

41

she was the person I was waiting for so I walked over and met her halfway. "Okay I can show you," she told me as she set off, walking back the way she had just come.

"How much is it?" I asked before getting too far.

"50 ringgit," she replied.

I made a point of stopping. "Oh no. I don't want to pay that much. I'm only paying 40 over at Roke Gardens." It was actually called D'Rock Gardens having seen the sign but no one pronounced it correctly and she probably wouldn't understand if I did.

"How long you stay?" she asked.

"Maybe four nights."

"Okay 40," the girl nodded.

I followed her past a pig tethered to a banana palm through winding paths up to the back of the village and, after three flights of concrete stairs, we were there, apart from the external wooden stairs attached to the side of the building leading up to the upper level. The top floor was given up totally to rented accommodation. Four rooms off a central corridor were all available. A large veranda spanning the whole length of the upper front of the building with a table and chairs looking down over, not only the village, but a large part of the big island, half a mile off the coast, was a good start.

She unlocked the door to the last room on the left and swung it open: it was an instant yes. In comparison to my current address, this was a palace. A double bed with bedding, two towels and a toilet roll, next to another single bed and an en-suite bathroom with clear running water.

"I will come back with my luggage tomorrow, okay?"

Back down near the jetty was the heart of the village. There were two street vendors on the corner across from the empty police station: one grilling sweet corn on a trolley cart full of hot smoky coals and another adjacent to it with a canopy, hand-made, rustic and wooden, selling sweet pancakes. A woman was stood in line waiting for her order to be prepared. I joined the queue and ordered one. An old couple, possibly man and wife, ran the operation together. The man took a cup-shaped ladle and scooped batter from a large plastic container on the floor, pouring it onto a circular hotplate. Then with the flat

42

bottom of the ladle, he carefully spread the batter with a circular sweeping motion. Next he added sweet corn in syrup from a tin with a spoon one piece at a time, spacing out each kernel with delicate precision. Then what resembled desiccated coconut was next, along with another unknown ingredient.

Starting to feel a bit rude, realising I'd been staring for far too long, I turned my attention and my eyes to a couple of buildings nearby with chicken-wire shelving outside, stacked with a small selection of goods for sale. Sun-bleached packets of savoury snacks and plastic bags with unknown contents sealed with rubber bands sat in rusty baskets. I turned back around to find the old lady placing my pancake, which by this time had been wrapped in a paper and put into a tiny plastic carrier bag.

"Terima Kasih."

"4 ringgit." I paid and quickly made tracks.

Fully aware time was not on my side, I set off marching back to Long Beach, whilst hastily opening the first sweet treat I'd had in days. I slipped the wrap of brown paper from its cute mini clone of a full-sized plastic carrier bag to reveal a folded pancake, sandwiched with warm dripping Nutella, pre-cut into bite sized soldiers. It was a given that blobs of sweet indulgence would squish out and slip in slow motion like a fat kid down a baby slide, over the greaseproof side of the brown paper sheet. Not once stopping for fear of the darkness, I picked up a strip, dangled the dripping morsel into my mouth, and bit off a large chunk of gooey pleasure. Chocolate heaven at the perfect time to fill the tank in readiness for the big return. There may well have been enough for two but my eyes were wrong if they thought they were bigger than my belly.

It quickly disappeared and, as I slurped up every last drip of a dietitian's idea of poison from the greasy sheet, my step quickened.

I'd become accustomed to the rustling undergrowth on this path, disturbing the odd ubiquitous baby Godzilla on my way past, but tomorrow had more than just lizards in store.

Somehow I made it back to my hovel just as darkness fell, laid on the bed and considered my transport options for tomorrow's move. 'Do I take my gear in the opposite direction to the jetty at Coral Bay in hope of a boat to the village, with no idea if or when it may turn up, or do I make the trip on foot again with full luggage and the likelihood of further downpours?' Thinking of downpours, I needed to find a better way of drying my ever-increasing pile of damp garments. I decided to grab the selection of damp pants, T-shirts and shorts and take them up to the roofed drying area.

On reaching the top step to enter the open-sided drying room, a small smoky light turquoise snake laid deadly still, zigzag, straggling two washing lines. It was either staring straight at me or asleep with its eyes open. Either way, this was a photo opportunity not to be missed so, after quickly hanging out my washing away from danger, I nipped back for the Nikon. I had no idea at the time it was a highly venomous male Bornean keeled green pit viper and that a single bite could potentially kill a human. I also had no idea if it would still be there when I returned but I shouldn't have been so pessimistic. This beautiful vivid green beast has the ability inflict a world of pain in a less than a second; he didn't need to hide.

On my return, his head followed me as I crossed his path to get into position, camera in hand. Since taking some decent shots of the Petronas Twin Towers at dusk a few days earlier, I decided to give it a go again using an acute ISO setting to draw in the light but these snaps were coming out grainy for some reason beyond my understanding. Then complacency got the better of me as I moved in just a little too close. He struck out, jabbing at the camera like a teenager flicking a rolled-up towel at his mate's bare arse in the changing rooms of the swimming baths. Luckily for me it was a warning rather than for real. Like when a boxer fakes a punch to draw out his opponent, it stopped short of its target. Heeded but not put off, I decided to use my flash, which meant a further trip back down to the room.

Before I left, I spread out my clothes into a better drying position then, from the centre of the drying area, I walked diagonally towards the steps and, in some ridiculous senior moment, straight underneath the snake, well within range of an easy strike. On realising my stupidity, I ducked, but it was a bit pointless. Had he decided to sink a pair of fangs into the back of my head, it would have already happened. I continued out of harm's way and turned to

find him staring at me with a look on his face like when your Dad catches you picking on your little sister. 'What a waste of good venom,' he thought, maybe. With no hospital on the islands, I might have struggled to find anti-venom, although locals tell stories of the extract of the root of a herb called Akar Cina Putih that is supposed to do the trick. Stupidly I'd forgotten to pack that, along with the dried water powder and the camouflage pills. Luckily for me, I got the only shot I needed, an image on the memory card, rather than one connected to end of a syringe. Today wasn't the day my story ended.

Assisted by the moonlight glow, I set off to my favourite restaurant for dinner one last time before the big move. 'Mmmmm, chicken sounds good,' I thought sarcastically with a smile as I bounded down the steps. Fires at three different locations along the beach proved life was more abundant than I first thought, as branches and dried leaves crackled under the red and yellow heat. The path to Grotty Bay was tricky to find in this direction, especially at night. An opening between two buildings lining the beach that all looked quite similar was hard enough to find during daylight so, without a torch, concentration was required to find the right path. Once through it was as easy as a politician avoiding questions to find my way over the hill to the other side.

In Shari-La, I ordered food but stayed in the foyer for the strongest WiFi signal. Opposite, on the sofa, sat a young man. I'd not noticed him at first, mistaking him for a local until he broke the ice.

"Hello, my name is Prem. Are you staying here?" he said. He was a gentle, kind soul, handsome and unassuming, of medium build in his late twenties. I recognised his accent as Indian and proceeded to explain my predicament, until Ali arrived with two identical plates of food.

"Chicken fried rice for you, sir, and for you. Would you like it here?"

"Yep, okay."

We were both sat on separate settees facing a large coffee table. "This is the best thing on the menu, I reckon, Prem," I told my guest as we sat up to eat, chatting about our jobs and our recent experiences in KL. "I am looking for some labour to work on a project back at home, if you know anyone who might be interested?"

"What is it?"

45

"I bought a disused church to convert into a home a number of years ago but, now I am getting divorced, it needs to be sold in order to give my ex her share of the estate we have built up over the last ten years. It's not completed yet and I need help to finish it."

"So is it help with the building work you require?" Prem asked.

"Well, yes, but mostly labour. I can show them what needs doing and provide the tools, travel and accommodation. There is around three months' work for two guys." The idea didn't ring any bells with Prem but we exchanged details and moved onto a different topic.

"Have you seen any of the lizards yet?" I asked.

"No. There are lizards?" He looked slightly distraught.

"Oh my god! These are the biggest lizards I have ever seen! Four-foot long and bellies like this," I gestured with my hands as if to be holding an eight-year-old around the waist.

"I'm scared now you told me that," he explained.

"Don't worry – they're more scared of you. Every time I see one, they scurry off into the bushes."

Prem was a software engineer living in KL. He was supposed to be travelling to the UK, Nottingham in fact, with work but it was cancelled at the last minute so he decided to come here to the island for a mini break. Like me, he had no idea how quiet it was going to be. That's what made him decide, like most others, to leave the next day.

"Have you not been snorkelling yet?" I asked as the resident cat sat meowing for scraps.

"No. I was talking to Ali about it. Did you go on your own?" I could tell by his tone he would not be happy going it alone down amongst the coral and the creatures.

"You can come with me in the morning if you want?"

He was a bit concerned about the weather for his crossing back to Besut the next day. "Maybe I will leave at 8 am if the weather looks bad or I can go at 12," he explained, although to be honest I didn't understand the logic in his thinking. The weather is either bad or it isn't.

Anyway I explained I would come over to the hotel at 9 am to go snorkelling and, if he was still around, we could go together. "You can borrow some of my snorkelling gear: I have two sets."

Although not what you might discribe as mountainous, both Kesil and Besar are abundant with steep inclines, and as far as I could see, everywhere other than the rocky coves, beaches and chalet complexes dotted around the shore line, was covered in forestation. It was November, rainy season, but there hadn't been much in the way of precipitation until last night's flooded room incident; now it wouldn't stop. Clouds were stuck to the hill tops like candyfloss on a stick and the rain was relentless.

Prem had decided to stay till lunchtime so it gave me a chance to show him the lime green, purple, orange and electric blue fish that had impressed me so much. I expected him to bottle it as he joined me in the water. He gave me the impression he was a bit of a wuss, but he was surprisingly okay. We saw lots of the multi-coloured specimen of fish and many others: so many in fact, that the sight of a large crustacean made a refreshing change. It was a hermit crab with a shell the size of my fist, clambering over the sub aqua landscape, picking at rocks like a long-nailed speed-typing secretary. The clever use of discarded shells as protection has always been a fascination to me. I watched and wondered if he was on the lookout for an upgrade right now.

Hermit crabs have a soft spiralled abdomen, so without the protection of their mobile home, usually in the form of a recycled snail shell, they would be easy targets to predators. Once they outgrow their armour, it's time to upgrade to something bigger. Up to 20 crabs have been known to gather together in decreasing sizes, waiting for up to eight hours for others of their species to take vacant possession of a larger shell, then they all move in turn into their respective new larger homes.

Bemused by the spectacle, an hour sped by like a speed boat, as we glided effortlessly past vivid orange clownfish sheltering between hypnotic patches of white-tipped ivory sea anemone, swaying rhythmically like the grass that dances off the hips of a Hawaiian hula skirt. A huge, pale brown, calcified disk of table coral is never too far out of view; its languid flatness, supplemented by sheer scale, creates another impressive reminder of nature's diverse aquatic beauty. Its constantly expanding eaves, unnoticeable to the naked eye, mark the outer edge of flat canopies that provide cover to schools of fry, a mass of minnow minors, primary students in classes of hundreds, learning and teaching alike, the benefits of sheltering under the cover of their sprat house, on the university campus of marine life, whose sprawling grounds are a vibrantly colourful, exotic, underwater garden, populated with topiary in the form of bright green brain coral the size of elephants' asses covered in a maze of zigzig patterns, interspersed with herds of stag horn coral, smatterings of antlers peeping over a rural hedgerow.

All too soon our short-lived friendship was at an end, for now at least. We exchanged details and said our goodbyes.

The rain had just stopped as I grabbed my damp, almost still wet, clothes off the line where the snake still perched. I stuffed them in a carrier bag so as not to dampen any other items and crammed them in the top of my rucksack. I'd decided not to attempt to get a lift so now water and waterproofs were a priority. It was going to be a gruelling hike and anything I could do to ease the pain could only be a good thing. I retrieved my phone, passport and bank card from the patio chair leg and my valuables from behind the drawer, made sure my water bottle was easily accessible along with a poncho in case the rain returned, and slipped the built-in rain cover over my rucksack because, although the sun was now blazing stronger than a bad boy yoot after pulling a 100 m wheelie down the main road of his council estate, brushing past wet undergrowth would still soak me and my luggage after a few minutes. Large at the back and small to the front, I set off yet again as the meat in a rucksack sandwich.

My ringgit was starting to dwindle so a cash machine or changing some of my stash of sterling would be essential in a couple more days. 'There's bound to be a cash machine in the village,' I thought to myself, as I reached the hole in the fence that I'd spotted at the top of D'Rock Gardens on my return yesterday. It saved a modicum of time climbing through onto the path rather than walking round and, with a steadily considered short gait, I edged my way closer to civilisation with each tentative step. As suspected, the vegetation was soaked, especially the banana palm. I unpacked the clear plastic throw away poncho and used it to cover my front rucksack for a bit of protection, tucking it down my front. The problem was I was already leaking like a broken tap and the impermeable layer tucked in against my T-shirt just served to exacerbate matters.

It's not long before you realise lizards are more common than cats round here and, if you don't see it first, you will hear its noisy waddling dash through a crisp carpet of fallen leaves, as he makes his escape; but I had just heard a noise that was different, quieter and fast. Almost instantly the sight of a massive lizard basking in the sun on the edge of the path three metres in front shifted my attention. They usually spot me first but it didn't take long for him to bolt after a second or two, just as a dragonfly the size of a small bird passed by my ear from behind holding a steady course dead ahead, droning along at eye level, like a Chinook helicopter on a distant skyline.

Suddenly I froze to the spot as the unusual slithery noise returned. A dark brown striped snake with the girth of a porn star slithered away from his basking spot on top of the bushes to the left, dropping down out of sight into the undergrowth. The noise, as you might expect of a snake moving, is quieter, slinkier and faster than that of a large four-legged reptile with limited movement. Moving on, I realised that was probably at least the second close encounter with a snake in as many minutes. From then on, I kept to the centre of the path as much as I could.

At measured intervals along the route, modern aluminium signs on tubular metal poles had been fixed into the ground with images of a Western man in running gear jogging, along with information on distance and calories burned. Yesterday I learned the path was not only non-existent in places but completely overgrown too; now the thought of snakes lurking around in the undergrowth just made matters worse when negotiating the assault course of banana palms, vines and the odd large tree blocking the path.

The rain held off as I edged closer to the village. I took advantage of the concrete benches dotted along the route whenever I saw one. If I sat on the edge, I could also squeeze on the rucksack behind me, temporarily relieving the weight off my shoulders. After the experience of yesterday's trial run, I knew to keep off the blocks on the hills and any green patches, but the added weight seemed to be helping to keep me stable. Once I reached the roofed sections of pathway, I knew I was close so now not reminding myself about the steps up to the digs would have been helpful, if not too late.

Past the concrete turtles and over the footbridge crossing the stream running into the sea, I heard the sound of clattering coming from a rubbish dump made up of dried banana leaves, ashes, old timber and scrap metal to the left of the path, next to a stack of sewer pipes. It was the sound of a metre-long lizard being chased over rusty tin by a bigger adversary. The victim hid in one of the lower tubes as a third beast, the attacker's accomplice, broke cover in search of the victim. There was no hanging around with the weight of this gear on my back so I didn't see the outcome of the skirmish. Small, medium, large or plain huge, you are never far from a lizard on the islands.

I'd made it to the path that meanders through the houses to the back of the village without collapsing but exhaustion was pulling at my eyelids like the effects of a night without sleep. Leaving time enough for a steady yomp was a serious consideration when planning this journey. Travelling at the pace of my first trip yesterday along something akin to a SAS training path would only have happened if my life depended on it this time.

One house had a full-sized Malaysian flag hanging from the porch roof next to a clever little six-foot long homemade metal washing frame on wheels, perfect for the rainy season, allowing easy switching between out in the sun or under the cover of the porch roof when the rain comes down. A couple of houses doubled up as shops along the route too. One selling snacks on the porch and the other selling bags of drinks tied up with rubber bands.

Close to the entrance of the second store, a machine with a horizontal metallic dish the size of a washing up bowl and a round rotating rasp the size of a child's fist in its centre warranted a second look. I was intrigued as to the purpose of this strange device resembling a candy floss machine turned onto its side. A young chubby girl knelt down in front of it and, as the rasp spun under the power of a crude set up of electric motor and pulley belt, she removed the flesh from half shells of coconuts by pressing them against the spinning tool, catching flaked morsels in a container between her knees.

Around the corner as the road reduced to a footpath, at the bottom of the steps leading to the digs, an empty cage the size of a dog kennel was now a podium for an impressive creature. It allowed him the vantage point his confidence demanded, to reiterate his authority at regular intervals beside a deep red banana palm flower, swaying gently like a disinterested stallion's penis beside the shimmering deep maroon and green plumage of a huge cock of the feathered variety, loud with youthful exuberance.

A slim, attractive, white-skinned girl with long blonde ringlets was hanging out washing on a porch. I had to make conversation, if only because it had been a while since I'd spoken to one of my own kind.

"Hello, where are you from?" I asked.

"Ireland," she replied.

"England. It's a small world!"

"Isn't it just?"

"Is there an ATM near here?"

"No. You'll need to go the mainland for that," she informed me.

"Oh, right no problem. I will probably see you around. Thanks, bye!"

"See you later."

'Shit!' I thought to myself, making the final push to the summit of the village. I had four hundred quid and enough ringgit to pay for my accommodation plus a couple of days' food. If only I had changed some cash while sat across from the money changing kiosk, sitting for half an hour in KL, waiting for the guys to sort out a local SIM card for my mobile phone. "Foolish," I said out loud.

The trek drained me so, like the battery of a rusty old jeep that refuses to start after years gathering dust under a sheet in the back of a barn, recharging was necessary. Seeing the top sheet folded down with two towels and a toilet roll placed out neatly did feel quite posh, especially having 24-hour electricity and plenty of sockets. I dropped my bags and got my head down for an hour, mid afternoon. After a nap I ventured out but this time in the opposite direction.

51

I followed a path across to the far end of town, past an old battered twin tub washing machine under a porch roof, rusty bikes, oversized satellite dishes and scraggy flip flops lined up on front steps. I spotted another block paved path leading up the coastal hill on through the edge of the jungle. A flat circular weaved bowl made of reeds laid damaged and discarded on the path as I passed. The strings attached to it were severed, no longer hanging, measuring or wherever it did. But, unlike the bowl, this path was unscathed. It had not seen the sort of monsoon damage that its counterpart at the other side of the island had sustained, and it continued to be fully intact as it dropped down to a hidden gem of a coastline, much cleaner than Long Beach or Coral Bay.

The lush, deep green, tree-covered hillside gave way to a milky powder sand beach with the odd gigantic dark charcoal boulder sitting between drooping holiday-advert palms. There wasn't a single human in sight, but I wasn't alone. A tiny hermit crab was sat motionless, hiding in its shell in hope that I wouldn't spot it. The trial of claw prints in the sand leading to the spot where nothing but it sat on a bed of otherwise perfectly smooth beige grain was a bit of a giveaway. I sat and waited it out till eventually, when it thought the coast was clear, so to speak, it popped up and dragged itself further along up the beach. If nothing else, it made for a great bit of video footage.

Being robbed is always a consideration to me when travelling, especially when travelling alone. Even with a prison-style security gate on the end of the corridor covering the exit to the porch, this was one of those properties, like most backpackers' accommodation, that wasn't as secure as I would have liked. If you are seen with expensive equipment, it's not hard for someone to find out where you are staying and then find a way in if they are that way inclined so, before I ventured out for dinner that evening, I gave it some thought. There were four rooms off one corridor and no other occupants. The keys to the vacant rooms were in the doors so I removed each room key in turn placing the key on the corresponding bed. I considered hiding some of my valuables in another room but, if it got rented out while I was out, that could be a problem. In the end I realized there wasn't a lot else I could do at this place to cut down the risk so I stuck my bank card together with my cash in my money belt and strapped it round my waist under my T-shirt. With nowhere safe to stash my camera, it was a bit of a risk leaving it while I went out but hopefully not flashing it around in public, and keeping it in a grotty carrier bag when I did take it with me, would help.

I sat at a bench at the side of the dirt track road running through the front of the village between the jungle and the turn off to my digs. There was a long building running parallel on the opposite side of the road. Still unaware it was the rear of a row of businesses along a waterside promenade adjoining the jetty, most of which were cafes, I dined, if you can call it dining, at the only place I knew to serve food. A little place next door to the shop. My seat was in front of a trestle table with a camping gas hob under a wok full of oil. It was a curved concrete bench seat and matching circular table out on the terrace. I attempted to order rice and fried fish with a spicy sauce that seems to be a favourite with the locals, but it wasn't on the menu so, living up to my Xbox gamer tag name 'TryOwtOnce', I went for the deep-fried sweet fish fritters, five for two ringgit. Although not at all healthy, they didn't taste half as bad as they sounded.

I was eventually to realise the jetty was the social hub of the village: a place to hang out, meet your mates and catch up. Guys would ride down on their mopeds checking out their mates' fishing haul, caught with novel improvised fishing rigs made up of a simple hook and line attached to an aluminium drinks can. They'd stick a sprat on the hook and try to lure a fish to take it by trawling the bait past their intended prey, emulating the movement of a fish by gently teasing the line repeatedly with, what I should imagine, comes from experience passed down through generations. After each mostly unsuccessful cast, they would wind the line back around the can then, while holding the base, being careful to hold the line in place, point the can in the direction of the intended cast with one hand, while swinging the hook, bait and a small amount of line with the other around their head in a technique similar to lassoing, increasing the speed of the revolutions until they created enough momentum to throw out the rig and at the precise moment letting go of the coiled line allowing the weight of the bait combined with the speed built up, to pull the line off the can. The whistle as it unwinds at speed is a testament to their skill in creating distance with the cast.

As I set off back to my pit, a five-year-old boy was stood at the side of the road holding something in his hand. He was screwing his face up while repeatedly sticking his tongue out then drawing it back into his mouth while spitting. As he walked off, he threw a fish to the ground. He had found out the hard way that this little rancid vertebrate, no bigger than his hand, was now officially cat food.

Very rarely do I find myself put about by spiders but, just as I was about to close my eyes and go to sleep back at my room, a tarantula's little brother appeared from nowhere on the side of the bed. My philosophy of live and let live went straight out of the window on this occasion as I imagined it crawling into my mouth to lay its eggs. I whacked it with my hat then looked for evidence of its demise but it had seemingly disappeared. I spread my search, looked behind me, under the bed; I even went as far as moving the bed and lifting up the mattress but nothing. It had vanished into thin air. I let it bother me for a while before moving on to worrying about my lack of ringgit until suddenly it was the next morning. I counted my ringgit again. After paying for my accommodation and the return boat ride to the mainland, I had thirty ringgit per day. I was hoping to manage on two meals a day at 15 ringgit each.

This time, equipped with my snorkelling gear, I returned to the beach that I'd discovered the previous day, making my way along the block paved path, hoping to see a monkey or two, a few fish and hopefully a turtle. No monkeys today but plenty of fish. Yellow-tipped, spotty, striped, dark, light, bright, dull: an amazing selection. I finned my way down the coast, heading away from the village on the lookout for turtles. It wasn't too far-fetched to imagine yourself floating above the landscape of an alien planet as I passed over a smattering of massive brain coral dotted around the seabed below me. One of these giant spherical creatures had enveloped the weirdest clam-like mollusc. Over time, having been attached to the coral for long enough for it to grow around it, all that was still visible was the opening between its armoured calcium mouth. A wavy opening that allowed it to poke out its flower petal, blue, wavy lips used to filter out algae and small organisms. Sensing my presence, the captive clam sucked in his hairy lips and clamped shut. If the spectacle of the clam on its own wasn't enough, this merging of two life forms was a truly amazing sight.

Protected by the stony coral yet still able to function, the advantage to the clam was obvious. If there was a benefit to the coral, I'm not sure; I suspect not. It is probably an example of a commensalistic, symbiotic relationship: a one-sided benefit with no harm to the host.

Table and stag horn coral are almost as abundant as the fish around here too. Less so are the patches of sea anemones that actually do provide a hiding place for clown fish, just like in the film 'Finding Nemo', in another form of symbiotic relationship called mutualism. They have an immunity to the sea anemones' sting by producing a protective mucus allowing them to hide from predators between the deadly swaying tentacles that might paralyse other fish. Both parties benefit from each other's presence. Receiving nutrients from the clown fishes' waste is what benefits the sea anemone and qualifies the relationship mutual.

If my body allowed, I would probably have stayed out all day but, after a couple of hours, I was in need of a rest. On the way back I knocked on the Irish girl's door to see if she could change me some cash. She wasn't able to help but we did chat about her job as a diving instructor on the island. She'd been here nine months up to now.

"Have you seen any sharks around here?" I asked.

"Oh yeah, black tipped and bamboo shark, yeah. The first time I saw one, I shit myself: it was around two metres long," she explained.

"Oh god! I'd have been the same." I added shark to my bucket list, along with turtles and monkeys, although maybe not one quite as big as me.

I decided to make the trip back to the mainland. My dwindling ringgit was a concern but also the lack of WiFi, and the fact that the local SIM card I had purchased in KL wasn't compatible, tipped the balance. With only one mast and one provider on the island, I needed the corresponding SIM for my smartphone. Without it I wasn't able to book and pay for the next leg of my journey, which was planned to be the Sabah region of Borneo, a destination I had been looking forward to visiting before leaving home. I'd presumed I could continue on from here across the South China Sea to Kota Kinbalu, the capital of Sabah, but after a little research I realised most routes use KL as the fulcrum point and this turned out to be one of them so back to KL for me.

All the tourists I'd met while here had turned around and left. Four Swedish girls went back the same day; the Argentineans went back the next day; and Prem only lasted a day too, although that's how long he had intended to stay apparently. After such an amazing day, I was just glad I'd not gone the same way.

Down at the jetty, I quizzed the boat guy about the time of the crossing the next day.

"You be here 7.45 am," he told me.

"Okay but I'm only going to get some money and coming straight back so I don't want to pay 50 ringgit," I explained.

"Okay 40."

"For both ways?" I cheekily enquired.

"No, one way."

'So two full days left,' I thought to myself. 'Kuala Besut tomorrow and then the last full day across on the big island.' On my way back to the digs, on the path where the Irish girl lived, thinking of what the big island might have in store, I found myself following two teenage boys, both wearing sarongs and fezzes, pushing a wheelbarrow each. I move to one side at the sound of a motor bike. It was an old guy riding slowly so as not to lose the wheelbarrow he was dragging behind him as a make-shift trailer. The sound of motor bikes is commonplace here, like the noise of cockerels, children playing and crickets. I'd still not got used to frogs' mating calls in the evenings though: like the sound of a rusty swing, slowly moving to and fro. The Imam's loudspeaker broadcasts aren't something you would easily forget either. Each night he starts with a gentle melodic song for around ten minutes until then the chanting begins. Initially at a slow whisper, he repeats these words, "Arr, billar, ting on la," gradually becoming louder and faster over the next few minutes.

Everything alive seems to be in abundance here, which is great when you have a snorkel mask over your face but it's a different matter at bedtime. The floor here was teeming with insects large and small. I started to resemble a used pin cushion and I thought, 'It's these little shits that are responsible: either these or bedbugs.'

The next morning, I passed the impressive, yet empty, police station opposite the start of the jetty, near to where the pancakes stall had been, and sat in the

continually busy, open-sided café forming part of the jetty. I killed time leaning on the barrier, watching needlefish skimming the surface of the crystal waters, while keeping an eye out for boats appearing over the horizon. I'd missed the first boat as I didn't wake up till 9 am, but realizing there would be others, I ordered food. After half an hour, at around 11 am, the Irish girl and her local boyfriend walked past and sat at the benches on the jetty. A few minutes later, a boat approached so I walked the 50 m down the raised concrete walkway connecting the cafe to the jetty. It wasn't a boat to the mainland, just a local guy going about his daily business, but it did give me the chance to strike up a conversation with the Irish girl and her boyfriend.

Sharp hilly peaks on the mainland were visible across the water, especially the mountainous areas to the left that continued into an opaque distant blur. Layered peaks, graduating lighter as they disappeared into the distance difsused by clouds and mist in the lowlands, reminded me of an oriental landscape painting.

The depth needed at the jetty for hull clearance of large boats intensified the colour and awe of the crystal-clear turquoise swell here. As I peered down, a huge shoal of tiny fish huddled together under a shimmering liquid lens, jostling to avoid the outer edge of a two-metre diameter living cloud, casting a continually evolving shadow against one of the concrete columns sinking to the seabed that formed part of the structure of the jetty.

"Do you know the time of the next boat to the mainland?" I inquired to the Irish girl.

"Yeah it should be around 12; we are going there too," she explained.

"That makes life a bit easier for me then. My name is Ian," offering her my hand.

"Megan," she replied, giving me a firm handshake.

I offered my hand to her boyfriend. "Ian," I smiled.

"Deathy," he replied giving me a shake. His long wavy black hair, friendly eyes, goatee beard, ripped black jeans and faded grey vest gave me the impression of a weed-smoking, guitar-playing hippy type. I managed not to react to the obvious British meaning to his name and left them to it.

Chapter 3
The Money Run

The boat to the mainland was late. The small crowd shuffled forward as he approached. I looked down as the skipper's mate threw a rope to a helpful youngster who pulled in the bow and tied off the vessel to a cleat at the bottom of the concrete steps. The boat was yellow with a light blue stripe, about six metres long with a canopy strung to a metal frame, blue PVC bench seats and a big pair of engines hanging over the rear. Although late, the two guys piloting the boat got off and headed for the café. "Tea break, Malaysian time," Megan explained as they headed off out of earshot. 15 minutes later the boat was almost full as we set off. This time I played it cool and just got on without mentioning the price like everyone else. This wasn't the same guy who I'd agreed price with the previous day so I fully expected a heated discussion when I offered him 40 ringgit but, as the boat arrived at the mainland, I spotted the woman behind me handing the skipper 20 ringgit with no change, so I followed suit.

"Terima kasih," I said politely as I passed over the cash and grabbed my bags, fully expecting a tug, but nothing.

Deathy and Megan let me follow them to where I needed to be, through the village to the bus station where the main shops were. We passed a taxi driver pulled up at the side of the road.

"Where you go?" he asked through the open window.

"The bus station," I replied.

"Okay I can take you," he continued.

Megan had already told me the ATM I needed was at the bus station a five-minute walk away. I told him; he laughed and looked away.

In these environments you can pay a big price for not being organised. Forward thinking, which is definitely not my strong point, is essential so I was quite smug that I had remembered to bring my passport:, a document required by foreigners when purchasing a SIM card in Malaysia.

Megan and Deathy pointed out the bank before heading into the bus station for the reason for their trip: a visa run to Vietnam. I walked up a flight of tiled steps, and through a pair of smoked-glass doors. Just inside the entrance, there were three ATMs in an alcove on the left, one of which was being repaired by a guy on his knees while further inside there were three rows of plastic seats fixed to the floor where you sit waiting your turn for the counter. I debated taking a ticket and a seat to change some cash but I imagined a half-hour wait just to be told they don't change money so I joined the queue for the cash machine.

While in line, I pulled the shopping list from my pocket I'd prepared earlier. Nail clippers, pens, SIM card, cash and a sharp knife for cutting pineapple, but I'd missed one important item: insect repellant. All went smoothly with the transaction and, to try and make sure I didn't end up in the same situation again, I drew out 1000 ringgit and headed for the shops. First I walked in what I thought looked like the sort of place to get me back communicating with the world.

"Do you have a SIM card?"

"No we don't have. Go to the shop past the restaurant," the shopkeeper told me pointing in the direction I had just come from.

Unlike my first experience of the town, today Kuala Besut was alive with exuberant traders, stall holders, food stuffs, sights, sounds, characters and colourful excitement. It was a market day so temporary steel-framed stalls, trolleys and a mess of organised chaos filled the back lane on the side street behind the bus station. Cooked food, fresh vegetables, fruit, fish and cold drinks, vended from stalls squeezed into the litter-lined road. A thousand tiny clamshells, trampled empty plastic drinks cups, tracks through squashed fruit, soggy paper and stodgy cardboard, from barrows and carts, covered the tarmac.

A woman, selling triangular bundles of folded green leaves stuffed with a mysterious ingredient, returned my smile. They reminded me of chewing mixtures I'd seen in Sri Lanka in the past, being sold by street vendors from trolleys in the bus station containing some sort of white anaesthetic chewing paste, with aniseed, tobacco and cinnamon. She waved one of the organic parcels in my direction so, continuing the same smile, I approached. There was a knot on the top of each package formed by wrapping the gathered-up end of the leaf around itself and back through a loop. As I untied it, I realized

59

it wasn't a leaf; it was a long thin reed that continued in one piece, wrapping around the contents to form a fat triangular pocket around two inches long. Further unravelling revealed the contents. It was a solid triangular morsel of sticky rice, quite greasy, salty and cold. I bought five for two ringgit but she gave me seven.

To combat dehydration, or just because they taste so good, Malaysian drinks sellers always seem to do well. I approached one such stall, drawn to the rainbow of colourful containers lined up in a row along the front of the stall. Now confident I had a good idea of what to expect to pay, I pointed to one of the large clear plastic cylinders containing a clear pale green drink that looked as if it had rectangular chunks of coconut floating around in it.

"This one," I requested.

"Two ringgit," said the vendor.

I handed him some cash and waited. A large metal bowl of pre-cooked string noodles with slices of boiled egg, sat on the vinyl floor-covering sales counter of the opposite stall, was begging to be bought by the foreigner who didn't want to miss any chances to experience the local culinary delights.

"How much?" I asked one of the women behind the counter.

"Two ringgit."

"Okay Terima Kasih." I handed over some cash.

They also had plastic-coated paper like the pancake seller on Perhentian Island but these guys folded it to make a cone, filled it with food, folded over the top, bound it with a rubber band, put it in a tiny carrier bag and handed it over. Noticing my interest in the food on the next stall, the drinks vendor decided to serve a local guy before me. He must have thought I'd be distracted for longer than I actually was. When I turned my attention back to him, he looked embarrassed as he handed the other guy his drink.

"Okay this one," he confirmed to me while pointing at my chosen drinks vat.

I nodded but didn't smile. First he took his ladle and stirred up the contents. I wondered what flavour the green drink was as I became temporarily mesmerized watching the morsels chasing the ladle around in circles, faster and faster, as he stirred. The new and unexpected drives my passion to travel so, when he ladled my drink into the plastic cup, the experience rather than the flavour was the most important thing. He put on the lid then slid an orange carry strap from underneath up towards the rim of the cup. It tightened at the top and had the feel of a thin plastic carrier bag. The strap incorporated a carry handle and did a great job. Surprising to think we don't have such clever little items back home. The drink turned out to be apple flavour and the coconut rectangular chunks of jelly, some brown and some white. As you sucked the straw, the chunks would follow up into your mouth, reminiscent of tapioca balls in bubble tea.

On a fish stall, two women stood opposite each other either side of a large wooden chopping board. One used a cleaver to decapitate eels while the other took the beheaded fish and ran a knife down each one's belly to gut them. A young guy saw me looking and didn't like my interest. Annoyed for some reason, he asked, "What do you want?"

"I don't know. Maybe everything," I replied with a shrug of the shoulders and moved on.

A few seconds later, a wrinkly old guy passed me at speed pushing a sack barrow overloaded with bulging hessian sacks tied up with string. He skilfully negotiated his way between a stack of wooden crates and a man bent down at a stall literally filling a carrier bag with chickpeas. The next stall boasted a mound of lychees large enough to make an elephant sick and the aroma from stalls further on with tasty looking pre-prepared food dishes gave me reason to stop and look. Whole fish coated in sauce, meat on skewers and fish kebabs.

One offering caught my eye. Chunks of glistening tandoori red, marinated food on bamboo skewers, chargrilled. "Is it fish?" I asked.

"Chicken," she replied.

"I'll take two." I pulled the first morsel off the skewer with my teeth, fat with a little meat. I spat it into the bag and tried another chunk, just the same and again a third time, until I dropped the rest of my purchase on the rubbish pile. Chicken it was not, pork maybe, but if it was most people here, being Muslim, wouldn't touch it so I never was quite sure. I get the impression some people use the word chicken as a generic term for meat around here. I spotted a tub of deep red sauce at the back of the cooked food stall that hopefully would liven up my sticky rice. "Could I buy some of this please?" pointing to the pot. The woman looked confused but after further gesticulating I got my spicy sauce in a little clear plastic bag with the opening folded over and a rubber band wrapped round to stop it spilling out, but she refused to take any money.

As I continued along towards the outer corner of the market, stepping over a smattering of discarded coriander stalks held together with rubber bands, a guy who stood over a large wok deep frying battered bananas said, "Hello!" with a broad smile. Beyond pak choi and okra hanging from the canopy of the stall nearest the corner exit, I could see the road and headed for it.

Each step further away from the market saw the noise and debris reduce. I walked back down the main street, past a couple of roadside street vendors. These premises were much more permanent: brick with corrugated tin roofs. Smoke from one stall lapped around its roof as the vendor fanned the coals of a chargrill with the aid of a hand-held weaved reed fan. He was burning coconut shells on one charcoal griddle and grilling skewers of something wrapped in leaves on the other. Two mopeds pulled up at his stall as a small herd of cows, seven in all, crossed the street unattended to graze on the verge at the other side. The same side, in fact, that a barefoot guy in scruffy jeans and ripped T-shirt, with a net on a long pole, picked off mangos one by one from a tree in the corner of the car park, the same car park I'd walked through with my new friends earlier. I stopped to watch with intrigue as he positioned his net over each fruit he found, usually hidden behind leaves, and using the rim of the net yanked down to detach each one. This skinny fella, after ten minutes harvesting, jumped onto his moped with a cleaver tucked in the back of his trousers and rode off with a carrier bag full of fruit between his legs and his dark, curly, matted locks flapping behind his ears.

I spotted many pigeons in Besut but the bird calls I could hear from the top floor of a three-storey building in the centre of town were no pigeon calls. Although constantly looking out for the source of the increasing noise as I approached, the only thing to come out of the rows of open windows was an incredible din from what sounded like a stadium full of screaming starlings. It wasn't till back home in England watching TV, purely by chance, I got to the bottom of the mystery.

Swiftlets make their nests from their own saliva, which traditionally has been harvested from caves in and around Asia to provide the main ingredient in the culinary delicacy: bird's nest soup. The dried saliva is said to have a texture of honeycomb and should be as stinky as possible. As demand has outweighed supply over recent years, loft farms started to spring up to cash in on the lucrative commodity. Amplifiers connected to large speakers blast out the relevant calls from the areas they want the birds to populate. If successful, farmers can earn a $1000 a kilo, while the original cave nests fetch up to three times that amount.

If it hadn't been for the guy with the net, I would never have noticed the mango trees in the car park but further on was a tree you would need to be blind to miss. At first glance, it looked like a sausage tree, which are as strange as the name suggests, especially the first time you see one, but when I took a closer look, it was something quite different. Its weird 40 cm dangling vegetation looked more like gigantic runner beans than super-sized bratwursts. Like something out of a fairy tale film, imagine a tree the size of a house where cricket bat-sized black peapods swing from the branches. I presume the pods were non-edible or the mango guy might have been in on the act.

Having procured all the items on my list thanks mainly to the two-floor department store, I hopped back on the boat. It was a different craft and a different skipper to the outbound journey. Most of the footwell floor space was taken up by recycled 25 litre, fuel-stained, translucent, plastic drums. Each lid was screwed down onto a plastic bag, presumably to make a good seal and stop the contents of what looked like diesel from leaking. I sat at the back near the skipper, facing forward, opposite the only other two passengers. There was a strong wind and the sea was choppy so we set off at a steady pace; still though the spray came up much more than previous trips. I got my clear plastic rain poncho from the side pocket of my bag and attempted to put it on while it blew around like a flag in a storm. After a couple of embarrassing minutes that felt more like five, attempting to locate an orifice to push my head through, it took a further minute to realise I was trying to fit my head through one of the sleeves. The two guys sat opposite kindly pretended not to notice my struggle as they became gradually drenched. The fatter of the two men kept wiping off the spray from his brown leather satchel each time it started to drip with water. Three quarters of the way there, the sea calmed but a heavy shower was coming in towards us. I held the poncho down over my knees with one hand while clutching the hood with the other as the skipper attempted to beat the rain to the jetty. He gave it all he got and almost avoided a proper soaking, if only for a two-minute jet wash at the end of the journey. Once again, I said thanks and handed the guy 20 ringgit with no disagreement.

With just enough daylight left for a bit of a walk after I returned to my digs to dry off, I set back off to the beach complete with camera stashed in a carrier bag to assist me in avoiding any issues involving little thieving bastards. Although much smaller, the beach immediately after the fishermen's moorings blinded Long Beach for its beauty. Unlike the other side of the island, debris didn't naturally wash up here so it was immaculately clean. Warm, golden, sandy grains tickled between my toes, soft and satisfying under foot, as I walked along the gradual convex curve of the snaking shoreline. Black Jurassic boulders, some too big to climb, divided sweeping palms from the dusty, caramel, powder terrain and intermittent yet perpetual white surf kept disappearing before my eyes.

This time I continued further around the coast, following another of the block-paved paths up and over connecting this to another beach. As I dropped down, an intriguing scene emerged between the trees. In the foreground a dog laid sleeping curled up on a rock, while behind a stunning and seemingly deserted sandy cove with a handful of wooden cabins dotted around the fringe faced the sea. Steep forest-covered hills towered down from above, disrupted only by the occasional chalet-sized stone sphere poking through the canopy, wedged in seemingly precariously yet timeless, balancing on their smaller counterparts. I spotted a further path up through the mangroves so I set off for a quick look.

A tall, skinny, roguish-looking local guy in his mid-thirties was chilling in a hammock 20 metres up the hill outside a cabin set back from the beach. I couldn't see him from where I was before but, as I approached, I said, "Hi."

"Hello," he replied as he lifted his head.

"How much are your rooms?" I inquired presuming they were his to let.

"50 ringgit."

"Oh! I'm paying 40 in the village for a good room. How about I give you 30?" I suggested.

Now up on his feet, he said, "35, you can have this one," making his way back down the path. He opened the flimsy wooden door of the room and showed me inside the cabin. It was in perfect location but very sparse, probably more so than Rock Garden and probably less able of keeping out the next torrential downpour, let alone the next burglar. Then there was the issue of transporting my luggage, which would probably involve a water taxi. Not wanting to upset the guy, I agreed to move over in a couple of days after my four-day block-booking at the blue house was over. After such an epic lie, I just wanted to get out there and set off back to the village having missed my chance to investigate where the latest path led to.

Within a couple of days, I felt almost completely settled. My recent worries were over; all that remained were minor concerns about the bugs in my room. After a dinner of Tom Yam seafood down at the promenade, I headed back the 300 metres to my house on the hill to sit on my veranda and reflect on the day. From here, assisted by a warm moonlight glow, I could clearly make out the concrete jetty across on the big island and a number of chalet complexes along the coast either side of it where I would be tomorrow on a full day adventure hike. After a few minutes thinking through a plan of action for the day ahead, surrounded by constant nocturnal calls emanating from the darkness, I joined my unwanted bed fellows.

Eyes closed and relaxed, laid in the darkness, the silence was broken by a rustling down on the floor next to the bed. I jumped up and turn on the light but all was silent again as I looked down from my vantage point, knelt up on the mattress. The noise could have come from a plastic carrier bag littering the floor but the mystery continued until seconds later when both me and the carrier bag moved with a jolt. Uncharacteristically, yet genuinely spooked, I grabbed my heavy notepad from the bedside cabinet and slammed it down onto the bag. The force of the draft threw out an object onto the floor. The gigantic spider from the previous night was back, yet still unharmed after my second attack in as many days; but now it was vulnerable, out in the open, on the retreat, sprinting for the gap under the bed. 'Maybe it was this snail-sized arachnid that was responsible for my polka dot complexion,' I thought to myself. More likely the ants but, even so, I didn't fancy sharing my room with anything big enough to be able to force open my eyelids and make me watch as he sucked out my cornea. I trapped him up against the side of the bed with the side of my notepad. The plastic hardcover chopped off half his legs and he dropped to the floor, frantically racing around in circles on the spot, no longer able to magically disappear before my eyes. Before allowing it the chance to work out how to escape, I finished it off, squashing it like the cockerel and the cat pancake I saw squashed to the road earlier at Besut. Panic over, I turned out the light.

I woke up early the next morning to find I'd been a buffet again. My elbows, triceps, feet, toes, lower back and legs all showed the same symptoms of itchy redness and swelling. Tea tree oil top to toe and a smouldering mosquito coil hadn't helped; neither had the fact I'd been to the mainland with a shopping list and forgotten to add insect repellent to it. The key was not to scratch but that was almost as difficult as getting used to throwing used toilet tissue in the bin when taking a dump.

I peered over the bed down at last night's crime scene. The spider legs were gone. What was left of his body was still stuck to the floor but the four amputated legs, that were clearly visible at the time of the attack, were nowhere to be seen. I wondered if I'd had another senior moment and cleaned them up without remembering. 'Maybe I did,' I thought to myself. I'd walked off twice from two different places without paying for drinks I'd ordered while on the island, having genuinely forgotten to pay. Luckily, neither time did anyone say anything to me: I remembered and went back to pay after a few minutes before they noticed. The squished spider torso was surrounded by tiny ants. Logical thinking always helps when, like me, you have a sieve for a brain. I realised it must have been the micro legion of insects to blame for the missing legs as I would surely have not done half a job clearing the spider's remains away.

Continuing from last night, giving careful thought what to take to the big island, I placed my smartphone, debit card, all my cash and the room key in my money belt and put it, along with a bottle of water and my travel companion, in a carrier bag. A khaki brown knitted monkey, made famous by TV adverts for PG Tips, a well-known brand of British tea, was the travel companion I referred to. He's a 15 cm, pot-bellied primate who's accompanied me to many places in the past. This little simian globe trotter has been spotted in the French Alps, skiing in Chamonix-Mont-Blanc; he even took a trip up the world's tallest building, the Burj Khalifa in the UAE, and has been off his tits at numerous British music festivals, most recently 'Boomtown', but more of that another time.

I headed down to the quayside café, bought a coffee and sat down. Three local guys were sat at the table nearby. I walked over and asked, "Do you know where I can get a taxi to the big island?" They all looked around while still sat in their seats. One pointed out a guy, Coke-can fishing off the jetty path. He was a small young man, around 25 years old, with a baseball cap and camouflage T-shirt. I walked over, stood by his side and watched as he pulled his bait through the water. A shoal of small black and white striped fish would chase the bait each time he cast in.

"See that one?" he asked while pointing down to a larger, white fish lurking behind one of the concrete columns.

"Yeah, I need a taxi to the big island," I explained. After a couple more attempts to lure the big fish out, he pulled the tiny sprat off the hook and threw it in the water. The stripy shoal now swarmed the food, instantly aware it was no longer bait. His hook was much bigger than I had expected it to be.

As he baited up once more, he spoke while continuing to stare down at the water. "It is five to go across but if you are only one then it is ten." He threw his line back in.

"Okay, I might wait to see if anyone else turns up," I explained. I set off back to the café but, within the distance of a few metres, realised I was being silly: like the time I told a crack dealer called Fox I would smuggle drugs for him from Jamaica. I turned around and walked back. It was the difference between £1 or £2. "Okay let's go," I proclaimed but he wasn't about to jump into action. I could tell he really wanted this fish so I waited a couple of minutes.

After a quick phone call, he told me, "My friend is coming," and, true to his word, after a couple of minutes, another guy turned up with a boat to the bottom of the jetty steps.

I climbed aboard. He made his way around the jetty and pulled in at the steps around the other side, literally just around the corner. A family with two young children, one around three and a baby in arms, came aboard. There had been a large police boat moored up across at the big island jetty for a couple of days but it had now moved on. I got the feeling they moved around showing a presence, staying over at different destinations around the area. I bet they have everything they need on board, like a home from home with prison cells.

There was another craft moored just off the coast of the big island: a large opulent yacht. Unbeknown to me, that's where we were heading. We pulled up alongside the impressive craft and the family got off. Before long we were off on our way, the last 300 metres my stop. This time, rather than pull up at the jetty, the young man ran the boat straight onto the beach. I got up and handed him five ringgit.

"How much is this?" he asked.

"Five," I replied. He just kept staring at the money in his hand saying nothing. His lack of communication was beginning to unnerve me so I said, "The guy said five ringgit if I went with the other people, or 10 ringgit if I went alone. OK?" Still he didn't respond. "OK?" I repeated, still to no response, so I got off.

Apart from the remnants of a bonfire, the beach looked just as much like the tropical paradise I had expected. I decided to walk up towards what I now know to be Shark Point. A decent-sized monitor lizard, large enough to give at least four cats a good fight, scurried off into the cover of the bushes at the back of the beach as I passed by. I was heading towards yet more ubiquitous giant prehistoric looking boulders randomly piled on top of each other of varying sizes, forming a pinnacle on the coastline, marking the end of the relatively straight beach and the start of a sweeping cove of even more outstanding natural beauty behind it. More gigantic stones, all either oval or round in shape except one, formed a second headland in the distance at the far end of the bay. However, one rock in this grouping, the furthest from land and the last thing before open water, was a strikingly different shape: one of a kind. It looked remarkably like the iconic image of a shark's dorsal fin breaking the water. Until now I presumed the name of this area derived from the amount of shark activity in these waters but it was now pretty obvious that wasn't the reason.

Today the weather was being kind, very kind. The sun's reflection glistened off the ripples off the coast, like candles at a rock concert. I felt the heat on my back radiating from a rock as I sat against it, sunbathing for a while before preparing to venture out into the bay for a bit of fish spotting. I needed to stash my money belt so I climbed up through, back down and under the boulders to find a decent hiding spot. You'll not be surprised to hear yet another lizard didn't want to make friends and ran off at the sight of a tattooed human clambering around amongst the honeycomb of rocks. I wedged my belt in the crevice between two boulders, well above the waterline and climbed back out into the baking sun.

The bay didn't look so shallow from dry land but once in the water it took some effort not to touch the coral with my fins on my way out to deeper water. A few metres out at a more comfortable depth, I pressed record on my GoPro and surveyed the area, slowly gliding up and down through the warm, slightly cloudy water. Everywhere I looked there was coral, unlike clownfish who needed a little effort to spot hiding in the undergrowth.

Just as I was deciding parrotfish were becoming as common as the birds with the same name, my gut wrenched and my eyes widened. Sliding in effortlessly from the distant hue: a shark! A real live bloody shark, around a metre long. After bobbing my pants for a brief, awe-inspired moment, a euphoric tingle passed through me as our eyes met. Quickly, I made a determined attempt to etch the outline of this adolescent killing machine's sleek contours to my mind, as that brief moment we found ourslelves two metres apart was washed away by time's relentless current. With an extended curve, its tail fin tapered back gradually upwards to a sharp point. Dark stone-cold eyes set into its long face and trademark dorsal fin poised to break the surface would leave no one wondering what its parents were capable of. It jolted its sleek grey head to the right and disappeared into the murky distance with a swish of the tail.

The encounter was over in a flash but hopefully I had caught the experience on film. The camera should have been on but I couldn't be sure as it was difficult to make out the tiny red recording light down here. As I re-lived the encounter in my mind, straight ahead was a turtle too. Based on the only other one I'd ever seen previously while on holiday in Mexico, close to the spot I proposed to my fiancée Kay 12 years ago, this was a toddler measuring around 40 cm in diameter. I attempted to retrieve the camera from my pocket again while I could still make out its lush, green, immature shell and wrinked neck. It held its position with a vigilant eye for a short while but, then suspecting I was up to something more sinister, it too put distance between us, quickly disappearing back into the fog.

Unbelievably, after hours bobbing around over the last few days in different locations with no signs of any of my bucket list creatures, two of them were ticked off in as many minutes. Anxiously peering into a foggy unknown, spooked by the first sighting, I considered the apposing emotions of the last few moments. The very real, shocking excitement and momentary fear of a close encounter with a shark had somehow enhanced the tranquillity of a fleeting glimpse of a young turtle crossing my path. Maybe there is some truth in people's suggestions that you cannot fully appreciate pleasure without the experience of pain.

Back on dry land, after collecting my valuables, I continued as far as the rocks at the far end of Shark Point would allow, cutting me off from the mainland as they drifted off out to sea and, with no sign of a block paved path up through the mangrove, I headed back the way I came.

Around half-way back along the straight beach from the point where the taxi boat dropped me was a concrete structure: a 20-metre stilted walkway with bulbous ornate spindles and chunky hand rails running parallel to the shore and with steps either end, providing access over and across a patch of boulders near the top of the beach. Over time, creeping vines had been allowed to weave their way around it. Now, almost hidden, partially enveloped by the jungle, all it needed was Harrison Ford cracking his whip to complete the scene. I'd dismissed it the first time, drawn to the dramatic rock formation up ahead, but this time I squeezed my way through the undergrowth and climbed the concrete steps. 'Probably here to provide easy access across the beach at high tide,' I thought to myself. Turning my thoughts to Tomb Raider, I imagined slashing a path through the undergrowth, machete in hand.

As I reached the top of the steps, there was a quick swish of leaves concentrated to one area in the trees above my head, followed by an animal call of some sort. 'Surely it has to be monkeys,' I thought excitedly. I reached for my phone, still surveying the canopy. "Oh yeeaaah," I said out loud in an American accent as a partially-hidden, brown, furry shadow crossed the canopy into the open. It was a male, probably not the Alpha but a decent size. He stopped at an opening in the leaves close by, sitting and staring while others in the troop broke cover and began to move in from the fringe. Five or six began to move inland. With a steady, considered gait, a mother sauntered over into the open and sat unfazed on a sturdy horizontal bough looking down, followed close behind by her infant. Then another male galloped in my direction. He continued overhead, passing over me while urinating. In this seemingly deliberate act, primate piss rained down onto the path close by, narrowly missing its target: if I was the target, that is. Still perched up on the branch above, the female joined in the dirty protest while her infant, clinging around her waist, watched on. Piss ran around the branch, dripping rather than splashing onto the concrete path, luckily for me not close enough to have the desired effect. The troop moved on through the canopy, up the hill inland. 'Purposefully pissing on tourists?' I considered, moving on myself back past the taxi drop-off point. 'I wonder if the Macaque finds the idea of squealing holiday-makers running away from their warm pissy showers as hilarious as I do.'

Past a couple of beach-front chalet complexes, a monolithic boulder blocked the beach. With no path around the obstacle and steep jungle hills blocking an inland route, my adventure seemed over. Up to this point while on the big island, I'd not come across any human activity, other than an odd couple of boats speeding through the channel between the two islands. With no help at hand, I decided to attempt to wade through the sea. It looked quite deep but this seemed the only chance I had to survey the rest of the island of Besar. Mainly made up of properties for the benefit of tourists, Besar proved much more difficult to get around than the little island, Kecil. The limited amenities offered by the locals in the village back on Kecil now didn't seem so limited. There was another thing I eagerly sought here. I'd seen a map showing a coast-to-coast path up through the jungle over to the far side of the island. Desperate to explore this route, I wasn't going let a bit of water hold me back.

I placed my keep-dry items in the carrier bag and set off wading, arms aloft. Reaching the other side of the boulder turned out to be much less of a struggle than I'd imagined it to be. Waist deep, with the occasional slosh under the armpits, wasn't much of a risk to life under today's conditions.

I was approaching the far end of the west coast, as the sun persisted in reappearing from behind the odd stray cloud. I ignored my aching legs and pushed on around the coast, towards the last place on this beach. A local man sat under an umbrella at one of a number of tables in front of a clutch of ramshackle buildings. Cheesy Euro trash pop music was emanating from a large speaker, peeking out from under a partially open roller shutter in the doorway of a converted wooden workshop. Without the odd advertising sign for ice cream and beer, the place would have looked more like the workers' yard it probably used to be. A scruffy retaining wall of sandbags along the beach front didn't help, nor the poorly constructed outdoor kitchen.

"We have beer," he informed me as I approached. It had been a week since I last had a beer and, as much as I convinced myself I wasn't going to drink for the rest of the trip, I continued along for around five metres before turning around. "Come, come, have a look," he said, while attempting to lift the shutter beyond halfway. Unable to slide up the door along its runners, he gestured to me to climb under, "Please, please."

Inside another guy sat behind the counter of his jungle shop, eyes fixed to his smartphone. There was a clear glass-fronted display fridge straight ahead with a small selection of beers. I chose a large Heineken at 15 ringgit, which was a complete rip-off especially as it was, at best, only moderately cold. I took it outside and, after a couple of minutes with the weight off my feet outside under an umbrella, the guy brought out a mug.

"For you," he explained, placing it down in front of me. It was ice.

"Thank you," I dropped some in my beer but within two minutes, the heat of the midday sun had melted it, diluting the brew. I drank it quickly, after adding further ice, to avoid watering it down any further. Needless to say it wasn't the best.

I was nearing the peninsula on the north-west of the island that I'd seen from the village previously but learning what lay beyond was my motivation to move on, as I said goodbye to the grotty bar with its shabby, broken, upturned boats and discarded frayed rope. Around the corner was another chalet complex. It felt slightly wrong, as if I was trespassing, as I walked along one of the paths between the wooden semi-detached cabins, three deep in places. This was by far the biggest complex I had come across so far on Besar, even bigger maybe than Rock Garden across on Kecil: well-established with a large central reception, restaurant and its own dedicated jetty. 'This place must be a gold mine in season,' I thought to myself. The geography of the landscape set this place apart. Here there was a much greater width of relatively flat land between the coast and the forest hills behind: the ideal spot to look out over the pristine waters, I suppose.

Painting the fence around of one of the chalets, a Bangladeshi-looking guy did a double take in surprise as he saw me approach. "Hi," I said with a smile, as I made my way past, still half expecting to be asked to leave. Through the chalets, I could see the beach coming to an abrupt end once again but this time it was much more dramatic. I walked as far as I was able along the beach in the hope I would see a way through but still there was nothing but deep water against a steep rocky shoreline up front, with a further pinnacle hiding the more distant coast a few hundred metres ahead. Wading was not going to suffice this time, made clear by the swell against the rocks. I'd got a difficult and potentially dangerous decision to make. Should I turn around, go back and enjoy the memory of the day I came across a turtle, a shark and pissing monkeys, all within ten minutes of each other at an amazing location with amazing weather? Or should I attempt to find a way through the turbulent swell to see what else this momentous day had in store, hopefully not involving the parents of the shark I'd met earlier?

Not sure if I might be spotted stashing my gear, I decided to wade out a little until hidden from sight of the chalets. I intended to stash my gear then attempt a swim along the coast. As I paddled deeper, the seabed was rocky and uneven. It proved too painful walking bare foot so I turned back and reassessed my options. "OK, put your flip flops on, Ian," I told myself.

Hindered by the constant ebb and flow, I tried again, edging along slowly over the rough terrain, arms aloft. Eventually, out of view of the chalets, I found a suitable spot and climbed up the crevice between two large stones. Finding the stash on my return required one of the attributes I was often woefully lacking – forward planning, that is – so choosing a monolithic rock as a marker was uncharacteristic of me. The second worst thing that could happen today, apart from being eaten by a shark, would be to lose my stash. Even having just half my leg bitten off while out at sea might seem preferable at the minute, until I realised I would eventually get back home after losing all my money, bank cards and passport and still be able to walk.

Up on the rocks, I tucked my money belt along with my mobile phone out of sight and climbed back down into the swell. After a short distance, I turned and purposefully studied the area before moving on, making a determined effort to etch the location on my brain, and then using my flip-flops as hand paddles, I made my way up the coast. Perpetually lifting then dropping, the sea revealed intermittent submerged boulders. I kept as close to the coast as it would allow, taking a wide berth around the rocky obstacles. Using the swell as a gauge, the sea seemed deeper than I had expected. I was swimming against the current, at times making no headway whatsoever, squally waves sloshing me back and forth. Caution was now required.

Long distances always look closer from afar. The realisation in this instance began to make me slightly anxious as I looked behind me. Much smaller than a few minutes ago, the big rock was still visible, but a long way back, yet my destination seemed to be moving in the same direction as me. Now, with no real sense of depth, other than a gauge off an increasing swell against the rocks, flailing my feet in the murky vastness felt as vunerable as a mouse in a snake pit. Without the flip-flops and fins I might not have found myself in such a foolishly compromising position. They proved to be really efficient.

'This might be a good way to fake my death,' I thought to myself as I pressed ahead with nothing better to occupy my mind. 'But how would I make my escape without the locals noticing?' I fantasised about leaving my belongings on the beach, taking a boat and disappearing with the insurance money but the truth is that even if I had wanted to, which I didn't, it would never have worked. The constraints of a close-knit island population and limited access made for a poor plan. Such whimsical thoughts about a hypothetical scenario might give you an insight into the sort of person I am but also it made me realise I was out there all alone, having not informed anyone of my adventure, for much longer than I realised. When something occupies your mind enough to make you lose track of time, it's easy to imagine half an hour to be ten minutes and I suspect that was the case in this instance. After a best guess of 30 minutes, I reached the point where I'd been hoping to see another beach, but it wasn't to be. Around the point, my heart sank as more of the same barren terrain stretched out further into the distance. This time the only sensible choice was to turn around and head back.

Although there was no sign of it, a quick turn for the worse in the weather conditions could easily turn out to be life threatening. Realising my vulnerability, I gave in and turned around. I looked ahead, knowing the furthest point I could see was only half the way back. I told myself, 'This is good exercise,' stretching out and widening my stroke. It's times like this it's best not to think about things: like when Ali, the guy from the hotel, saw a couple of long scratches on my leg, caused by walking through thorny creepers on the path. "Ooooh! Jellyfish?" he enquired as I got out of the sea after snorkelling.

I expected the swim to be more tiring by now, given the effort I was exerting. Adrenalin must have played its part. As I continued, my thoughts drifted off once more. Memories of little sharks, turtles and monkey piss helped to take my mind off the marathon return leg. Unharmed yet slightly bewildered, I eventually reached my stash. As I made my way back towards the chalet complex, the Bangladeshi guy was still painting the chalet fence. By the amount of times he looked up as I approached, he wasn't expecting to see someone like me around at this time of year.

"Hi, do you know where the path is to the other side of the island?" I asked as I got close. He didn't understand and pointed further in to the complex. I followed his instructions to a group of people around the corner. Three more maintenance guys and one girl were stood talking. I repeated the question.

"Okay" said the girl. "The jungle trek?"

"Yes," I replied. Surely that was it and if not it had to be worth a look.

"It is the rainy season," she kindly informed me. "We don't recommend you go because of rain and you should wear shoe okay?"

"Oh! Okay that's fine. Thank you," I said, not wanting to upset the girl, but I wasn't finished yet. I continued along the concrete path towards a large building in the centre of the complex where an older guy was stood in a doorway. I greeted him with, "Hello!" He smiled and returned my pleasantry. At that moment I noticed a monkey sat on the path three metres in front of me. I fumbled around for my phone to take a snap from the steps of a communal building that could have been a restaurant.

As I did, the old guy warned me, "Watch out, monkey!" I looked around. The guy was pointing up to the single-storey shallow-pitched, corrugated tin roof where around another ten of the troop were sitting together, one of which was almost directly above my head on the guttering a metre above me. I moved back, under the canopy.

"Is it pissing?" I asked, while gesturing with my hands in front of my crotch, pretending to do a wee.

"Mmmm," he replied, nodding in agreement.

'I knew it!' I thought to myself. 'Dirty little bastards!' "Do you know where the jungle trek is?" I continued.

"Yes. Behind the entertainment, down the path," he replied.

By now the monkey down on the floor had walked across to a palm tree at the corner of the building and climbed up to join the others on the roof. I tried to get photos but the sun was too bright in the background. The troop moved on and so did I, heading towards the so-called entertainment; what he meant by that I don't know because all that was behind was yet more chalets. I followed the path around behind the back of the chalets until I found a little sign next to the gate in a green chain-link fence: 'jungle trek' it announced.

I didn't like the idea of carrying my snorkelling gear on the jungle track so I doubled back to the closest chalet and tried the door. It was unlocked. I went in and had a little nosey around. The bed had been lifted and put on its side, otherwise it was empty. There was an en-suite so I stashed my fins and the rest of the gear I didn't need behind the toilet and set off back to the trail, double checking behind me that no one had seen me coming out of the chalet.

All was quiet as I made my way through the gate into the jungle. The path started on a gradual uphill gradient, tree roots providing natural steps. The only sign of the path's direction at some points was the sand that had been laid down. As it wound its way up the hill, the gradient increased. A rope tied from tree to tree as a handrail was provided to aid your ascent for a few metres. I grabbed the rope and pulled myself over a couple of slippery boulders.

Large exposed roots and overhanging branches all added to the challenge now, but the worst thing had to be the spider webs. Although beautiful in the morning dew, each one a little marvel of engineering, you'd be lucky to travel two metres without demolishing one with your face as you negotiated the path. Unlike at home where a quick swipe of the hand obliterates all those hours of delicate work, webs around these parts are made of tougher stuff, like northern men. Their industrial-strength silk tickles the back of your ears and neck as they eventually give way under the pressure of a human's head ploughing through it. I decided to use a stick rather than my face to remove the little annoying traps, and the constant irritation they caused. A swiping motion not dissimilar to the action of chopping a path through undergrowth with a machete helped but didn't quite get rid of them all, so I altered my technique. By waving the stick round in circles in front as I walked, like some weird Harry Potter spell-making weirdo, I pretty much eradicated the problem.

As the path began to descend, to the left and partially hidden by the undergrowth was a murky vivid green pond, almost luminous. You wouldn't want to swim in it, unlike the basking prune-skinned reptile I disturbed while approaching. It's not too hard to spot a lizard when it throws itself into a pool of water like its life depends on it. Much better at swimming than diving, it was across and gone, into the undergrowth almost quicker than the displaced water took to come back down to earth. Once over the next hump, I noticed a major obstruction further along the track as it headed downhill once more. A huge tree lay across the path. It had uprooted and fallen from the hill that sloped left to right, coming to rest at right angles across the path. Although not all was visible, what I could see of its length was enormous. Had it not come to rest at waist height, passing the obstacle wouldn't have been such a task. Its trunk, of around half a metre in diameter was perfectly straight and true, even the gaps between the bark were regular and uniform. You'd think it was a fibreglass prop from a photo but far from it. This lump was real all right and the only thing shifting this monster log would be a chainsaw or a herd of elephants. I ducked under, through the undergrowth, after taking a photo of a monkey sat straggling the fallen giant, with its trunk tapering off behind him into the distance.

My kids, Bailey and Isabella, love the concept of Monkey keeping in touch with them while accompanying me on my adventures. I had not seen them for a couple of weeks, only managing the one chat on the phone up to now, in the airport at KL while waiting to fly to Kota Bahru. Every other time I had attempted to call, it had dropped out. Monkey's messages and photos provided an important link. Sat on the edge of the speed boat waiting to travel to the island, on the beach on driftwood next to giant shells or here in the jungle sat on the giant log, Monkey always kept in touch.

At the bottom of the hill, the track met a river but, rather than crossing over, it followed its meandering bank. The flow navigated its way around rocks near the far side of the water, probably broken shards from the king of all jungle boulders shadowing them from behind. More like a cliff than a boulder, smeared black markings dripped like melted candle wax, etched by the effects of time, petered off towards its base. Holding its own metre for metre up in the canopy, standing firm as a gentle-giant reminder of prehistoric days gone by. The trees thinned as I continued along a flat section of ground, giving way to more bushes and shrubs. The track turned into an ankle-deep stream as I began to put distance between me and the jungle hills. A steadily flowing water course now led the way.

Signs we were getting closer to civilisation started to come to light. A chain-link fence to the right stood partially detached from its posts, too old to do the job it was originally put there to do. It had the feeling of an area restricted by the authorities such as a sewage plant or a reservoir, but I could only guess as long grass was all I could see on the other side. I wondered how I would remove a leech if it attached itself to my foot while wading through the stream. 'Apparently you can burn them off. Do I have a lighter?' I thought to myself.

My wandering mind quickly returned on hearing voices up ahead. A large compound came into view on the left where two men were shovelling gravel into wheelbarrows from a large pile in the yard. Bushes growing along the route, either side of what was a definite stream rather than a path, blocked the way at some points. A machete would have been my tool of choice at this moment in time, if I had a choice. Pressing on, I saw one of the guys pushing the wheelbarrow through the yard. I tried not to let him see me as I passed as I couldn't be absolutely sure I was on the right track. The possibility I might have drifted off the path did cross my mind as walking along a stream did seem a little odd.

I didn't hear anything further from the guys as I crept forward, literally going with the flow, until a row of buildings appeared up ahead. It turned out to be beach-front tourist accommodation. I walked between a clutch of dark teak chalets on stilts, onto the beach and found myself at a large cove around 500 metres long looking out to an infinite ocean with a small wooden jetty and boulders again, peppering the distant headland in both directions. Patches of chalets of differing construction methods lined the beach. I looked round at the sound of a child's voice in the distance and noticed a couple of hammocks hanging under one of the trees on the fringe of the beach.

I walked the length of the beach. First to the closest, left-hand side, then back past the signs of life to the far end. I strolled up the shallows paddling my way through the gently lapping waves, thinking of the money the boat owners must make in the height of the season. Not even I would be foolish enough to attempt to carry my luggage along the jungle path. The only alternative to get here could only be by boat and this beach was about as far from the village you could get. Reliance on a boat for transport would give the locals a strong hand when negotiating fairs. Plenty of holiday accommodation means plenty of tourists and plenty of tourists means plenty of money. By now I was alongside the hammocks.

I looked up and said, "Hello." A group of locals were relaxing in the shade.

"Taxi? Water taxi?" a woman shouted from under the tree.

"No thanks," I replied waving my hand up in the air with a dismissive shake.

I could see there was nothing else of interest as I neared the end of the beach but I continued to the absolute end. Why I did that I don't know. Maybe just to say in my mind that I had completed what I started. Conscious the locals would be watching me, I stood looking out to sea at the end of the beach rather than turning straight around. It didn't quite seem so pointless that way. I felt a little bit daft turning around and retracing my steps while being watched but my mind soon moved on to other things, like where to go on next on my Asian adventure.

Bali was an option since bumping into an American woman drinking Chai outside a roadside café in Brickfields. She was a writer who'd fallen in love with the place while on holiday and now lives there full time. Not forgetting the main reason for being here, to visit Borneo, I came to Perhentian by chance while researching areas of interest in Malaysia's other province, the one separated by the ocean: the northern half of an island mainly made up of Borneo where unspoilt beaches and Orang-utan can be found. If you threw Thailand, Vietnam, Philippines and Indonesia into the mix, I was left with the nicest of dilemmas.

Reaching the jetty, I walked along the uneven wooden slats out over the water to the end, where one of those boats used to ferry people to the mainland was moored up. This vessel had only one engine though. As in other beach locations around the island, areas of the sea had been cordoned off by means of ropes threaded through floating buoys to separate boats from people swimming and snorkelling.

I couldn't believe I didn't feel hungry, since all I'd had since waking up was a cup of coffee. It must have been 3 pm now and not even the slightest rumble of the tummy. My water consumption, as you might expect, was a different kettle of fish. I brought a litre bottle with me from the digs and it was now almost gone. 'Time to make tracks,' I thought. I didn't bother walking to the absolute end of the opposite beach this time; instead, I took the path back to grab my stash, past a couple of lizards fighting in the bushes behind the chalets. 'I hope monkeys can't open doors,' I thought, as I waded back up the stream. This time I found a branch with others still attached to clear a web-free return path, twirling as I walked. I imagined turning up back at the other side holding something resembling a giant candy floss. The return journey didn't pose the same levels of web browsing as in the outbound journey: in fact, it went without incident. With no drama to recall, apart from the odd uphill slip, eventually I was back through the gate.

My snorkelling gear was stashed in cabin 32. The chance the door might have been locked since I had left earlier was a niggling thought. 'I'll ask the nice old guy to open it for me. He will understand,' I thought as I approached. I tried the door; it opened. My aching feet reminded me of the long day it had been so far as I made it back to the jetty with daylight to spare.

I laid face down on the hot concrete, watching crabs over the edge on the stanchions at the waterline. I'd not noticed my eyelids closing, until I woke to see them still picking at the barnacle encrusted structure. A rally of blinks allowed me the time to watch them feed claw to mouth, for a few interesting moments. Alternating left then right, rhythmically, like a slow-motion marching band drummer. I looked towards the noise of each boat's outboard motor skirting the coast of the little island every few minutes, following it with my eyes in hope it was coming my way, but none of them did.

The only sign of life here was two locals burning prunings on the beach nearby as I arrived, but now one of the guys had disappeared in a boat. Increasingly conscious that darkness would render my attempts to flag down a ride almost impossible, I walked over to the guy that was left.

"Hi, I need to get across to the village," I explained.

"How did you get here?" he quizzed.

"I got a water taxi this morning."

"Why no phone number?" he asked.

"I didn't realise I would need to get their number. I don't have the number," I explained.

The other guy returned with the boat mid-conversation. He stopped just off the shore and seemed to be cleaning the inside. The guy on the beach shouted over to him and they talked in Malaysian, shouting back-and-forth over the water.

81

"He can take you," he said. "It will be 10 ringgit."

"But I only paid five to get here," I reported.

"Yes but it is late. It is more when it is late," he explained. There seems to be a selection of reasons to find to rip-off tourists, but I was happy to pay the extra quid given the situation I found myself in.

Conscious of being bitten again in the night, I slept on the top bunk of the room opposite. My bites had become more than just an irritation and, no matter how much tea tree oil I lathered on, it didn't seem to make any difference. I was swinging towards the ants being the culprits as I had never been bitten anywhere near as much in other situations while in the company of mozzies. The truth is I will never know for sure but sleeping in the bunk next door turned out to be a good move, as I woke up at around seven 7:30 am, to find no more damage had been inflicted. I had a quick shower, packed my stuff and headed out for one last circuit around the village, camera in hand before the noon boat to the mainland.

My bus left Kuala Besut at 8:30 pm and, as 12 pm was the time of the last boat of the day to the mainland, I was in for a long wait. I took one last look at the far end of town where the path to Long Beach began to see if there were any further reptile scraps. This time no fighting lizards but a group of people gathered around a wheel-barrow caught my attention.

As I walked up, an old guy shouted to me. "Fish?" he asked.

I drew in for a closer look, telling him, "No thank you."

The wheelbarrow was half full of fish of numerous species, including one I recognised: parrotfish. It looked too colourful to be considered food in my eyes, like eating something out of a tropical fish tank.

"Can I take a photo?" I asked the old guy whose wheel-barrow it was, holding up my camera in his direction to make sure he understood what I was saying.

"No, no photos," he insisted, as one of the fish gave a burst of energy, flapping up into the air in a last-ditch attempt to escape its capturers. How fish can survive after being drawn from the sea, into a boat, brought back to land, put in a wheelbarrow and fetched to this spot is quite remarkable.

I remembered Megan telling me how nice parrotfish tasted when I described one to her that I'd spotted snorkelling. I'm pretty sure given more time on the island I would've been negotiating a price for one of those colourful creatures. Itching to take a sneaky snap, I forced myself to leave without the shot, as one guy delved around to find more of the same species of silvery white long bodied fish to add to his bag. Regretting my compliance with the photo ban, I stomped off towards my accommodation along the back route through the village. "I should have just took the fucking picture."

The village was a maze of pathways running parallel to deep concrete gullies, there to direct the monsoon rains away from the properties. Although there was the odd wider path, most were just about wide enough to squeeze a moped past a wheelbarrow. One such path I took heading back towards my digs that I'd not been along previously had a wooden drying frame of crude construction at chest height over the gully opposite one property. A barefoot, bare-chested man of around 60, wearing a blue sarong, had been stood over the frame as I approached, spacing out fish in tight rows on a board. Each neatly butterflied creature measured about 20 cm, long enough fish to warrant a picture laid side-by-side so, now sat on the step, I asked him if he would allow me the opportunity to record the image. He agreed, although the flies didn't much like the intrusion. A black mist of insects lifted up into a cloud as I came close, then quickly returned down onto their banquet once they realised I wasn't quick enough to catch them. It's commonplace to see children carry fish between their fingers here, three per hand, not dissimilar to milkmen back home in the eighties dangling bottles between their fingers. I was starting to get the feeling these guys got a little bit sick of fish. 'No wonder the lizards move so quickly,' I thought as I pressed the shutter on my camera.

Time on the island was almost up: lifelong memories made and lessons learned – never let a monkey stand above you unless you are under water; never go on a jungle trek without telling someone; and don't get too close to snakes.

Chapter 4
"Singa-bloody-pore Sir!"

The bus station at Kuala Besut had a number of rows of metal seats fastened to the ground under an opening in the centre of the building, overlooked by small offices located each side of a covered seating area, each with a kiosk window where passengers could purchase bus tickets from a company of their choice, and leave your bag for the day if you are cheeky enough to ask. On payment of the fair, you receive a printed till-roll ticket with an allocated seat number.

"You want up or down sir?" the lady inside the office, sat tapping a keyboard, asked.

"What is the best?" I enquired.

"I think up."

The quality of its transport infrastructure is a good indictor as to the state of a country's economy, so varying forms of transport when backpacking is as much a cultural experience as it is fun. I'd not yet had the pleasure, so had there been a track, a train would have been my preferred mode of transport to the next port of call. I was travelling to Singapore on a budget AirAsia flight from KL. All routes out of Kuala Besut involved a bus ride so I plumped for the eight-hour overnight sleeper to the airport, saving me the cost of a night's accommodation.

The novelty of convienience shopping compunded by a sustained lack of such an amenity while on the island lured me towards a building set back 50 metres from the main street beyond the market. About to take advantage of the unrivaled variety offered by the only supermarket within a half-hour drive, a childish excitement quickend my step. A can of mango juice, an apple, a tomato and a small packet of chocolate flavoured biscuits shaped like teddy bears should easily see me through till breakfast, especially bearing in mind I had planned for my dinner to commence an hour before departure. I ate at a restaurant on the corner just the other side of the car park from the bus station when I was here previously. It seemed to be the most popular place around. As you might expect, its tables were undercover, providing shelter from the elements come rain or shine, but open sides to the road at the front and car park to the side felt unusual to a Yorkshireman accustomed to locks and shutters on commercial buildings. Inside, past heavy circular concrete tables and matching curved bench seats, through towards the rear was a tabletop buffet where you could be served from a selection of bowls by waiting staff. That didn't appeal today, so I went for a dish from the menu popular with locals: boiled rice with sauce, grilled whole fish and a side of pickled salad. Washed down with a hot lime tea, it filled a hole and at a price far beyond reasonble.

With 15 minutes before the bus was due out, I moved back over to the steel seats in the bus station. A line of three gleaming double-decker coaches were now parked up out front, in stark contrast to their shabby surroundings. Signs on the windows boasted HDTV and WiFi but once aboard the reality was slightly less impressive. None of the items advertised, apart from a double USB charging point, were available or working. I found my seat upstairs. It was a large comfortable recliner on the row directly behind the front seats, next to the window. With no fold down table like on a plane, I hung my carry-on bag on the hook on the back of the seat in front and settled myself for the trip. As we set off the bus was less than half full and no one had yet took the seat next to me. 'Yes! Two seats to myself!' I thought while plugging in my phone charger. With very little to see outside in the darkness, I kicked back and removed my flipflops.

Ten minutes in, there was another pick up. The sound of footsteps coming upstairs turned out to be a mountain of a man. He stopped and looked towards my seat briefly then moved forward, sitting on the seat in front. 'Thank god for that,' I thought. I often say, "Thank god," but only as a figure of speech as I'm an atheist. Two minutes later we were on the move again, as was the seat in front. The big guy reclined his seat sharply, trapping my carrier bags to my knees. He turned and said, "Okay?" but he didn't wait for an answer, just quickly spun back round, put his feet up on the front rail and settled down to sleep. Still with no neighbour after two more pickups, I prized myself out of the window seat, swapping across nearer to the aisle.

Now more free to move once again, I started to notice the chill from the air-con. Like when a southerner tries to do a Yorkshire accent, going overboard is what tends to happen with the air-con on public transport in hot climates like this. I suspect it's a nice change for locals not to be sweating their boobs off but it was a bit like travelling down the motorway in a car back home in winter with a broken heater. As you might expect, I didn't get a great deal of sleep but still the journey went surprisingly quickly.

Before long, I was trying to work out how to get out of the bus station. I could see people walking along a raised walkway towards a building on the right but the only way up was by escalator and that wasn't working. I walked to the kerb to cross the bus lane to the next platform. On spotting me, a guard shouted down from the walkway. I didn't understand what he said but he gestured for me to use the broken escalator. I stood confused for a while so he repeated his instruction, waving his hands to encourage me closer to the stationary equipment. Eventually it dawned on me that you might need to activate a movement sensor to bring it to life.

In the terminus building on the upper level, airport-style electronic notice boards displayed times and destinations, one of which was my airport shuttle train. One lift and two escalators later, I was outside the barriers at the ticket office. With six hours to kill, there was no rush to scan the notice board and move on. I sat beside a young Malaysian family with a baby in a buggy in the waiting area and gathered my thoughts. The limited amount of sleep on the coach was starting to catch up with me. Although I didn't imagine falling asleep here, prolonged sitting brought on a vacant haze so I bought a ticket and moved down to the platform where I could get my head down. With two rucksacks used as a combined mattress and pillow, I caught up on a little sleep against the concrete stanchion under the stairs until my train arrived. From getting on and finding a seat at the second stop, this early morning rush hour train was rammed after two more stops.

I sat back, eyes closed, hoping to catch up on a bit of sleep as the plane sat motionless, purring on the runway. The primary reason for my impulsive purchase was the price of the ticket. It was the cheapest of my preferred destinations but I had no idea what to expect of the city state, other than the memory of a scene in a film set in the 1920s, where a young girl refers being sent to 'Singa-bloody-pore, Sir'. Soon trees flashed by, the nose lifted and the tarmac dropped away.

Passing through passport control at the other end and I looked for the cheapest mode of transport: a bus. The stop turned out to be underground in a sprawling concrete basement. As I waited, I planned my day. Having had a glimpse through the plane window as we made our approach of an impressive harbour with a huge building resembling a curved cruise liner, I knew what I wanted to do first.

The stop after getting on, there was a quick search by the police. One walked up the aisle, looking left, then right, at each passenger in turn as his colleague watched from the door. After finding nothing untoward, they left. After multiple stops along subterranean roads with double yellow lines like at home, the journey through the airport made its way up into the daylight, on its way to my connection with the Mass Rapid Transit system. The MRT, the less shabby equivalent to London's tube trains, is the jewel in the crown of Singapore's public transport system. You'd think a state-of-the-art underground rail system would connect up to the airport, rather than having to take a connecting bus, and you would be right. I wouldn't be making that mistake again.

The MRT was right there under my nose all the time. Automated ticket machines, positioned in the concourse of each station, with destinations selected by touch screen was the only way, apart from vaulting the barriers, to get past the lines of turn-styles. From here you could load up a card with credit for multiple journeys or pay for a single trip to pretty much everywhere. If the MRT was anything to go by, this city was going to be sleek, modern, clean and efficient. The nearest stop to my new temporary home, Footprints Hostel, was at Jalan Besar, a ten-minute journey.

Granite floor tiles in modern geometric designs and bright stainless-steel benches met me as I alighted the carriage, through sliding glass doors that lined up with the carriage doors, forming part of a clear barrier between the track and platform. Wider than their London counterparts, these carriages were fitted out with blue fibreglass seats running along both sides, with one red priority seat near each door. Video screens set into the wall between the top of the window and the ceiling advertised universities, banks and posh cars with route information superimposed in the bottom right-hand corner of the screen. The odd public information message would be slotted in the schedule every few minutes too. One such message you would not see at home was of people covered in dust and blood escaping the scene of a terrorist attack, running through a tunnel towards daylight, with information on what to do in the event of an explosion. If anyone would take their eyes off their smart device for a few moments, they might have noticed the penalty for molestation too. According to the poster, you can expect two years and a good caning.

Up an ear popping four escalators to ground level, I took my first glimpse out through the concourse of the area that was to be my home for the next few days. Across the dual carriageway were two restaurants on opposite corners of the road leading to my digs, facing each other: Yong Kee seafood restaurant on the left and an Indian buffet café opposite. Past shabby, red plastic patio chairs surrounding well-used, round, white melamine tables, spilling out from the Chinese restaurant, I spotted the hostel on the corner up ahead, past a household electrical item repair shop and a bar. A few other hostels could be found around here, but the one on the corner of a crossroads, opposite another Indian café was mine.

15 Singapore dollars gets you breakfast and a dorm bed in a room shared with seven others, a locker, bed sheets and pillow case, which is handed to you at reception for a $20 deposit or your passport, whichever you prefer. Towels and padlocks are also available for rent, for a small fee.

"Okay, so the code for the bottom door is 4747 and you are in room 302 on the 10th floor," the young portly Chinese lady informed me from behind the counter on reception.

"On the 10th floor," I repeated. "Do you have a lift?"

"Lift?"

"Yes an elevator."

"Strong man, you will be fine," she explained.

So, sandwiched between two rucksacks, I turned away with raised brow and headed off in search of my room. Bare concrete showed through on the central, most heavily used areas of red-painted stairs leading up to the rooms. Large black self-adhesive vinyl blooms and foliage at the top of each flight of stairs contrasted against white emulsion walls but the second floor was as far as the stairs went. Thankfully, what sounded to me like the 'ten floor' was probably meant to sound like the 'top floor'. I pushed open the door and room 302 was right there. Further doors lined the 15 metre corridor, dormitories along the right and utility rooms to the left.

Signs were I wouldn't be alone as I pushed open the door with my foot to reveal a smattering of possessions in an otherwise unnocupied room. There were a few bags dotted around, a mobile phone charger plugged into wall socket, clothes on hooks, draped towels, a tin unit housing of lockers and four sets of chunky, yet slightly rickety, tubular framed steel bunk beds with mattresses and covers held down by elasticated bands stretched over each corner. I made my bed then investigated the tin cupboard, situated at the side of my bed. Three rows of three doors were provided to house more valuable items. Each had a swivelling catch with a hole for a padlock that lined up with the corresponding hole in a plate fixed to the frame. I chose the middle locker in hope that it might be ever so slightly less simple to prize open. Breaking in would have been a doddle given the inclination but that was more likely to be burglars rather than my fellow travellers. On the wall, next to each bed was a shelf with a reading light and a socket above it over four clothes pegs.

My phone was now in desperate need of a charge but, rather than have to wait for it, I came up with a cunning plan to allow me to go out and explore while leaving it behind. I gave the impression my charger was plugged into the wall socket while unconnected to a device by using two chargers, one plugged into the wall connected to my phone hidden under the pillow, and a second charger hidden under the pillow, apart from the unconnected end of the cable out in plain view on my bed.

Still yet to meet any of my bedfellows, I headed back to the MRT with a spring in my step. Without my smartphone to help me, I repeated in my head, 'Jalan Besar, blue downtown line,' over and over as I descended back down to the subterranean platform in an attempt to find the stunning architectural landmark structure so I glimpsed from the window of the plane. After a quick scan of the underground map, the stop named 'Bay Front' at the end of the line, seemed the obvious choice.

On arival, I made my ascent behind an American guy chatting to his young son. I overheard him mention he was heading for the Bay Front so I followed covertly. We exited the station into a delicately manicured, horticultural rollercoaster of exaggerated grassy mounds rolling alongside a busy road beyond a flat, wide, immaculately-paved, pale cream granite terrace, home to a centrepiece of water jets rising from the floor in its centre. Its crescent of fountains projecting up at graduated heights, synchronised to create a dancing ripple effect, provided a cooling spray and a splash of entertainment as the man and boy marched by with purpose.

Unlike the area around my digs, here in the heart of the city, wealth has weaved a golden thread of opulence into the fabric of society. To be overwhelmed by a ubiquitous flare at every turn is a pleasure rarely afforded to visitors in other cities. The city cruises along un-rushed but at pace, managing somehow to balance the pace of life required to sustain this lifestyle while retaining a peaceful charm. Downtown, nothing is spared the VIP treatment, even bins and benches often look like commissioned one-off pieces in this high-gloss city state. Take, for instance, a nearby gleaming curved brass bench seat installation, around 60 cm wide, curling up at its edges, arcing over itself, tying in a loose top knot, then back down to meet up in one continual twisted ribbon.

I found myself speculating about the lifestyle of my unwitting guides. The Dad was around 35 years old, a slim Causcasian with jeans, checkerboard Converse pumps and well-groomed facial hair. I imagined him driving his VW camper on family surfing trips between his job as a high-flying software developer as I followed across the road to a further pedestrian precinct, where a grid of denim-clad rancher types, kicking up boot heels and dothing Stetsons to twangy guitar riffs, thumbs hidden in leather waist-coat pockets, shamelessly pranced around in an abhorrent public display of tasteless indulgence.

I continued, following into a gleaming multi-storey glass hive, where a honeycomb of shops and stalls selling confectionary, electronic gadgets, clothes and shoes buzzed with activity. Up numerous escalators and through the exit at the opposite side of the precinct, I broke off my pursuit once I'd been led to this vantage point over a barrier down through thin air, across a gusty bay to the island of Sentosa.

From the right, a panoramic vista begins with a virtually seamless transition from infinite cloud-smattered sky to open water, where distant ships shimmer as specks in the haze. The ocean draws in to skirt the island across the harbour then disappears from view under the bridge connecting the mainland to my left.

Stumbling onto this scene alone would have been ample justifiction for visiting the outer fringe of the city but, stood beside an outdoor kids' play area on the third floor promenade, I noticed what seemed to be an outdoor attraction: a smattering of oddly-coloured random structures suggestive of some sort of kids' theme park on the opposite bank. From up here I could see a long covered walkway leading to it on the left, around the edge of the bridge. There was a more direct route to the other side too. A cable car, shuttling gondolas back and forth high over the water, connecting up with further cable routes across on the island. Making the most of my geographical error, drawn to the intrigue of brightly coloured, contorted metal structures, I headed for the walkway, down two flights of stairs, then along the covered path parallel to the road bridge. A huge rotating globe standing 4 metres high with the words 'Universal Studios' was surrounded by a seemingly endless queue of people. Out of curiosity, I followed the line of bodies snaking around for 200 metres, to turnstiles not yet allowing entry to whatever further attractions lay beyond. Maybe if my kids were here it might have been different but otherwise it held about as much appeal as sauntering in front of a hefty shopping trolley being pushed along by a 12 year old on a sugar high. Whatever it was, it didn't appeal to me, neither did the next few minutes strolling through child-orientated, corporate, money-spinning attractions until, that was, I came across the entrance to the cable car.

15 Singapore dollars buys you a seat on both of the two cables: one heading back to the mainland high over Keppel Harbour where I'd just come from,

directly into the top floor of a skyscraper and the other down to the beach, which is where I headed first. Gliding silently over a tree-lined hillside with a soft sway, I passed over something reminicent of an obese, dwarf tower crane. Had it not been for the giant lettering plastered down its side saying 'Bungee', I doupt its shape alone would have alluded to its purpose. The four unfeasibly long zip wires starting from a hillside to my right that ran under the cable car, out onto the beach, were a much more obvious amenity to spot.

Around the pulley wheel at the stop for the beach on its perpetual journey, I jumped off the gondola, heading for a closer look at the bungee, via a 7-Eleven store under the cable tower for a takeout beer. The beach almost passed as natural, but there was a slightly synthetic feel to it. I passed a couple of busy open-air restaurants on my way, enclosed by trellis and creeping plants, before reaching the big scary elastic band with the power to make some people lose their bodily functions. For the benefit of those with frayed nerves, it was positioned directly over a swimming pool just in case its not the only thing that frays.

Immediately adjacent to the pool was an open-air dance floor where a small group of late teens were dancing in the eye of the storm to Euro-trash pop music, within a noise-cloud that thundered out from a PA system, soaking the ears and holding the attention of all nearby with their impressive moves. I sat alone on the sand to drink my beer and followed with my eyes as they danced their way across the beach, making me realise this was probably their job. 'Where do you get a job like that?' I pondered, until a genuinely petrified scream resonating from the direction from the obese baby tower crane snapped me back into the moment. I watched as a girl decelerated loudly, nearing the pool, becoming silent then screaming briefly again each time she recoiled. After spending a couple of minutes looking down, fighting the natural instinct to conserve life, until finally taking the irrational step to euphoria, her moment of feeling on top of the world would come, but maybe not until her feet were back on solid ground.

A reminder of the ongoing tradition of maritime trade passing through the port, I scanned a clutch of bulging cargo vessels, top heavy with containers, sitting just off the coast. The backdrop looked odd against the resort, albeit manmade. My industrial musings offshore instantly returned to more immediate recreational activities, on hearing excited voices shout out across the sky from behind me. Two guys riding the zip lines gave out a protracted, "WOOOOHOOOO!" simultaneously accompanied by a metallic whirring from the approaching pulleys, giving an audible location of the progress of a ride that may probably otherwise have gone unnoticed. They raced towards platforms on a pair of blatantly obvious manmade islands, 20 metres off the coast.

Palm trees set in sand-covered, crescent moon-shaped islands faced back to the mainland in an attempt obscure the floating reminders of ongoing commercial activities, blotting the landscape beyond. Very little daylight remained so I began to head back. Half-way back was a further cable car station connecting the two lines. I got off here and joined a surprisingly large queue, waiting for journey to the top of the skyscrapper. Holding more interest than its beach activity counterpart, this queue filled the stairs leading up to the entrance, turning back on itself below the stairs for a further 20 metres. It may have been down to timing as it was now dusk and many buildings were beginning to be illuminated across the bay, creating an evening skyline worthy of a photo or two from such a vantage point. Families, having probably been here all day, must have timed their exit to coincide with the sun going down, in order to enjoy the last experience of the day, before making their way home.

Outside the line dancers were long gone, replaced by small groups of people gathered to enjoy the fountains in the pedestrian precinct brought to life by coloured lighting enhanced by absent daylight. Sleep was long overdue but I wasn't going to miss the opportunity to sit in the darkness on the manicured turf mounds, alongside likeminded individuals and lose myself in the dancing water for a few mesmerising minutes.

My dorm at Footprints was full when I arrived back. Most of the guys lay in their beds chatting quietly but jumping straight into mine was far too antisocial. This was our first meeting so battling a head fog of fatigue, I exchanged the minimum amount of pleasantries before allowing myself a crash out for the count. Three Spurs fans, mates in their early twenties from London who'd been doing charity work building walls in Thailand, two other English lads backpacking together, a young Nigerian man there for work and one sheepish Malaysian guy were my latest bedfellows.

I found myself wide-awake by 7:30 am the next morning, which happened to coincide with the start of breakfast. As you enter the building from the street, the reception desk is straight ahead stretching across most of the back wall. There's a seating area to the left where you can kick back and watch TV and kitchen area to the right with three tables and bench seats, partially separated by a glass screen. You could help yourself to toast, cereals, tea and coffee. Sweetened processed food seems to have considerably more sugar in lesser developed counties. At home, we are gradually being weaned off it for health reasons, but breakfast here was noticably different to back home. With two types of breakfast cereal on offer, you could choose small, round, sweet chocolate balls or the sweeter yellow clusters. Even the sliced bread provided for making toast or the peanut butter didn't get away with it. In fact, the only thing not sweeter than it usually is back home was jam.

The kitchen was crowded with Malaysians but not young backpacker types like you might expect. These Malaysians looked a bit out of their depth, like it was the first time away from their village. This was an older crowd, traditionally dressed in headscarves and ankle length robes. You could help yourself to toast, cereals, tea and coffee. I stood in hope of finding a seat spotting an old lady detaching a piece of kitchen roll one perforation at a time, pinching her fingers carefully each side of the perforated line, eventually removing one piece from the roll, while an old guy sitting nearby ate toast with a knife and fork. This was my respite before I was once again the one standing out, oblivious of the etiquette of foreign cultures.

After a quick freshen up, it was time to head off out for a second attempt to find the iconic landmarks I spotted from the plane. Marina Bay, not Bay Front, was what I'd been looking for, I was reliably informed by the girl on reception. Back downstairs after a quick shower and once over with the toothbrush, a party of Philippino youths where gathered around the TV, some huddled on the sofas and the rest on the floor, watching a Harry Potter film as I was leaving. "Just because you've got the emotional range of a teaspoon doesn't mean we all have," one of the youths read out loud from the subtitles, proving his ability to speak English by repeating Hermione's speech.

Back past the restaurants on opposite corners at the end of the street, I crossed the road to the station, inserted my money, picked up my ticket and placed it in the reader on the gate, wherein the mechanical flaps opened up to allow me through. Pretty simple really, unless you then go through a further turnstile on the row to your left and end up back where you started, ticket spent, fumbling in your pocket for change for a second ticket. Eventually down on the platform, I waited amongst commuters, eyes glued to mobile devices.

Three minutes is around the longest amount of time I had to wait for an underground train in Singapore, which is nothing compared to the extra time you add to your journey if you get on the train going in the opposite direction like I did a couple of times. Beautiful women are everywhere in Singapore and, luckily for me, I reached my stop before I got caught staring. I'd never get lost if my location-finding skills matched my ability to spot a beautiful woman but they don't, especially not down here. Underground stations emerging into shopping malls can cause confusion when you are not familiar with your surroundings as there are no landmarks to guide you, just passages in all directions leading to who knows where.

After eventually finding daylight, I headed across a main road looking for something of interest. It brought me to the drop-off point for a posh looking place called the Marina Bay Sands Hotel. Between valets and wannabe baronets, I picked the nearest of the numerous automatic glass doors, into a jaw-dropping foyer around 30 metres wide. Like the inside of a colossal skeleton's ribcage, the internal cavity of the building was made up of two wide asymmetric curved legs that lean in on themselves, gradually almost meeting briefly 23 floors up, before arcing back out to the 55th floor. Looking up at a spiky, metal, matrix, abstract chandelier the size of a passenger jet filling part of the void above my head gave me an unworthy feeling like perhaps I wasn't rich enough to be there. I checked around to assess if it was a public space. There were scores of people preoccupied with hotel related issues so I wandered further through unchallenged.

The space turned from lobby to atrium, stretching the full 250 metres of this section of the building. It was dissected by a footbridge in its centre, running across at right angles, out through a clear glass section of the third floor towards the gardens by the marina. I skate-walked with sliding feet along a gleaming cream marble floor, past a restaurant that might discourage the practice of asking for ketchup or wearing flip flops to dinner, dwarfed between rows of three-metre-tall plant pots each weighing over a ton. Past boutique shops, a casino and walkway linking to a nearby mall, I reached the opposite end of the cavernous expanse. Then, outside, a red Ferrari sat waiting to be rented for the day alongside an equally special looking, canary yellow head turner.

Other than a busy road I didn't spot a route to anywhere appealing so I retraced my steps back through to reception, past the colossal check-in desk and back out from where I came to continue onward from where I diverted off a few minutes before towards another busy carriageway. After a few hair-raising moments crossing the busy road at a point with no crossing, I caught my first glimpse of a forest of circular, metallic, flared-top funnel frames resembling alien space trees, covered in natural foliage, that might easily have inspired set designers of futuristic films such as 'Avatar'. There are 18 in all of these so-called 'supertrees' whose trunks rise up with a graduated girth then splay out at heights of 25 to 50 metres, some connected by walkways. Supertree Grove is one of many attractions here at the Gardens by the Bay. Between specimen trees, pergolas and roofed canopies, I began to catch glimpses alluding to the brazen architectural majesty of the vessel whose foyer I had just stumbled upon.

I joined a steady stream of visitors, sauntering along a labyrinth of pristine landscaped pathways. Paradoxically, with distance a picture emerged. I noticed a further two towers, identical looking to the one I had just stumbled upon. They were holding what resembled a curved cruise liner aloft in the sky. Imagine each building is a cricket stump with the bales, or Sky Park in this

case, balanced on top. I'd just stumbled on the foyer of the most expensive resort ever built, a stunning structure boasting 2,561 rooms, a sky deck longer than the height of the Eiffel Tower, with a record-breaking 220 foot cantilever at the bow end. Don't bother to count them; take my word for it – 250 trees and hundreds more shrubs and bushes complement the area up there that's not taken up by the world's largest infinity pool.

Back down at ground level, ponds with fountains, tree-lined paths and landscaped knowles, covered in patches of brightly coloured blooms, provide a tasteful space to enjoy the skill of the craftsmanship required to produce marble carvings of elephants, lions and camels found amongst palms and exotic plants. I moved on towards a steel arc peeping out over the canopy ahead that could only be some sort of building. I passed a raised circular marble seating area surrounding a Moraceae tree, better known as a Bengal fig to you and me. Its vines drop down to the ground, take root, then gradually form its own dense mini forest.

The curve of steel I'd spotted turned out to be the world's largest columnless glass house. With a name like the Flower Dome, you don't really need an explanation as to its purpose. Beyond fat-trunked baby baobab trees and vine-covered archways, another smaller steel and glass dome also became visible: the Cloud Forest. Like two huge metal armadillos paired up by a central covered lobby, sitting on the edge of the riverbank, they are structures of different sizes yet closely related in shape and form, like a mother sat by her resting child. You can buy entry tickets or travel down the escalator to the riverside walkway from the open-ended lobby, or just appreciate the blend of artistic flare and architectural skill that has created a series of curved steel beams running parallel to each other, resembling partially transparent metallic creatures, with glass panels around four metres wide filling in the parallel gaps between the beams, sealing the structure to allow a man-made tropical climate to flourish inside. Tiny plants to large palms, suited to the manufactured eco-system, thrive in the Flower Dome, while the Cloud Forest boasts the world's tallest indoor waterfall at 30 metres.

Down the escalator to the path by the river seemed the obvious choice to progress from here. On the lower level, a designated area marked out with a yellow-lined box on the side of the path had numerous bikes and scooters offered for short term rental. Scan-and-go bicycles from four or five companies not only provide transportation but variety and competition too. Most interesting to me though were the electric scooters, an unusual mode of transport about to become common place in the UK.

Sitting conspicuously across the water on the opposite bank was Singapore's answer to the London Eye. The Singapore Flyer, as it's known, is Asia's largest observation wheel offering great views back over the skyline. Still just following my nose to see what's around the next corner, I took a route along the riverbank, sharing the path with Chinese tourists, cyclists and clusters of nippy electric-scooter kids. I approached a footbridge across the river but, as with most things in the city, the Helix Bridge, as it's known, is no ordinary bridge.

Buildings, shops, scenery, hotels, landscaping, restaurants, landmarks and architecture. If you insert the word amazing in front of all the above, it should give you an idea of what makes Singapore special, and the Helix Bridge is a prime example. Its name alludes to its form. Six stainless steel tubes running parallel to each other spiral across the water, connected by smaller brace bars supporting a footpath running through the centre but, rather than the obvious straight route, it gently curves left. A number of viewing platforms along the way on the concave side offer the ideal spot to take in the best view of the city skyline yet. As the river widens out into the marina basin, the cluster of skyscrapers behind it are impossible to miss, as is the designer shop on the left with a difference. Chrome rectangular fingers curve around from a central point like a giant hand holding up an imaginary ball. It reminds me of a 1970s modernist sofa chair for a giant but even this, boldest of statements, doesn't steal the show as behind lies the Marina Sands Hotel from a different elevation and an obscenely large mall.

Every few minutes, traditional dark cedar wood junks with paper lanterns swinging against the swell circle the harbour carrying sightseers. A nautical tour of the city on a classic dark wooden vessel with a steep abrupt stern and elevated deck seems slightly out of place in this ultra modern opulent world. Maybe that's exactly why they are so popular. Ancient looking vessels framed against a wall of real-estate giants are hard to miss.

Aching feet and hunger convinced me to head back towards the hostel: in the same area there's an abundance of cheap quality food outlets. Back home I might splash out on a rare rib-eye and a nice bottle of Côtes du Rhône on occasion, but not here. Like Santa's belt, my money needed to stretch and I didn't want it to be to breaking point, besides backstreet cafés hold much more excitement and intrigue to me. Nando's don't sell the kind of food you still remember six months later; not that I ever go to Nando's. The fringe of the Indian quarter near to my digs was a bit frayed around the edges. A battered van with welded modifications to carry extra cargo or passengers was parked up outside a second-hand computer shop, the floor cluttered with open carcasses of dead PCs, empty card slots and frazzled motherboards, parially hidden behind closed vented shutters, while beside, alleyways with boxes and broken bikes chained to homemade shutters added to the mess.

Sat at the table nearest the footpath of an Indian café, on the opposite corner of the crossroads to Footprints, I ordered chicken Biryani breakfast/dinner: RM6, from a scraggy double-sided A4 laminated sheet given to me by the waiter. Obviously I wouldn't dream of having it for lunch – that would be disgusting, like eating with a knife and fork – even if the meal did cost the equivalent of £1.20. There's always a wash hand basin for pre- and post-meal ablutions somewhere close by. But, unlike at home, it will usually be found outside the toilet, on a wall at the edge the eating area for instance. The importance of hand washing needs no explanation when eating with fingers. Well aware of this fact, and the one where I must never use my left hand to stuff food in my mouth, I gave my hands a quick once over then, sitting alone at a table for six, I filled my time watching 'Mr Bean' on the TV fixed high up on the wall.

Three guys with straight black hair, dark faces and bright white scleras, wearing long-sleeved shirts with collars and flip flops, joined me as I waited for my food. The last local Indian restaurant I'd been in was Brickfields in KL. It had a similar feel and pretty much everyone, apart from me, ate with their fingers. 'Not this time,' I thought as my food arrived to a titter from a 'Mr Bean' fan sat at one of the inner tables.

"Chicken biryani diner," he explained, as he placed a generous plate of moist meaty rice and a separate bowl of curry sauce in front of me.

Promptly delivered and smelling as good as it looked, I thanked the man, poured part of my source over the rice at one edge of the plate, and mixed it with the fingers of my right hand. It's a strange feeling to have hot food covering your fingers when you have been brought up to use cutlery, even more so to then push it into your mouth. Little by little I poured the sauce onto the edge of my rice on the plate, mixed with my fingers, brought the food to my mouth and pushed it in with the back of my thumb. It was pretty messy for a beginner like me but so satisfying and hugely memorable. Halfway through my meal the three Indian guys, who'd joined my table earlier, received their food along with a plastic container of cutlery which all three proceeded to delve in for forks and spoons. Let's just say, if you don't like being self-conscious, you would not have wanted to be me at this moment. As always though, no one looks in disgust or talks behind your back. They just get on with their lives and leave you to it.

This was the fringe of the Indian quarter. The street leading away from my accommodation headed towards the heart of the community so, with belly full, I decided to take a closer look and washed my hands ready to leave. "Thank you. That was good," I explained to the guy on the till, as I paid my bill and headed towards the busier end.

The street was dark, dry and warm. I headed towards a late-night grocery shop a few metres up the street. A man stood straddling a bicycle parked outside the shop without dismounting, chatting to his friend as he emptied boxes of fresh produce inside. I squeezed past along a narrow aisle, my back against the massively over-stocked shelves scouring for exotic titbits. Unknown items, packets and tins were crammed into space well beyond its means but, despite such a selection, nothing jumped out.

Moving on towards the T-junction at the end of the road, most of the shops I passed were still open. One had a bucket containing bunches of peacock feathers twinkling in the moonlight breeze, while a pair of enormous yet still only half-size brass tigers, along with numerous other sculptured creatures, spilled out from another. The road intersecting at the junction was much busier, long and dead straight. Six-metre-wide illuminated displays of multi-coloured lights were suspended across the carriageway every 10 metres as far as the eye could see. Each section identical to the next, spaced out at equal lengths, creating an eye-catching tunnel effect tapering off into the distance. It reminded me of Christmas back home, but there were no bells or sleds on these illuminations; instead there were oil lamps, flowers and leaf patterns in green, purple, white and red. Whether or not this was a constant feature of this street, or a temporary Diwali treat – like the delicate lotus flower displays I'd seen in some foyers made from different colours of dyed rice, painstakingly poured onto the floor in petal shaped formations – I will never know.

Here was the main hub for shops. Every other building houses a shop but not like the community-orientated backstreets of jewellers, cafes and grocers. Shops here offered more souvenir-based products: sunglasses, toys, fridge magnets and fragrances. More of the same up ahead was my motivation to turn around and call it a night. Just one last thing before turning in for the night though: to download an electric scooter app to my smartphone while in WiFi range at Footprints reception.

The weather was shit the next day, dark clouds and the occasional ten-minute downpour, but it didn't matter. Monsoon or not, the electric scooter ride was on. I heard voices in French coming towards me from behind as I stood waiting to cross the main road. I turned to see two men and a woman, all riding yellow OFO rental bikes towards me. I recognised the distinctive colour as we had recently had a rollout of the same bikes with a black band on the frame back home in Sheffield. I attempted to translate their chat in my head as they passed by onto the main road but my French is pretty poor, especially when spoken at speed. 'Open the dog?' I thought deliberately wrongly, joking to myself that they may be referring to an old David Bowie lyric 'ouvrez le chien' that for some reason has been stuck in my head ever since seeing him in concert many years ago.

I was heading back to Marina Bay for a bit of mildly exciting electric scooter fun by way of the MRT again. This time I tried a different stop that brought me out slightly short of my destination on a pedestrian precinct between two tall towers. I could see the iconic cruise liner sailing through the sky in the distance so only an idiot could get lost from here. No... I didn't get lost! There was a rental bike parking bay on the other side of the water, just past the Helix bridge, where I knew scooters were available for rent. It was past a couple of bar-restaurants and a kiosk also advertising electric bikes for rent. The kiosk was not yet open: too early according to the sign on the window.

Towards the bridge to the other side of the marina took me past a rectangular pontoon covered in astroturf and marked out as a football pitch, floating in the quieter side of the marina opposite a mini grandstand. It seemed a bit weird to see a floating football pitch so I checked it out on the net later. It was originally designed as a temporary venue ahead of the completion of the national stadium, making it due to be obsolete by 2012, but it wasn't till two years later that the stadium opened doors on the 30th June of that year. Five years on, and it's still there, hosting pop concerts, sporting events and providing seats for the annual Formula One Grand Prix. It's the world's biggest, apparently, with 200 separate sections that can be reconfigured into different shapes to suit each event.

Within ten minutes, I was stood over a scooter, attempting to scan the bar code on the handlebars over and over, until I realised the app wasn't going to work. "Fuck!" I said quietly out loud whilst alone on the path. "At least the rain has stopped," I thought, consoling myself as I turned around. My back-up plan was to return to the kiosk near the floating football pitch. "By the time I get back to the kiosk it should be open." It was but only just, as a man was removing an advertising board from inside as I approached. A few documents, signatures and a payment saw me off and away. Exchanging knowing looks from other grown-up kids riding around and passing each other with slightly embarrassed grins, I shot along the Helix Bridge heading back to Supertree Grove.

My first experience of the gardens was mind blowing but I'd just scraped the surface. With many paths still undiscovered, I headed back for a closer look. For me, an electric scooter was the perfect way to explore the rest of the sprawling gardens and beyond. A series of paths lead you over hills in bloom, curving around lily ponds and thought variegated canopies. It's a horticulturalist's dream. Vast diverse gardens, made up of an area of land reclaimed from the sea, invite you to browse areas such as the Heritage Gardens with themes dedicated to Chinese, colonial, Indian and Malay cultures that might sound slightly boring to some, but you'd be wrong. 50 million visitors and counting tells its own story. My hour was ticking down fast so I wound on the throttle.

I found an estuary feeding the marina from the opposite side of the water. Colonial buildings, some old, others reproduction such as the scaled down copy of St Paul's Cathedral, peeping through from the distant skyline gave the place a historical feel. I took a route over a Victorian-looking, ornate, cast-iron footbridge riddled with flat cross-braces and hand hammered rivets onto a cobbled path by the river. I followed it up-stream into seafood heaven to the sound of a latent Big Ben chime. Restaurants lined the waterfront route, each sharing their own section of covered, riverside, alfresco-dining terrace, sandwiched between the river and the cobbled path. Waiters with menus tucked under their arms, waiting to convince passers-by to eat, stood by the side of bubbling glass tanks, partitioned off into separate sections outside each establishment, where live seafood from around the globe awaited its fate.

I made a mental note to come back for a closer look later and continued my explorations along the path. Back towards the marina, a statue overlooking the bay on the edge of the water was drawing a crowd. I slalomed my way through tourists for a closer look. It was a white 70 ton, 8.6 metre tall, stone statue of a mythical creature called Merlion, with the body of a fish and head of a lion. It's a famous landmark where wedding parties pose for album photos with a constant jet of water flowing into the bay from its mouth. My time was almost up, so after a quick photo I made my way back to drop off the scooter just as the heavens opened. Luckily, I was just a couple of minutes away and there was a restaurant with a canopy adjacent to the scooter kiosk. I pulled up and waited but there was no respite. After a couple of minutes, I had no choice but to brave another soaking.

"Was it good for you?" the young man enquired as I pulled up.

"Brilliant, thanks."

"You can like on Facebook, please?"

"Yeah, yeah. I will." I ran back to the restaurant to sit out the rain with a beer.

The seafood restaurants I'd found nearby while out on the scooter were at a place called Clarke Quay on the Singapore river. After the rain I walked up for more booze.

Scores of illuminated signs, food menus and Chinese lanterns hanging from terrace roofs fill your eyes with interest, while across the water, colonial buildings with Georgian windows and grandiose pillars take you back in time, contrasting with the Sleek architectural marvels taking centre stage in the opposite direction. The domed roof of the replica St Paul's Cathedral once again peaks out from behind waterfront buildings on the opposite bank from here; while to the left much further back, a cylindrical sky scraper makes its mark, boldly standing alone on the distant skyline. Further left still is a square building, quite low to the ground compared to its width like a giant box, but its most striking feature is the disk-shaped upper section plonked on top, resembling a 1950s sci-fi spaceship. The traditional sightseeing junks glide through here on their way to Marina Bay, past clusters of beer-drinking business men.

I found a seat at a table next to one such group just as a waitress dressed a quartet of Asian high-fliers in thin polythene aprons, slipping one over each man's head in turn then tying it behind their backs. An Australian man was the last to join them. He made his apologies while shaking hands around the table and in no time won them over with his confidence and knowledgeable chat, quickly turning his attention to the negotiations. He talked of unique situations, time scales and negotiated terms.

Lights came on around the bay as daylight faded. The seafood display tank

outside this establishment had name badges in each section: Alaskan king crab, Australian king crab, Canadian crab, Lala clams, Indian green lobster, oyster and black sand clam. A childishly cunning display of rainbow lighting illuminated the balustrade of the footbridge at a turn in the river further up stream. This was the point the landscape turned slick once more, with slanting glass-roofed arcades and mood lighting in the distance.

It was obvious the businessmen had previously come across the seafood cracking tools provided on their table, a variation on nut crackers used to open crab shells. Noisily splitting open the exoskeleton of dead decapods, minutes after being boiled alive, the men shared the delicately flavoured strands of flaky white meat. The world's biggest claws could not have protected them from that scalding pan of water. From shell crunching to number crunching, they removed their clear plastic forecourt, fuel dispensing gloves and laid down their tools. It was clear there was big money involved here, as the Aussie businessman talked of Megawatt deals to smiles and agreeing nods. From nowhere, disco music in the distance suddenly increased in volume, as an eighties throwback western guy on a single-wheeled Segway, wearing shorts and sweat band, wove his way past the restaurant, down the cobbles into the distance. It was time for me to move on.

I passed a place of worship at of the end of a road on a corner on my way back. High walls with elaborately detailed, decorative cows sat up high on the copings left you in no doubt: this was a Hindu temple. There's no mistaking Hindu temples – where else would you find blue-faced boys and elephants with pot-bellied human bodies? The entrance doorway had a smoky blue, extremely steep, hipped roof that glowed under subtle effect lighting directed up from below. Tiers with scores of tiny sculptures of bare-chested men holding swords, others with turbans, loin cloths and handlebar moustaches, women holding ornamental sceptres and a miniature statue of Ganesha were all stacked up, layer upon layer on all four sides of the roof, topped off with a wide-eyed, double-tusked, demonic head staring down. 'How far is India from here?' I thought as I moved on.

With one eye on finding bargain flights and an open itinerary, I felt pressured to

105

continually be on the lookout for the next leg of the adventure. If cost hadn't been a factor, I'd have loved to include India, China, Australia or Thailand but it was. It was the reason I was in Singapore for that matter, so no complaints thus far. I had come across an international ferry terminal tagged on to the mall at Bay Front but my limited investigations into the appeal of its destinations off the south coast consisted of taking a picture of the departure board and having a quick look on the internet if any area was worth visiting; it lead to nothing.

Although I fancied a change of modes of transport, flights were looking likely again. My rule of thumb for the price of flights was based on recent experience, around the 40 quid mark, so when a flight to Kota Kinabalu in Malaysian Borneo came up at around this amount, it put a stop to my indecision. My original intention was to visit Borneo, mainly because it sounded less touristy, off the beaten track, and so far my plans had deviated somewhat. Research back home prior to the trip told me KK, as it's known, was the starting point for further adventures with the attraction of a national park off the coast in the form of a cluster of islands, a 10-minute speed boat ride away, so the flight was booked.

Chapter 5
Zoku Lifestyle

There's nothing like the internet for booking all things backpacker. Pretty much everything is cheaper on the net, if you do a bit of work. Competition and search engines with databases indexed on cheapest first make life easier in that respect. Zoku Lifestyle in KK was up there on my search for bargain accommodation but it looked too good to be true. Advertised as new, the photos backed it up. Scatter cushions, beanbags, cool furniture and stylishly adorned shelving drew me in – that and the 35 ringgit per night price tag. I booked a couple of nights to start with.

Apart from Milano and a couple of others, AirAsia is the top dog airline operator around here. It was their flights I was to take next but in the airport my rucksack didn't want to check in. I'd used the interface to check myself in and receive my boarding card but checking in my bag didn't prove so easy. After a while an AirAsia rep came to my assistance and soon got to the bottom of my problem. I had missed the checkbox, and subsequent additional cost, of a bag to be stored in the hold. This was to be the start of a chase back and forth against the clock to resolve my issue, starting with a queue at the pay desk. As I reached the front some five minutes later, I was informed that I needed to go to check-in.

"Down here sir. Over there." The lady pointed in the general direction of the centre of the airport so off I headed, looking out for the distinctive red signs. I was looking for a manned check-in desk. It took less time to find than to get to the front of the queue. Time was running down on departure.

"Sorry, sir, you don't have any baggage allowance on this ticket," the assistant told me once I'd reached the front. "This bag will cost you $60," she continued.

Holding in my disgust, I attempted the nice guy 'please could you help me?' approach, not one of my strongest attributes. "Oh I'm so sorry for any inconvenience," I grovelled. "I didn't realise. I must've missed this requirement when booking online. Please could you help me as I don't have a lot of money.

Is there anything you can do for me to make it cheaper please?" I explained, giving her a sullen smile.

She didn't reply, except for a stern look, which continued as she tapped the keyboard. She paused, then tapped again. 'No news is good news,' I thought, as she typed some more. These are the situations where it's best to say nothing and, as hard as it was, I managed not to speak. "I can do for you the online price this time at $30."

I don't usually manage to sweet talk anyone into giving me what I want but this time it worked. "Thank you. Terima Kasih."

AirAsia were no longer held in high esteem in my eyes though. Even with a 50 percent reduction, I felt ripped off. The internet booking form wasn't clear. Ryanair prompt you numerous times with options for additional extras like paying for allocated seats but, with the prospect of exploring KK in a couple of hours, my thoughts moved on to more enjoyable things.

The destination airport couldn't get much closer to the city. A Grab car got me to KK Times Square in ten minutes but couldn't pinpoint the accommodation. Knowing I was close by, I let the driver go and set off on foot in search of my new temporary home. Times Square has three blocks of nearly identical buildings, stood parallel to each other, creating a semi-enclosed pedestrian grid. I walked through looking for an obvious sign until I'd reached the last block but I couldn't find my bed.

I sat at a table out front of a Chinese restaurant to check my booking details and find the exact address, which was an ideal opportunity for a beer. I asked a young Chinese lady sat at the next table if they sold beer. With a friendly demeanour, she got up and approached the waitress, following her inside. After a bit of Mandarin chat, she nipped back over to my table. "I ask her if any promotion for beer," she explained. "Maybe they have."

"Thank you. Do you do you know where Zoku Lifestyle Hostel is?"

"Do you know address?"

"The address is KK Times Square but I need to find more details," I explained.

The waitress came across with a PDS, showing a deal for one large Tiger beer for 15 ringgit. That was a great deal compared to some places around.

"One bottle please" I requested.

Now with a chance to relax and gather my thoughts, I removed my Malaysian phone from my pocket, pulled my hand luggage and camera bag close and set to, looking for further info. After a couple of taps of the screen and a quick scribble, Zoku's details were in my notebook. The beer came with a silly little glass holding maybe a quarter of a pint maximum. With two gulps I finished my first glass and called Zoku's number but voicemail kicked in.

"Block F, level two," I read out quietly as I got up and approached the helpful lady. She was sitting with a man, a friendly looking full-set Chinese guy of around 40. My appearance was met by another beaming smile. "It's block F," I told her.

More Mandarin, this time between the sitting couple, then the guy spoke.

"I know this place, my friend's place," he told me. "It is capsule hotel I think."

"I'm not sure; only that it's called Zoku," I tell him.

"Okay I show you. Finish beer then we will go."

"Thank you, my name is Ian," holding out my hand for a shake.

"Robert," he told me as our hands clasped.

Worrying never helps a situation but it's easier said than done when you are alone and surrounded by the unknown. That bit of anxiety I wasn't able to ignore dropped away like a broken lift on hearing Robert but you can't be sure what to expect in these situations until it's done so I finished my beer quickly. Robert picked up my small rucksack and I followed him back from where I'd just been. On the corner of the central covered area between two of the buildings was a desk just plonked there: nothing else, apart from the man sitting at it. Either he was a security guard, whose uniform was in the wash, or just resting – it was hard to tell. He was overlooking an Indian café opposite on the corner of the next block, the start of my block.

"Where you from?" asked Robert.

"England, and you?"

He laughed. "I am from China. My business is here," he explained.

"What is your business?"

"With my brother we import," he vaguely replied.

Further down past a couple of empty shops was a launderette, a dive shop, then the entrance to block F.

"You speak good English."

"Thank you. It is here," he told me, dropping my bag to the floor.

"Thank you, Robert. I will buy you a beer when I see you next time."

"Goodbye."

A flight of stairs led up to a landing with a lift. Shortly after pressing the button, the lift door opened. A name at the side of the button for the second floor said 'Zoku Lifestyle'. Each building in Times Square has five floors. Eight square pillars clad in black granite hold up the buildings to the outer edge of the complex, providing space for under cover seating, while the ground floor of the internal block is populated with shop units. Openings in the centre of each block at ground level allow pedestrian access straight through the middle of the complex, without the need to walk all the way around. The gaps between the buildings are covered with glass roofs to keep you dry in the rainy season. As much as four metres of rain can fall each year and most of that is between October and February. Each building shades the other and the gap between them allows the potential for breeze to pass through.

The lift door opened at the second floor to reveal a clear glass door to my right, held tight by an electromagnetic lock. There was a door bell but, before having a chance to press it, the lock buzzed and I pushed open the door. By now it was late, around 10:30 pm, but a helpful young Chinese lad was on hand to greet me behind a small L-shaped custom built reception desk, to give me the necessary instructions, show me my room and, of course, take my money. 73 ringgit for two nights was a steal, at around £6.50 per night. I had a modern, clean, sturdy bed, washing machine and dryer, stylish furnishings and breakfast included.

Between the chill-out area at the far end of the room, a light coloured, chunky, wooden galley table with bench seats filled the space between reception. It fit the room perfectly, as did the shoe rack to the right of the front door, and everything else for that matter. An impressive use of space, combined with subtle decorative detailing, gave me the feeling a female interior designer

110

may have had a hand in this fledgling business. Grey high-gloss kitchen units along the back wall, on the opposite side to the dormitory doors, filled the back wall between reception and the drying room doorway, then a modern wall unit, with randomly sized openings, housing books, games, plants and ornaments, looked down over scattered bean bags and a stylish Scandinavian designer chair. At the far end of the room, behind a screen wall, a bank of lockers big enough to store a full rucksack overlooked a row of toilet cubicles. Beyond that, a long, dark grey stone, designer trough, four-man wash-basin ran along the wall to the left, with a mirror above it and a shelf with toothbrushes and hair products. The laundry was on the right and a row of four showers through the back.

A tall, young, Arab guy standing at the dining table said, "Hi." The rapport was almost instant: his confidence and enthusiasm for similar interests became obvious as we exchanged pleasantries.

A pretty, young, mixed-race English girl sitting in the rocking chair reading, also said, "Hi," and so did a young, curly-haired, German lad in the bean bag next to her.

After further chatting with Saeed, the Arab, he revealed his desire to dive at the islands off the coast of Semporna, which involved either a long bus ride, expensive Grab ride or flights to a place called Tawau. Within minutes we had become travel companions, booking flights that would depart in two days' time.

Saeed was from the Yemen but he lived in Saudi Arabia, as an electrical goods salesman in a large store, living with his Mum and Dad, selling air-conditioning units and PCs. "I would like to go to the island hopping also," Saeed informed both me and the German exchange student whose name I never got. Let's call him Fritz. What?! Okay, Daniel then!

Daniel was studying in Singapore under a student exchange agreement between the two countries. The top five percent of students from Singapore get the chance to study in Germany, as did he to Singapore studying electrical engineering. This allowed him opportunities for mini breaks on weekends such as this one.

"Island hopping? Is this the national park off the coast here?" I enquired.

Daniel was noncommittal about the island hopping but he enlightened me nevertheless. "It is five islands; you can see from the coast called Tunku Abdul Rahman marine park."

Daniel's expression remained calm and unfazed as Saeed butted in quickly, "A beauty spot. You buy a ticket from the office in town."

Having travelled alone since leaving home, I was glad of the company so agreed to get up around 8:30 am to walk over to the tour operator's kiosk for the boat across to the islands.

The next morning the two of us walked over the road after a breakfast of cereal, toast with peanut butter and three coffees. It was by far the best hostel yet. Through Times Square, across the main road and a bridge over a river running into the sea, we were ten minutes into a half-hour walk. Slightly overconfident but both feet firmly on the ground, Saeed was refreshingly forthright, bubbly and happy. He didn't want to miss a thing and could come across as slightly pushy in his quest to maximise his travel experience, I was to learn.

"Where did you come from before this?" he asked as we walked along a wooden decking promenade on the shoreline.

"I just spent a few days in Singapore," I explained.

"It was good?"

"It's an amazing place but you wouldn't want to stay for more than a few days. It can be a little bit expensive after you get bored of cheap Chinese and Indian food on the outskirts of town," I explained.

"I heard this," he replied.

"Usually I prefer more of an adventure, somewhere unspoiled and unknown, like the Perhentian Islands."

"Perentian! You have been? Where did you stay?" he asked excitedly.

"I stayed at Rock Garden at first. The locals pronounce it Roke Garden, at Long Beach."

"Yes I know Long Beach. When did you go?" he continued.

"I was there for a week just before Singapore. The snorkelling was the best I have ever done."

"I did go there also. Did you go to Philippine?"

"No, not yet, but I am thinking of going," I explained.

112

"Yes it is very good. Philippine is good also but diving is good. I have been last year."

We continued around the back of a hotel, through a line of waterfront bars, passing stacks of chairs and a row of shisha pipes on the way. Past three markets, first the food market, then one selling gifts, crafts and scarves, then finally the fish market, just before the outdoor patio table seafood restaurant area. Jesselton Point was next and that's where the ticket office was.

The name of the area comes from a man called Sir Charles Jessel, baronet, barrister, magistrate and businessman. The city also had the same eponymous name until 1968, when it changed to Kota Kinbalu. This was the place the British North Borneo Charted Company was formed in 1881. Sir Charles Jessel was granted exclusive rights, by royal charter and with military support, to exploit the region's natural resources. The empire on which the sun never sets, or the British Empire as it was more commonly known, once controlled 24% of the Earth's land area and held sway over 412 million people: that was 23% of the world's population at the time.

The ticket office felt like an old London bus station. An antique English square building with six kiosks along one side and desks lining the opposite side of the room, all with pushy sales staff and wood panelling. There were two shops on the far wall and bench seats filling the central area. Daniel wasn't around at breakfast time so we presumed he had decided not to come and stayed in bed but here he was, sat on a bench.

"Hi, are you coming to the islands?" I asked.

"Maybe, I don't know. I don't have a long time," he explained.

"We didn't think you were coming when we didn't see you at breakfast," I explained feeling slightly guilty.

"I wake at 7 am and went for a walk to the sea."

"You can come with us to snorkelling, for maybe three islands," Saeed offered.

"I don't know, maybe," he replied.

It felt like he'd wanted to be left to it so we did just that. Saeed did a deal to hire a mask and snorkel, ferry us to one island for two hours, then move onto a second island two more hours, then back where we started.

Daniel caught up with us outside making our way to the jetty: "I am coming."

I followed behind as they chatted, passing through a couple of alfresco cafés. Redundant wooden stumps breaking the surface are all that's left of the old pier, once used to move staggering quantities of rubber, rattan and honey. Their rotted tops stand defiantly to attention alongside concrete columns that took over the job over more recent years. An open roof covers the first section of decking up to the point it stops and turns left for 30 metres. A row of shops and cafés situated between the ticket office and ticket collectors' gates, take advantage of the passing trade, as a steady stream of tourists collect their life jackets and clamber down the gangplank onto the bright orange floating plastic speed boat mooring pontoons, interconnected like a giant jigsaw.

Although many companies run from here, the boats are pretty much the same, around 10 metres long by 2 metres wide. The fibreglass hull incorporates bench seats down each side and a stainless-steel tubular framed canopy that shades passengers, similar to the boats in Perhentian. Stick a 200cc Yamaha outboard engine on the back and you have the typical island-hopping craft. Each boat holds up to 16 people, providing a steady stream of income for the local economy. The benches under the shade of the corrugated tin roof on the jetty catch the breeze if you're lucky on hot sunny days, like today. The shelter benefits people not only waiting for the island-hopping adventure but passengers waiting for the ferry to the island of Labuan too. Although still Malaysian, you need to pass through immigration, showing your passport or ID card to get there. With whispers of tax haven, the place has connections with offshore banking apparently and diving is said to hold some hidden treasures here also.

As the next pair of boats raced off towards the islands, top heavy with Chinese tourists, a stray cloud gave a brief respite from the steadily rising sun. Another boat moored up after a return journey and a guy with an armful of luminous orange life-jackets made his way up the gang plank towards us, signalling our time to move.

An entertaining 10 minutes watching similar boats all sprint in the same general direction and we were at the wooden jetty of Mandukan Island. A straight run of around 100m of timber decking led to the beach, which for me was the most impressive thing about this place. Poor snorkelling and shabby beaches, Mandukan did not appeal. The national park status afforded to the area seemed to have worked against an island trampled by the constant flow of tourists. The odd person attempted to snorkel in the murky shallows but I didn't see the point after five minutes. I opted to spend the rest of my two-hour slot, chilling on a sun lounger.

A gorgeous, black-haired Taiwanese girl in a red bikini stood under the shade of the palms at the back of the beach. She seemed to be alone. Having been for a wonder on his own, Saeed was making his way back over to the sun beds where we were laid. I watched as he walked across and stopped at the girl. They sat chatting in the shade for a while before she stood up and posed for photos. One leg bent with pointed toe, she pouted at the camera with the sea as her backdrop. After a few shots from different angles, Saeed handed back the camera and came back across.

"Do you have a girlfriend?" I asked. Saeed just looked and laughed, without answering my question. "Did you get her phone number?" I inquired.

"No, we just talk. She's here on her own, on holiday," he told me.

The recent experience of Perhentian Island had dulled any shine there may have been left off this poor, exhausted, tourist hotspot. The need for a mini break was no more evident for the so-called 'protected island' itself than the holiday makers that leave their daily mark. Next, for our final port of call, we hopped over to the island of Sapi. A 25-acre, tree-covered mound alongside its close neighbour Gaya, breaking the surface of an otherwise flat aquatic landscape 7km from the mainland. Here is home to 2-metre-long monitor lizards and a troop of kleptomaniac macaques, apparently.

The two neighbouring islands become connected by a sand bank at low tide and feel much less spoilt than their shabby big brother. Time flew by like a swallow on the wing as I strolled collecting images of driftwood benches and tilted palms, while trawling ankle deep and bare foot in the lapping waves. Suddenly it was all over.

On the mainland, talk turned to food as I noticed the buffet was closed on the pier. "Do you want eat?" Saeed asked Daniel.

115

"I don't mind, but I can eat any time," he replied, in his usual slightly high-pitched, yet typically German accent. "There is a burger place around the corner or the outdoor seafood place down here," he continued.

"Seafood sounds good to me," I told him.

Saeed agreed with my preference so we passed by the burger bar and a large black police speed boat with three engines moored up at its own little jetty along the footpath on the sea front. Thick square concrete posts, cladded in timber with a pair of heavy chains dangling between each one, provided a barrier at the drop-off down to the sea. A sculpture saying 'I love KK', with the word love replaced with a heart shaped symbol, in shiny chrome 3-D letters, stood on a granite plinth near the road, then just beyond was the start of the restaurants.

Swaying gangplanks, coloured wooden hulls with white hand-painted registration numbers, cumbersome anchors, frayed flags fighting to break free of their lofty tethers, and tatty clothes straggling makeshift lines. This was the image of nine fishing boats, moored up in a line, next to a row of permanent steel-framed gazebos on the water's edge on the right-hand side of a path, between a further two parallel rows of canopies on the left. At around 3pm every day, staff begin unstacking folding tables and plastic patio chairs, placing them in rows under the shade of plastic-coated tarpaulin roofs.

We wandered around looking to find a deal. A young girl chopped up ice with a cleaver, while her boss, a beautiful 30 year-old woman, set out her stall placing giant shrimp on her display table. All around people began to lay out fish and seafood, on beds of ice outside each establishment. A tray of huge oysters piled high waited to be sold alongside a large set of balance scales, as little by little the area filled with tables and chairs.

A teenage boy with a black baseball cap picked out fish from a large storage box, placing each one out with great care and precision. The fish were roughly all around the same size: 40 cm long. Grouper, white snapper, red snapper, parrot fish, baby stingray and tuna laid side by side, wide mouthed and milky eyed, waiting for the final end from grill to mouth. A guy fanned the coals of a grill trolley, raising the heat on lines of mini squid kebabs, each stuffed with

116

spices and its own tentacles. Parallel incisions across their bodies opened up as the hot flesh shrank to reveal a tantalizing snippet of their inner delights, awaiting the person handing over 20 ringgit. A whiff of garam masala passed through the air, as bums started to be placed on seats. Three Muslim men, in ankle length gowns and embroidered skullcaps, were one of the first groups to take a seat.

Each open kitchen has its own set of tables with different coloured plastic tablecloths that define each of the sections. Orange, white, yellow and red. Bunches of fresh herbs provide a foliage backdrop behind crab, lobster, scallop and a strange, large, stripy sea snail called a carnot, with a shell the size of a cantaloupe.

After one full circuit of the stalls, Saeed asked, "Which fish was red snapper?" at the stall we first looked. The young guy threw one onto the scales. "How much for this one?" he asked.

"Ten."

"No, no my friend. Too expensive," he argues playfully. "What do you think?" he asked, looking round at us two.

Remembering what I was told many years ago, I explained to Saaed "I once ordered red snapper on a beach BBQ in Thailand and the chef told me white snapper was better. Before too long the white snapper was on the scales instead, along with a small portion of squid.

"Okay we give you five," Saeed tells the guy with the scales.

"I cannot. The price is ten."

Banners with coloured images of plates of food swayed in the breeze, attached to the outside edge of the gazebo roofs. One read 'Salamat datang ke gerai' then underneath 'Welcome to stall'. A trolley full of yellow Calor gas bottles rolled past as another jet gained height in the sky above our heads, then banked left, out to sea.

"Okay seven. Halas, halas," the guy turns to his senior for approval.

"Okay? Yes?" says Saeed once more, now looking for confirmation from the boss guy. The boss nodded in agreement.

"How do you like it cooked?" the youngster asked. Unaware we might be asked such a question, we looked at each other for inspiration.

"How about grilled with garlic?" he suggested.

"Mmm? That sounds okay. What do you guys think?"

We agreed to take his advice and took a seat to wait for our food to be cooked; all the time Daniel didn't talk about what he might eat, until we sat down. "Do you have fried rice with vegetables?" he inquired.

"Yes I can do."

"That's good for me," he said. "I am vegetarian."

I ordered an iced lemon tea and looked around.

A 12 year-old boy held down a crab with one hand, then lassoed a claw with nylon twine with the other, wrapping the twine around its body, back around a few times, until finally tying it off around the last claw, thus disabling its weaponry. He repeated the process on each one in the bucket at his side. My lemon tea arrived in a tall clear plastic glass, hot to the touch yet full of ice, with a sweet minty tang. A pair of middle-aged tourists were drawn to the front display. The guy picked up a lobster and held it up in the air. Around 20cm long, its body was plain and completely overshadowed by two unfeasibly long, thin, deep blue claws and tentacles each twice the length of its body. Then our food arrived.

The white snapper was still in one piece but butterflied into two fillets, with a light covering of red sauce on the flesh. We tucked in, sharing turns at scooping out morsels of flakey white meat, but the truth is it wasn't as good as I remember. A disappointing result this time but an eventful day all the same and, with flights to Tawau to look forward to the next morning, the letdown was soon forgotten as we walked back with full stomachs.

The alarm set for 6:30 am, we got our heads down back at Zoku where a couple more new faces become our fleeting neighbours. AirAsia came out cheapest again so onto the red and white jet for the continuing adventure. Completely led by Saeed's judgment, we were heading for the islands off the coast of Semporna for diving and snorkelling respectively. Saeed had a divers license and was keen to cram in as many dives as possible in the first two days. "Because of a build up of nitrogen in your body, you cannot fly for around 18 hours," Saeed explained. Not expecting to be doing any diving myself, due to a lack of license, this dilemma was not my concern.

118

In under an hour we were there, stood outside arrivals on the kerb at Tawau airport looking for transport. "I can check price of Grab car," Saeed explained, pulling his smartphone from his pocket. Semporna was just over an hour's drive away.

"How about taking a look at that nature reserve with the world's largest tree?" I suggested.

"57 ringgit to Semporna," said Saeed. I wasn't expecting so much and, bearing in mind the giant tree was in the opposite direction, it was a good job we had travelled together. In a flash of inspiration, Saeed said, "What about hiring car?"

I didn't give it a thought as they tend to be too expensive but, with two car hire desks behind us three meters away, it was worth a shot. "I've got my British license in my wallet."

"I have my license also," he explained.

We went to a counter each but there was no one around at mine. On hearing a conversation, I joined Saeed as the man told him, "We can only accept international license. Sorry." But Saeed, being the determined kind of person he is, would not take no for an answer and badgered the staff while I left him to it, sitting on the curb looking for travel options on my smartphone.

I noticed a guy talking to Saeed. "Hey Ian! This man friend has car we can take."

"They can bring it here?" I asked. He turned and asked the man.

"Yes, no problem. License, no problem," the stranger explained.

"Cool. Job done," I told Saeed. The guy was charging 60 ringgit per day. 120 for two days was around the price of a Grab from the airport and back.

"Yes this is much better because we can come back to the airport at the right time," Saeed explained excitedly. We now had free reign to come and go as we pleased.

We asked the guy to make the call to his friend and after a quick conversation, he turned to us and said, "Yes okay ten minute." Then suddenly, literally seconds later, out of the blue the car hire guy had a change of heart and agreed to let us have a car. I can only imagine they didn't have a vehicle available so, rather than tell us, they made it look like it wasn't their problem by refusing to accept our licenses, then a car turned up just in the nick of time. It was all very strange but we made our apologies to the man who made the call and reverted back to the kiosk, as it felt like a safer option. I became the designated driver, as Malaysian traffic drives on the left like at home. Saudis drive on the right so it made sense for me to take the wheel. A decision I favoured, as I prefer to be the one in control.

Here you can fill your tank for a fraction of the cost it would be back home. A full tank was only 20 ringgit; that's around £4. We headed for what is described as the world's biggest tree attraction before the digs. Snacks in hand, Saeed settled down in his seat and put his phone on loudspeaker. Ed Sheeran was the first track to rattle its way out of his tiny tin can speaker but it was better than nothing. A Yemeni guy living in Saudi playing Ed Sheeran, seemed strange to me. I expected some random upbeat flute warbling tune. Saeed had around five similar favourite songs on repeat so, when the satnav directed us through a large set of open gates into an empty car park at our destination half an hour after pulling out of the petrol station, my ears were glad of the respite.

Three Chinese teenage girls were walking back past the ticket office as we approached. "How was it?" I asked one girl.

She looked around at her friend and her friend replied. "Yeah okay. Do you have socks?" she asked.

"No why?"

"There are leeches," she continued.

"Oh, yeah I see."

"What is leeches?" Saeed asked. I tried to describe them as a worm or bug, but still he wondered.

"They attach themselves to your skin," I explained.

"And they look like bug?" I sketched one on my notepad and showed him.

"They suck blood," the girl added.

Because I didn't want to get stung into paying for my big bag on the plane again, I was travelling light. The only footwear I had was the flip-flops I was wearing, no socks or long trousers either. Saeed had trainers and socks but he also had shorts like me. Undeterred yet slightly apprehensive, we paid the entrance fee. In exchange we received a photocopy of a map of the reserve, showing the location of the world's tallest tree at 88.2m tall, a hot spring and two waterfalls. The only issue up to now, apart from the lack of reasonable clothing and footwear, was the photocopied map. It was of extremely poor quality to the point it was a bit useless.

The path started in good repair. A raised wooden walkway guided you through the first few metres, where I almost stood on a millipede the length of my foot. I tried to get a photo but it didn't like it and adopted its defensive stance, curling up into a spiral. Then soon after, a similar looking beast crossed our path. Like its longer cousin, this one had the girth of a sausage, but it was much shorter with a segmented toughened shell. He had also curled up at the sign of trouble but in a much more effective way. At the first sign of a predator, he would roll into a perfectly round armoured sphere.

Five minutes in, the only indication of the correct direction to follow was the path worn by previous visitors and it didn't get any better later. We entered the park around lunchtime and, after hiking through, around, up and over, for half an hour, it was becoming obvious a full day would better suit this activity. The place was vast. Exposed tree roots doubled up as natural steps on the steepest sections as we marched onwards to our first port of call: the giant tree. Some of the specimens we were passing on our way must have come close to the record. Here the largest trees tended to be the ones with a strange wing roots, like baggy ships sales, on the lowest section of trunk.

"Can you hear that, Saeed?" It was a chainsaw up ahead in the distance – an electric chainsaw, not the usual petrol driven type. "Do you hear that?"

"Yes I hear it."

"Is that a chainsaw?" I asked.

"I think bug," he replied.

'There's no way that is a bug,' I thought to myself. The noise intensified the closer we got to the source but weirdly it didn't get louder. Further along the path, the sound now seemed like a distant machine but in the opposite direction. I would have bet my shirt on it not being an insect but I was wrong: this was no chainsaw.

We came across a rigid ribbon vine crossing our path a couple of times, although I'm sure it has a name other than the one I just gave it. I'd not seen anything like this before not even on TV. Around an inch wide, it would peek out from behind a tree trunk and curl its way loosely for many metres aloft into the canopy like a sprained overstretched organic spring. As you might expect, the humidity was off the scale and leaves the size of tennis rackets littered the floor.

I had been coping quite well in flip flops, until the first leech appeared from nowhere on my shin. "Shit!" I shouted, grabbing it with my fingers. I pulled and stretched it but, still attached, it slipped from my grip.

Saeed turned around, "What is it?"

"Fucking leech!" I exclaimed.

Stories of leeches needing to be burned off, or smothered in salt, as the Chinese girls had suggested, didn't bother me at the time because things like that only happen to others, yet a parasitic slug had actually somehow attached itself to my skin for the sole purpose of stealing my blood and I couldn't get it off. That freaked me out, especially having neither salt nor a flame at hand. I tugged once more; this time it detached, but only as far as between my fingers. Shaking as if to dry my hands after washing with no towel didn't work either. The little sucker was still attached. A firm flick is what eventually ended our symbiotic whirlwind relationship.

Now I had a good reason to concentrate on spotting the danger, I noticed them on stalks of vegetation at the edge of the path at calf height. Like a child struggling to reach a stationary Tarzan rope swing on a hillside, they wait fully outstretched towards the path in hope they can grab on to an unsuspecting victim – to great success bearing in mind the amount of times it happened. Gradually after the next four or five parasites were removed, one at a time as they attached, it became much less gross, almost normal even, and in little more than an hour, we were posing for pictures at the main attraction, swamped by a trunk you could hide a van behind. It was the same species as most of the colossal trees we had passed on the way, but this gentle, old, majestic giant, the Burj Khalifa of the forest, is more than just a tree. It stands strong yet humble, as a gently swaying symbol of nature's ability to create structures worthy of worship, silently offering a spiritual lesson to all those who care to take an interest into the wonders of life and its harmonious

122

concurrence with time when unhindered by human interference. At around 15m diameter at the base, its trunk, like a timber highway leading to the sky, travels up through the canopy, where distant branches are stroked by passing clouds. The path leading here ends at this point so, after the time it took for photographs and open-mouthed staring, retracing our steps was the only option. We reached an intersection eventually and checked the time. "I think we cannot go to waterfall and hot springs," Saeed informed me.

Darkness fell at 6 pm here, one hour earlier than mainland Malaysia, so we had to make a decision. "I have seen many waterfalls," I explain to Saeed.
"Okay hot spring I don't know," he replied.
"Yeah let's do that if you don't mind?" I enquired.
"No problem."
The path seemed endless at times. A 20-metre ropebridge over a river helped to break the monotony but, beyond that, the path turned increasingly muddy again and the amount of leeches increased with it. After double figures, you stop counting and caring so much for that matter; one thing to avoid was getting wet. Mud between my flip flops and the soles of my feet was causing them to slip from under me as I walked. Keeping one eye on the terrain coming up and one on my lower legs for leeches, I would stop when I needed, if not to place a dry leaf under my foot for traction then to remove another parasite. The sound of babbling water increased in volume as we moved along. Maybe we would see a waterfall after all, even though this was the wrong path, but disappointingly it didn't happen. Not as disappointing as the hot spring though.
When we reached the spot we had marched 45 minutes to find, it was a massive let down. The path had found its way to the riverbank once more at a point where a shelter had been erected. A crude wooden bench with a corrugated tin roof was a sign this must be the point we were meant to reach as the path stopped here. I climbed the hillside ahead to double check we weren't missing anything but nothing else was around, just a tributary to the right off the main river, stretching back 20 metres, with a strange pale blue tinge and slight whiff of sulphur. The same pale blue stains could be seen

around a patch of rocks about a metre above the water level too where a tiny stream of water was seeping out. I attempted to reach the source of the contamination by wading through the ten metres or so. Saeed had long since lost interest and was stood in the shallows of the main body of water admiring the view.

"You can see something?" he asked.

"No not really. But I'm going to try and get over to the rocks over there to see how hot it is," I replied.

Boulders laid under the water here were spiky, pitted to the point it was too painful to walk on them barefoot. Corroded by whatever had turned the whole area into a scene out of a sci-fi film. Halfway between the spout and the place I'd left my flip flops, the pitted rock became too painful under foot so I asked Saeed for his help.

"Can you throw my flip-flops please?" I asked. Now reunited with my footwear, I continued. The closer I got to the source, the thicker the sediment became until each tentative step clouded the water more and more with a pale blue cloud, further hampering my progress. I reached the source to find nothing particularly different. The water was very slightly warmer, nothing more. All in all, quite a disappointing leg of the journey, especially bearing in mind the prospect of running the leech gauntlet on the hour-long hike back.

Quick checks for the blood sucking a little shits migrating up my legs would be carried out regularly on the homeward leg. I lifted my leg back, checking my calves almost every other step, de-leeching as required so I couldn't believe I'd missed one when I felt something on the back of my leg, halfway back along the path. If unnoticed, they work their way up to a warm spot to feed and one had slipped by undetected. After removing the stray, I checked under my shorts. It was clear but things were about to get worse before they got better.

I pulled up my T-shirt and found two, well dug in around my belly button. They must have been under there a while as they did not detach like the others. They'd had time to draw blood and, when we did eventually part ways, there was claret. "I need to strip off as soon as I get out of here and check I don't have any more," I explained to Saeed, imagining the task of removing leeches from my balls and arse crack. Saeed had managed to avoid as much unwanted attention as me, probably down to his socks and trainers. Back at the car, I immediately did a full body leech check, which surprisingly turned out to be clean. It didn't stop me from imagining the feeling of them for hours after though, quickly turning round to look every few minutes like a cat with fleas.

On our way back towards the accommodation, I could have eaten a lizard. We passed a KFC. "Are you hungry, Saeed?" I asked.

"Yes I can eat."

"I might call to KFC if you don't mind?" I asked but of course he didn't mind. I spun around and turned into a row of businesses on a road running parallel to the main road. KFC was on the corner on one side but another place caught my eye. A more traditional restaurant was on the opposite corner and it looked quite busy. Saeed preferred the idea of this place also so we walked in and took a seat near a young man preparing roti at a trolley stall in the front corner.

It was a pleasure to see his skilled craftsmanship in action. He threw a thin film of dough in the air, spinning as he threw, aiming to land sticking to the metal surface of the counter. After landing he then pulled it out and stretched it further over the surface. Next he dipped his fingers in a bowl of oil and drizzled it over the flattened dough, finally folding it over until it resembled the shape of a sausage roll. These he had collected in rows to his left and, as an order came in, he finally rolled out the dough once more, making a round pancake around 25cm wide. The roti here were one ringgit, or 20p in real money, and for that you got curry sauce and a watery dahl to dip it in.

"We have these all the time in my country," Saeed said. "They are expensive here though. We pay half this amount," he continued. Undeterred, he placed an order. "We will take two," proclaimed my companion. "Why so expensive?" Saeed asked. He did not receive an explanation but we did receive a world class roti.

After final preparation, he transferred the doughy discs to a hot plate by his side where they bubbled then crisped. He could fit around four at a time on the cooking plate and, once done, they went back on the stall for the finishing touches, literally. Stacked on top of each other, he slaps the stack from the side, sliding his hands along the work surface into the pile in a clapping motion, turning the pile each time, to even out the battering. As it's squashed, the height of the pile increases, then he separates each roti, pulling it back out into its original shape and serves it up on a segmented steel plate with sections containing the accompaniments. Anyone who knows some culinary skill will know how hard it can be to turn the simplest ingredients into a mouth-wateringly more-ish morsel and he did just that, with the perfect combination of crispness and soft moist yummy underbelly.

Drinks here were also a revelation. A drink not dissimilar to Ovaltine but better called Milo is popular hot or cold. Best I think cold, it can be purchased here for two ringgit. The cold one comes hot, in a glass topped with ice and a straw but be warned – if you like malty drinks, it's going to take some serious willpower not to keep ordering more at these prices.

Fed and watered, we got back on the hunt for our digs once more. It had been dark for a while at this point but driving was easy, as pretty much all the signs were the same as back home. Saeed played the same block of tunes off his smartphone as Semporna drew closer. Saeed had also sorted the accommodation for us both while still at Zoku. It always feels much more of a task when I attempt such jobs so to look at his phone screen and agree with his choice of hostel got my vote. It seemed like a two-minute job to him. Coral Home was now our home. For the two nights we would stay at this rough and ready coastal town, gateway to renowned dive sites off the coast. The islands were a 45 minute speed boat ride away, the best of which, Siperdan, was restricted to a strict quota, unless you were prepared to pay a premium for that quota to be overlooked.

Finding the digs wasn't as difficult as getting inside. "Hey it's good you opted for a free parking space when booking," I told Saeed. It seemed a bit pointless at the time of booking, as we didn't have a car, nor did I think it might be the case, but once gain the boy did good.

After 20 minutes attempting to gain entry, the door eventually clicked open. We were greeted by a young Chinese lad, who informed us we had no booking and the only room he had was a double with one bed. We reluctantly agreed to take it but further pestering led to a twin room eventually. The only drawback was having to wait until it was made ready. This place was quite small and a little grotty compared with Zoku. A brown, aluminium sliding patio door met you at the top of the concrete stairs at the entrance. On the door was a sign saying 'NO SHOES' and a rack to leave them was provided on the top landing. Inside a table next to the door was where we would be eating breakfast. A sofa bed against the wall nearby had a pale blue quilt cover with a scene of clouds, hot air balloons and a caption saying, 'It is a full white cloud in the night shy'. Apart from the desk and work surface, there was nothing else in the room other than a corridor leading to the bedrooms. Toilets and showers left something to be desired, but they worked. You could find them around the corner, past the desk in the opposite direction to the sleeping quarters.

We opted to nip out for a while and come back when the room was ready so we dropped our bags and jumped back in the car. All streets, regardless of their location, looked like back streets here, especially under the cover of darkness. Luckily for Semporna, the islands drew a steady flow of tourists wanting to experience life under the waves. A four-wheel drive truck pulled up in front of us as we were about to pull out. Suspecting it might be the owner of the digs, we held back. A big Chinese guy and a woman got out, heading for the stairs.

"We have a booking!" I exclaimed, as I made my way back over.

"Okay yes. We just have to make up the room," his wife informed me.

"You going diving?" the man asked.

Saeed's ears pricked up at this remark. "Yes. Do you know the price?"

"How many islands you want?" continued the guy.

"I don't know, maybe three."

"Okay you can go to Mabul or...?" He paused hoping to hear another option.

"What about Sipadan?" I asked. I knew very little about diving other than Sipadan is one of Jacques Cousteau's favourite dive spots.

At 99.96% under water, you might call it the tip of the iceberg, although you're not about to need your big coat here. Sipadan is the summit of an

127

extinct, submerged, volcanic cone rising up 600 metres from the seabed, peeping out just above sea level, neighbouring the island of Mabul. Even though it's a disputed territory between Malaysia and Indonesia, that's not the reason armed guards police its 30 acres of natural splendour. Pristine forest, overlooking picture perfect powder sand beaches, drifting off beneath a foaming azure fringe, drops away into a turquoise expanse. Hidden below the surface lays the asset they protect.

Enforcing the strictly limited and highly lucrative permit scheme implemented by the authorities, it's this sub aqua world that attracts divers from around the world and without a permit you don't stand a chance. Sipadan has been mentioned as the best dive spot in the world according to one well-known diving magazine, rubbing shoulders with the likes of the Galapagos Islands and the Great Barrier Reef. One thing that's much less subjective is the honour of being Malaysia's undisputed number one dive location. These subterraenean terraces covered in an abundance of vivid coral and vegetation teem with unfazed marine life accustomed to regular intrusions by humans. The potential for up to 50 metres visibility in the dry season and a diverse variety of around 400 species combine to offer the potential of spectacular views of huge fish in big shoals, if you can afford it.

"Oh no, you cannot. You need booking many weeks to go there and it is very expensive." Surprisingly, Saeed had not heard of the place.

"Why is this?" Saeed asked. Although I'd not known him long, I knew being told he couldn't do something would just make him more determined and I was right. "Why not Siperdan?" Saeed badgered.

"They have only a small amount of people can go. It is the best place," he explained.

"How much to go Siperdan?" Saeed was starting to become more abrupt than forthright.

The guy laughed nervously. "You cannot," he repeated.

"Okay, how much other place?"

"If you go to other islands, you can pay 350 ringgit."

"For how many dives?"

"Three dives," he told Saeed.

128

"Is it okay for me to dive? I don't have a license," I explained to the guy.

"No problem," he told me.

"I can dive?" I asked excitedly.

"Yes, no problem. You can do fun dive."

"Where is booking?" Saeed continued.

"You can go to jetty. There you can book, but maybe they close now," he explained.

Me now eager to dive, and Saeed now eager to go to Sipadan, we thanked the guy for his time and quickly headed down to the sea front to investigate further.

We reached our destination, around 1 mile away, by passing through the busy main trading street. No shiny bright shop fronts drawing you in around here; this was a traders' patch. It reminded me of the wholesale markets back in Sheffield. Rusty wheelbarrows, cardboard boxes and scruffy wooden tables stacked up on the pavement, waiting for the next working day to begin. Down at the waterfront, a covered boardwalk had its entrance at the roadside. It ran out at right angles to the road for at least 100 metres over the bay on stilts with a roof covering the whole length. Empty scuba tanks sat waiting for exchange under the sign at the entrance. Plants draping down from hanging baskets and benches lining the way invited you in. You could be forgiven for forgetting where you were for a minute; that is until you look directly across the road on the footpath opposite.

This was the stomping ground of child hawkers, selling seafood out of plastic washing-up bowls, dangling from nylon twine. These living creatures, sloshing around in three inches of water, were traipsed up and down the street by girls, boys and youths, from as young as five years old. They competed amongst each other to convince every passer-by, apart from the police, into purchasing crab, lobster, sea snail, fish: in fact anything that could be caught nearby, you could buy here.

Just before a row of shops selling souvenirs and snide goods at the far end, the boardwalk branched off to the right. This was where the dive shops were. There was a clutch of four shops, each with racks of wet suits hanging from coat hangers outside, and a couple were open. We inquired at a place called

Blue Ocean. It was the first on the right. Observing the 'no shoes' sign, I slid the glass door open and walked in, up the two steps into the office. A chubby Chinese girl sat behind a desk did her best to answer Saeed's barrage of questions in the reception office, mainly consisting of why we could not go to Sipadan. After a while her boss, a young dark-skinned Chinese guy with an approachably round face, came to her assistance from his office. Saeed began to repeat his questions.

"Why we cannot go to Sipadan?" he pressed.

"Only a small amount of people can go," explained the boss.

"Sipadan, I can go."

"You can go okay," said the boss. He'd had enough. "1100 ringgit," he explained.

"1100 and I can go?"

"Yes." That shut him up. Compared to the 300 ringgit to go to the second best dive site, Saeed decided not to shell out quite so much and negotiated a deal. He paid 300 ringgit, for three dives, because he had a license, and I paid 330 ringgit for two dives as I needed a dive buddy.

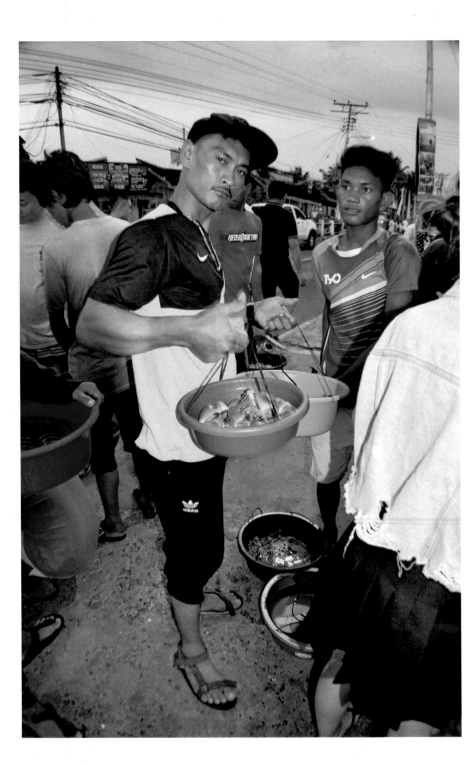

Chapter 6
Not Sipadan

N ext morning at Coral Home, the alarm went off at 7:30 am. I woke up, first feeling confused, then thankful. I'd slept alone in my own bed, albeit in a small twin room with plain white walls and no windows, but it was preferable to sharing a double bed with a man I hardly knew.

This room was nearest to the dining area: one of six off the main corridor. Two single beds were pushed into opposite far corners from the door, parallel to the longest wall, with most of the rest of the width taken up by a bedside cabinet each. With just enough room to swing inwards, I opened the bedroom door to find food left out for breakfast in a self-service bin. Three cold fried eggs on a plate, under a curved clear Perspex display lid, hinged at the back, with bread for toast, beverage ingredients and water dispenser with hot and cold options.

We were instructed to be at the dive shop by 8.30 am but we had both been sluggish to rise. Half the way through making toast and coffee I checked the time and realised we'd be late if we didn't cut breakfast short.

"It's ten past eight you know."

"It is past eight already?"

"Yes, ten past: we need to leave now. We have 20 minutes to get to through town to the jetty."

I necked my coffee, stuffed a full egg in my mouth and rushed back to the bedroom. Saeed followed; we grabbed our things and left. My fins had not been used in years prior to arriving in Malaysia so, glad to be putting them to good use, they would make their way into the boat later, along with my camera and full facemask-snorkel combo that I treated myself to back at home.

Outside the warmth of the morning sun glossed over the shabby surroundings, like a fit supply teacher in a remedial class. We jumped in the car and turned left at the end of the road, heading down into town and straight into stationary traffic on of the main trader's street. Daylight had brought this place to life. The shutters were up on a line of wholesale warehouses on the right, while

131

bulging hessian sacks, wooden crates and trollies leaned against the back wall of what looked like a market along our left side.

With no option but to wait, entertainment was provided by a gang of over-exuberant teenagers pushing a fleet of modified wheelbarrows, upgraded with metal strengtheners welded onto their axle braces and around the top lip of their trays, piled high with boxes of goods, each being relayed from one business to another. Full loads needed a little care, but once their barrows were empty, the lads raced back as fast as their fake Adidas flip flops would allow, competing for the testosterone-fuelled title of fittest fool of the day.

One lad had a problem manoeuvring what was obviously the heaviest of all the loads of this round. Maybe his eyes were bigger than his muscles when he made the regrettable decision to allow his vehicle to be overloaded to the point it caused him to lift then drop it again a couple of times en route, before stopping and looking around with a conceded expression as his colleagues sprinted back past looking for the chequered flag. One lad pulled his barrow alongside on his way back and attempted to help; hoping to prove to be the strongest, he lifted the barrow, dropped it again and left the lad to work it out for himself.

We started to make a little progress along the street and eventually lost sight of the lad and his plight as we crawled past a bulbous-nosed old man wearing a shabby cloth cap parked at the side of the road. Sat arm resting on the open window, he waited, back wheels slightly hidden by their rusty arches in a light blue battered 1980s Toyota, whose opened boot lid retained a mountain of fresh fat watermelons. After a further five minutes in the crawling traffic, he also disappeared from view as we neared the end of the restriction, which turned out to be the junction to a roundabout that we could have approached from the same direction as the traffic that was causing our delays.

At the waterfront, no one batted an eye lid when we turn up 15 minutes late; they were all too busy setting up for the day. Two young Chinese girls who'd booked to do snorkelling were sat waiting to come along with us today also. They'd already gone through the process of finding a wetsuit and signing the relevant paperwork so now they sat giggling with their hands over their mouths pretending to be meek and submissive.

I was stood beside the wetsuits hung outside, next to a large plastic box where the fins were kept, as one of the young guys who looked very happy not to have been left behind from an over-manned operation, came over with a smile as big as Donald Trump's ego. "You pick your size?" he quizzed while pointing at the rack. A red and black one, medium, with a snorkel motif and Chinese writing on the front, is what I tried on. It was a good fit so I left it on to the amusement of the staff. Not wanting to back down too much after realising no one gets suited up till later, I dropped the suit to my waist while everyone else had slipped back into their shorts for the journey. We also had the pleasure of not only signing a disclaimer but a non-disclosure agreement too.

Although the jetty had a nice feel to it, the water around it didn't, especially against the roadside. An armada of plastic bottles bobbed around in a Mexican wave of waste on the shoreline in a brown speckled soufflé fringe. There is an improvement as you head out to sea but there's almost always a bottle somewhere in view. A clean-up campaign in November 2019 yielded 60 kilos of plastic waste from the shoreline on Sipadan and here too there's a real need of some similar treatment. As in so many other areas of the world's oceans, there's an issue here that's impossible to miss.

The wind in our face and a snowy white blizzard of surf in our wake, we pressed on with the 45-minute journey toward the first dive site, or at least that's what we thought. Without notice, although it was probably planned and not mentioned, we stopped at a sand bank island made up of a long stretch of sandy beach, around half a mile long, with pretty much nothing else other than a property at the far end that was out of bounds. Shells, snails, clients from rival boats and the odd blue starfish was about all there was.

"Okay you can look here, but you cannot go to the house. It is private, okay? 10 minutes, you can take photo." We had joined three other boats and, like us, they'd all intentionally grounded on the sand bank as a temporary mooring. The area over the top of the long sandy bank dropped back down to a lower level of sand beyond. Still wet from the previous high tide, it stretched out 200 metres in front where people stood in little groups, dotted around taking selfies. As is the norm around here, they were mostly Chinese but there was the odd westerner and Yemen too.

I noticed a cone-shaped shell different to most I had seen before. I picked it up, spotting a curved hooked section of shell on the edge of the opening, the same curved feature as the giant ones with a smooth pearlescent pink internal layer you can find for sale in shops. As I held the baby ornament between my fingers, a thin tapered snail partially slid out of its armour, turned itself back round to the point of the obstruction, namely my fingers, and attempted to prize itself out of my grip, using the thin tip of its tail to wedge in between its shell and my finger. Eventually, after a few attempts it gave up and retreated back inside.

Saeed had wandered off on his own, as had I, but when we were called back to the boat he was nowhere to be seen. He had gone to the far end of the island and was oblivious to the calls to move on but, just before the need for a search party, he could be seen making his way back over. Trying not to look guilty, he jogged the last couple of metres. "Look," he said, holding out his hand. It was an electric blue starfish, moving around sloth-like over his fingers. Two minutes later we were gone and the starfish had a long walk home. Next stop Mataking Island.

This place had a jetty but we were not afforded the privilege of running and jumping off the end into the sea like others were doing as we arrived. Nor were we allowed to moor up there either. A rival dive company either owned it or had done a deal to rent it so we anchored just offshore. Saeed was the first to brave the murky depths, leaving a trail of bubbles on the surface as he descended with his buddy. This spot was far from one of those crystal-clear stretches of water with amazing visibility but you could still make out the needle fish skimming the underside of the surface. A harmless, timid, thin creature with a needle-like snout, unable to harm anyone, apart from the sixteen-year-old boy who was stabbed through the heart and killed by one accidentally while swimming in the dark one night. At around half a metre long when fully grown, they tend not to be alone. Usually found in shoals of three and above.

One of the guys working on the boat had tattoos, one of which was the same as the Buddhist tattoo on my back. He was shaved bald, in his late 20s, with a pot belly paunch but his endearing personality was his biggest attribute. Even

134

without the knowledge of what it was they were saying to each other, it wasn't hard to grasp that he was the one who would be invited to parties. Although softly spoken, he didn't go unnoticed. He got around the no-smoking ban by keeping his lit cigarette hidden inside the top of a small glass bottle with a little water in the bottom at all times to stop stray burning cinders doing any harm, even when taking a drag. I showed him my tattoo.

"Ooo yes, now you must go back and thank them for their protection it has been giving you," he told me in his soft, slow, determined tone, smiling and nodding in encouragement. "Then you will get more good come back to you," he continued, with more smiles and nods.

It was 15 years since the Buddhist tattoo by the monk in a temple near Bangkok was done, so maybe he had a point. It was made up of nine zigzag lines pointing upward. The middle one was the tallest, reaching my lower neck, each finished with an arrow on the top. They sit above two grids of squares, each with symbols inside. The whole thing resembles some sort of building: a temple maybe.

"Do you know any Thai?" he asked.

"Yes, I know a little."

He spoke a few phrases, but nothing I understood so I told him what I knew. "Mi jep - no pain; Nic noy pric – not too spicy' sip son baht – 12 baht." That was pretty much my full repertoire.

"Want to dive?" The guy with the big grin who asked me to try on the wet suit at the jetty asked.

"Yeah."

"Okay let's go." He explained the procedure. We were to make our way into the shallows and perform some tasks. "First remove the mouthpiece, while on the water, okay? You take out like this," going through the motions as he talked. "Bend over like this, bring arm around and up. Come up with other arm and put back in, okay?" I nodded then followed suit, just as another scream and splash came from the jetty. "Okay, now mask," he continued. I needed to show I was capable of removing water from my mask as the need arose by blowing down my nose, while holding my head back and pressing the top of my mask, to create a gap at the bottom. I did it, just as he asked. "Ok let's

135

go. Here." He gestured for me to come closer. I felt the tightening of my vest against my torso and instant buoyancy as he inflated it with some sort of valve. "Ok, follow me," he ordered. We moved out into deeper water.

To avoid coral damage, our boat's anchor was carefully dropped at around two metres, 30 metres out from shore, just at the point the seabed started to drop away quickly at 45 degrees. I didn't understand the purpose of the inflatable vest, until he deflated it slightly and I felt myself sink a little. Now I know it provides the means of controlling your depth. The BCD (Buoyancy Control Device) comprises of a vest with an internal inflatable bladder and a control valve connected by a short tube. He released some more pressure from my valve and we started to drop gradually down to around five metres. As we dropped, the pressure on my inner ears turned to pain, worsening the further we descended. Flaring my nostrils and clenching my jaw produced a crackle closely followed by a relieving stereo squeak in my ears that immediately did the trick.

Under the ocean, sights and sounds combine to create a profoundly different experience. The ocean teems with soft noise here. Randomly timed subtle pops, clicks and snaps, reminiscent of a distant crackling bonfire, swirl around combining with muffled, distant, cosmic buzzes unlike anything on land. Alien noises that provide a poor sense of distance compared to noises on dry land. The terrifying muffled squeal of an outboard motor approaching for instance, always feels much nearer than it actually is.

The usual suspects nibbled away at the rocks: parrot fish, sweet lips etc, nothing too big though. Bigger fish seemed more wary and would shy away quickly if they crossed our path. My guide pointed down at a turtle resting next to a rock directly underneath me. I tucked my head down to my knees, kicked up with my legs and paddled my fins to descend for a closer look. Not before I got to within touching distance did he cruise away with effortless grace. It was a good size, maybe 50 cm, but its parents lay ahead.

Constantly drawing air from a tank initially felt unnatural and a slightly scary, especially under five metres of water. I didn't expect it to take more effort to pull air from the tank than breathing normally but, after a while, along with the intermittent muffled babble of air racing past your ears to the surface, it eventually becomes the norm. There's far too much to occupy your mind, like scary predators at the top of the food chain with as many teeth in their mouths as cards in a deck.

Up ahead he gestured towards some rocks but I didn't see a thing. Drawing closer until within touching distance, he pointed again and there it was. The snout and gaping crescent jaw of a moray eel hiding in the coral with literally just its face visible from out of a crevice. I moved in for a close-up of the dead eyes and dentistry, which serve as quite a deterrent from poking your fingers near its face when you're close enough to see the bed of nails it uses to turn prey into pin cushions. They don't look any prettier or less scary in real life, even with the gormless, almost lifeless expression. It's as if they think, if they open their mouth and stay still, you can't see them.

They say – whoever they are – time flies when you're having fun. Well, down here, time races by faster than a dolphin down a water slide and unbelievably our time was almost up. Just as we were surfacing, Eagle Eyes spotted something else. A group of three or four spherical concrete objects, each around the size of a space hopper, hollow and full of large holes, were sat on the seabed, like the dead skeletons of WW2 naval mines. I presumed they had been placed there deliberately for the benefit of people like me. Hiding inside one was a lionfish. Highly poisonous, they are easily recognisable due to the covering of spiky tentacles, providing 360-degree protection. He was around 15 cm long. I held my hand out towards the hole to provoke a response to no avail. From time to time I would get the okay sign to which I would reply back with the same signal: index finger and thumb tips touching in a circular shape. This time though, I got a different sign. "It's like a finger, pointing to the moon. Don't watch the finger."

While ever anyone is in the water and the boat is stationary, the tubular stainless-steel ladder with rope wound around it for added grip stays hooked over the rim of the boat, dangling into the water, only to be lifted and rested on the bench seat when the boat is moving. Getting back on board without it would be a nightmare. Saeed was back on deck when I climbed the ladders. With no buoyancy, the weight of the tanks takes some effort to get back up on board. A row of blind holes, designed to hold the oxygen bottles in place, are situated towards the front of the boat, at either side, set into the bench seats. The trick is to locate the bottle into the hole, while still strapped to your body. Docking is best done efficiently to avoid embarrassment.

"How did it go?" I asked Saeed, as my bottle dropped into place on my third attempt.

"Good," he replied, but his voice told another story. He would have been heard by the entire crew had he given a derogatory comment but I knew him well enough by now to know he was lying.

It was the turn of the Chinese girls to enter the water next, giving us a chance to eat lunch and chill for a while. Included in the price and provided by the organisers, each of us received our own plastic containers. A tray with lid and varying sized compartments containing rice, chicken, vegetables and gravy. They'd been loaded on board this morning, along with towels, bottles of water and an urn of the best green tea ever, as it was the only green tea I had ever actually liked.

Dive site number two was first on the afternoon's itinerary. A quick ten-minute blast and we dropped anchor again, this time at Pom-Pom island. Back on with the wet suit, fins and mask. We entered the water for my last dive. The guys told us the turtles move around each day to feed, then rest in regular spots. This must have been one of those spots because they were scattered around in groups every few metres, laying up against large rocks or slotted into crevices. As I scoured the watery landscape, I noticed one large guy up to my right, around 70 cm, then two more straight ahead, then more still, until I counted six together. The Daddy of the bunch, at around 120 cm, had two long sucker fish attached to his back. As I approached, we briefly made eye contact then, with effortless grace, he raised himself and his passengers out of his seat and glided around my head in a majestic arcing curve, all the time within touching distance. In seconds, our brief close encounter was to be over. Like a miniature Starship Enterprise leaving its docking station, he banked round and slowly vanished off in the abyss. Either a well-known hotspot, or just plain lucky, my turtle count on this second dive was 30 plus, more than I could ever have expected. A day to remember and, to top it off, a bit of sun and fun back on board with my new mate.

138

The boat had a solid fibreglass cabin with windscreen and a door leading to a tiny front deck area. It was out of bounds while moving but, with dropped anchor, through that door led to the ladder up onto the roof. It was time for a bit of our own variation of jetty jumping. As I climbed back on board after my first dive, the chubby lad with the bottle in his hand again pointed out a beautiful Chinese girl on the beach 25 metres away.

"When you dive you should shout, 'Hello sexy lady!' in Chinese. Okay?"

"Okay!" I agreed and quickly climbed back up. He told me what to say so this time I shouted loudly, "Hai, xing gan nu laaaannnng," before I hit the water. If nothing else, the crew were amused.

The weather for me was ideal today, not so much for Saeed though. There's something about living in a country that's always dry and hot, reaching 50° in the height of summer, that puts people off, plus he was already quite dark skinned so sunbathing wasn't going to appeal that much. Saeed is the sort of person who isn't going to turn down an opportunity to have some fun though. He took a turn climbing up onto the cabin roof and also joined in the coached shouting in Chinese to the lovely lady, while performing an impressive back flip. By the time we got bored with the laddish acrobatics, the Chinese girls were back on board, with tails of exciting underwater adventures and big smiles. We weighed anchor and set off back.

With one day left in Semporna, the flight back to KK from Tawau airport was tomorrow evening: this meant no dives tomorrow due to the build up of nitrogen causing potential issues at altitude so, with limited options to fill our last day, we considered another day out on the islands.

"I will look on my phone to see what else there is we could do," I told Saeed back at the digs.

"I want dive again. If I go early morning, it is okay to fly later?" he tried to convince himself.

"Is it worth the risk? What about these caves?" I said, showing him my smart phone. I'd typed in things to do in Semporna. A cave system that is home to thousands of bats and swallows came up on the search. Apparently they share the cave, using it at different times of day, as the bats leave the birds return. Quite interesting until you read the reviews of the overpowering stench of shit.

"Maybe we can do this, or waterfall?"

"Back at the nature reserve?"

"Maybe, I don't know."

"Why we just do snorkel at the islands. We can do deal for cheap price," he explained, but I was swaying towards something cheaper. We could have gone back to the nature reserve, braving the leeches once more, in search of the waterfalls that eluded us the first time around. Saeed handed back the phone. "I think I do snorkel." It wouldn't have been too hard to go our separate ways on the last day but snorkelling wasn't so expensive. We negotiated the price down to 130 ringgit so I decided to go along.

Apart from the jetty to the islands, the only other good thing that we came across in our brief visit to Semporna was a couple of busy restaurants close to the jetty, just past the car park opposite the dive shops. Nothing here comes close to the aesthetic of the western culture so forget the image that springs to mind and visualise four business units of equal proportions in a rectangular concrete building sat alone at the side of a road, more in keeping with a British warehouse than retail space, with a flat roof, roller shutter doors and a frontage on three levels, each as wide as a footpath, stepping down from the main floor, over a metre off the ground, to street level. Tiled in poor quality white ceramic tiles with more chips than a diced potato. These steps run along the full length of the building, continuing round either side. A three-metre-wide area between a dangerously deep open road gully and the bottom of the steps was filled with alfresco dining furniture.

A Muslim-run restaurant, offering roti at one ringgit, was the first you came across on the nearest corner to the car park. It drew in a smattering of customers but then there was the busiest place by far at the opposite end, sandwiched between two empty units. This was a Chinese seafood restaurant with those tanks that hold live fish and seafood but there's not just one or maybe two bubbling tanks full of fresh flapping fins and clamping claws waiting to be slaughtered here. Although relatively expensive, large groups of diners would share food and each other's company around plastic patio sets. As if in competition with each other, mountains of crab, fish, cockles and sea urchin would take centre stage as sharing platters. Eating here costs double or more than other, cheaper cuisines around but it didn't stop the tables filling up to almost 100% capacity tonight. People loved this place, especially the Chinese. I promised myself a seafood feast one night so this seemed like the perfect time.

We drove into the car park and got out just as the child street vendors were scampering in all directions. Some dashed past us up the road, holding their bowls aloft, sloshing the contents while making their escape. They were running from the police. I presume street selling is illegal and maybe they were in the country illegally, afraid of being repatriated. Whatever the reason, they weren't hanging around.

After the ones on the way back from the nature park, I couldn't resist a roti from the Muslim restaurant, even with the idea of a seafood feast. I made it my starter, moving on to the Chinese seafood place for my main course. From the outdoor eating area, I climbed up the long steps that ran the whole length of the block to the tank displays. Crabs in the low tank nearest the till and urchins in the low tank opposite. A walkway between the tanks was the route used by staff through to the rear kitchen hatch where they would pass wriggling baskets of hand-picked creatures to the kitchen staff with customers' instructions of how they should be prepared.

Further tanks were stacked on the till side on two levels. White tiled concrete with glass fronts, they held further fish, lobster and shellfish. On the white ceramic tiled floor of the upper level, I picked a lobster from a tank. All the tanks where roughly the same size, around a square metre, with bubble pipes to oxygenate the water. Each lobster was individually trapped, encased in two halves of a 2 litre Coke bottle. This way they were unable to fight each other before being scalded to death. Scores of bottles filled the tank, each containing a deliciously tasty prisoner.

Randomly I pointed out the victim to the waiter, who placed my lobster in a plastic basket. "Anything else?" he asked.

"How much is this one?" I enquired, pointing at the basket.

He put the lobster on the scale. "38 ringgit."

"Okay I will have a crab also." He dipped in and grabbed a crab from the tank, holding it with his fingers on the side of its body, dropping it in my basket.

Wanting a closer look, I went to pick up the crab but, as I grabbed it, the guy quickly said, "No!" just as the crab gave out a scream. I had picked it up by the wrong side, clasping my fingers on its eyes. It's weird to think the waiter would be concerned about the treatment of a creature that's about to be dropped in boiling water. I completed my order with six large shrimp at a total of 86 ringgit and made my way to an empty table down below.

Once sat down, I realised I had forgotten to order sea urchin. I had seen the spiky pots on tables with what looked like a white moose or soup inside and, having never experienced the taste, I needed to go back up the steps. "Also one of these," I said while pointing in the tank.

"How do you want it cooked?" he asked. I tried to explain what I had seen other people eating but I don't think he understood.

I returned to my table just as Saeed made his way from the roti place. As a Muslim, he was well met by the staff there, especially the girls. He would laugh and joke with them, teaching them Arabic words for plate, forks, etc. I'd left him flirting with the girls when I came to order my seafood supper.

"Did you order food?" he inquired.

"Yeah, I have treated myself tonight. Crab, lobster, prawn and urchin!" I proclaimed.

He browsed the menu. "I think I will have seafood noodle," he explained.

I saw people with bottles of beer on the tables but it wasn't from here. "Excuse me. Where can I get a beer?" I asked a passing waiter.

He pointed to the bar across the street. "This one," he said. They did take-outs so I nipped across while waiting for my food.

I hadn't experienced any flash floods on this trip but, if the rain gullies were anything to go by, it was bound to be an exhilarating experience. Some were covered with grates but not the one I needed to cross. I jumped over it, around the puddles and between the constant stream of slow-moving traffic, like a real life version of the retro Frogger game.

As I returned to the table, the sea urchin was the first of my order to have arrived but it wasn't prepared as I had hoped. Alone on a plate, a spiky bowl with a slice of lemon straggling the rim but nothing else. I peered inside. There were lines of flashy gel striping through the inside of the shell corresponding with the stripes of colour on the outside. I squeezed in the lemon and scraped down the first section of watery gel into the bottom of the shell then onto my spoon. With a taste of bitter oyster and no real texture to speak of, it was never going to become a favourite. Although I made sure not to waste the food, urchin the world over can breathe a watery sigh of relief, safe in the knowledge I won't be ordering it again.

It's a time-consuming job dissecting seafood so, having finished his meal and noticing I wasn't half the way through mine, Saeed said, "Okay I am going to the other place and leave you to enjoy your food."

"Yeah that's fine. I will come and find you when I am finished," I replied, while working out how to tackle the lobster. I say 'lobster' but technically it probably wasn't lobster after all. It didn't have tentacles, nor did it have the flappy fantail associated with the classic premium crustacean. This creature resembled a grub made up of articulating sections, each with a paddle to its underside for propulsion and a stripy shell. Although not quite as nice as its posh cousin, I would have it again. The main drawback was the mass of micro compartments of cartilage between the meat. The same could be said for the crab also, although if I had bought a bigger size, that might have helped. The shrimp tasted the best by far, although to me shrimp means small prawns. These were definitely nothing like small.

I struggled my way through the last of my dinner, while being entertained by a young Chinese couple having a tiff on the end table. The icy atmosphere radiated across as they sat in silence, whilst I put the finishing touches to a model of Mount Everest made from my plate full of discarded seafood shells. Then, still without a word, the woman got up and walked off anxiously. As she disappeared up the street, I'd still got a shrimp and half a crab to go. I was becoming ridiculously stuffed but this is not the sort of food I would waste. I forced the remainder of my dinner down, paid the bill of 98 ringgit and set off to find Saeed.

As expected, he had an audience of teenage girls and didn't want to leave in a hurry, one of whom was proving how well she could sing. Song complete and goodbyes done, we headed towards the jetty back to the hire car. One of the street kids, a gangly fourteen year old, was stood up to his waist in the sea, under a veranda of a shop on the water's edge. I watched as he dipped under and picked urchin from the sea, one after another, hardly moving from one spot. At first I thought it was easy pickings but, after giving it some more thought, I realised he must have tipped them there to hide them from the police and now the coast was clear, so to speak, he was retrieving his stash.

The decision had been made to snorkel the next day on another trip to the islands with the Blue Ocean guys. We made tracks past a path of fruit stalls near the junction in the road where we turned right heading for home. There were a few buildings and a decent sized, yet grotty-looking, hotel overlooking the jetty.

An old Chinese couple had checked into Coral Home as we arrived back. The wife was quite chatty and full of stories from her younger days: living in London with her friends. Although outspoken, she had a warm personality, as did her husband. The next morning, they were up for breakfast at the same time as us. We shared the table and a better selection of food stuffs. Rice with flavoured sauce wrapped in a banana leaf and green pancakes rolled up with a sweet coconut centre were left out under the clear plastic cover today.

We arrived at Blue Ocean around 8:30 am, with no notice or booking, to the disappointment of a Chinese guy, sat waiting to go diving with his wife.

"Are you are diving?" I asked.

"Yes," he answered, looking surprised. "Are you diving?" he asked, with a disgusted look on his face.

"No today we are snorkelling because we have a flight later. We were diving yesterday. Have you dived before?" I asked.

"Oh yes," he replied with a snigger as he turned his back on me in disgust of my obviously ill-informed query.

'Fuck you,' I thought, walking off. The bloke not only thought he was better than me but expected that he would have the boat to himself with his wife until we turned up to spoil his private charter.

First stop today: Mabul Island.

As Mabul came into view, lines of wooden cabins on stilts could be seen from the boat. Beautiful displays of flowers and plants cascaded down the wooden pathways that interconnected the properties. Traditional Chinese

ornamental cabins with sword-shaped hip detailing, jutting from the edges of the apex of saddle-shaped rooftops, with ever decreasing sized roofs stacked up on others like giant wooden Christmas trees.

At the jetty on a crystal blue sea, teeming with sprat and fry, we alighted and walked up the steps to a roofed deck on the corner of the complex. The quality of the teak walkways, fencing, cabins and roofs gave you a sense of privilege but that's to be expected at 1000 ringgit per night for the cheapest cabin. Walkways heading in numerous directions were constantly populated with rich Chinese holidaymakers. A steady stream of foot traffic and the odd golf trolley taxi was typical here. Blue Ocean had a deal with the water bungalow resort. An admission fee was payable for any non-residents of ten ringgit with a free bottle of water: a price anyone would be happy to pay, until you realise the only way to get to the actual island is along the 150 metre path leading to dry land and on that dry land live a community of Pilipino Gypsies who, although obviously more in need of the money, didn't receive a single ringgit. Saeed and I, along with one of the Blue Ocean guys as a chaperone, headed for the beach where the staggering contrast in lifestyles was soon to become obvious.

An elder walked across the beach in our direction as we reached the end of the jetty. She wore what resembled a large turban of bright floral fabric and continued past, under the jetty and into the distance along the beach to our left.

A testament to the amount of times our guide had been here previously was the way he negotiated his way around the knackered boat, gap in the wall, huge rusty engine and general debris on his way through to the dusty settlement. In front stood two parallel rows of cabins; the gap between them created a natural sand lane running through the heart of the village. Close by, two six-year-old girls sat on the ground barefoot between a grid marked out in the sand with lines of small plastic items, bottle tops, sticks and tiny plastic toys. It wasn't a game, more like a fantasy village. 'Quick! The children must get to school before they are late!' I imagined one saying to the other as they repositioned the items one by one.

By the lack of reaction from the locals and the fact there were a couple of makeshift shops on the track, we weren't the first to leave our sandalprints in the sand. Up ahead an open-fronted hut sheltered rustic timber tables, each crowded with underwater treasures. From the contorted lips of spikey white conches, hordes of gaping, pearlescent, pink-gloss mouths seduced the eye, while carved stone turtles and sharks' teeth necklaces, dangling from crooked purlin poles, added to the attraction. Despite the impressive size and extensive choice, I fought the impulse to own a tactile oversized memory I would later regret and continued towards the heart of the village. The two girls followed, soiled palms turning upwards, outstretched in response to every glance.

On the opposite side, another shop caught Saeed's eye and, as he browsed a scuba bottle pendant on a display amongst an array of hand carved trinkets, the owner's porky little boy, also around six years old, pushed both girls simultaneously in the chest whenever they came too close, turning around arms folded each time with a glint of satisfaction in his eye, content with the ease of his task. A turtle and scuba bottle pendant purchased, we continued up the street followed by what now was an increasing crowd of barefoot kids. One with a frayed fish net and flower pattern dress; others wearing shredded hem shorts and cockroach vented vests; but, contrary to what their dishevelled appearance might suggest, they all seemed happy and well.

On either side of the main street, more buildings, mostly residential, shared the outskirts with tat, tethered livestock, palms and vegetation. After 60 metres, we turned left at the end. A cat napped undisturbed in the shade of an adjacent roofed staircase leading to another home across the path. Playing under the veranda of one home to our near left, alongside sharp rusty corrugated tin, a cage, gas bottle and broken bicycle, kids with sticks stopped and smiled as we disturbed both their peace and the scorching sand under foot. Past a teenagers' hangout of a makeshift sports ground complete with basketball court, we returned to the start of the main street.

About to turn our backs on a relentless cycle of poverty, incomprehensible by those privileged few, a world away on the nearby luxury resort, I checked my wallet for ringgit. Six notes, one for each of the bare foot urchins following

close by, was perfect. Past a pile of discarded coconut shells, I took out a note and handed it to the closest kid, oblivious to the imminent melee. Suddenly I was ambushed by a crowd of desperado minors and. as I reached back into my wallet in an attempt to swiftly see the job through, three kids attempted the same, pulling and clawing at my now raised arm, quickly backed up into a scrum by an outer ring of raging kids. I pushed out, prizing off their soiled talons, forced into bellowing a fierce warning. "No, NO!" I repeated, with an increasing severity of aggression, likely to rouse anger in any testosterone-fuelled parent within ear shot.

It worked briefly, until the money came back out. This time I stood back and attempted to pick off each kid, passing a note each while fighting off others. Now with all allocated notes gone, some kids hung back with a stunned ecstasy, gazing in awe of their tightly grasped prize, while the unlucky ones continued to swarm regardless of my empty wallet. Nothing but continued bellowing deterred them, so that's what happened. Eventually things calmed down to the point I could bring the troop in for a group photo. Saeed obliged with my camera. Me and ten kids holding the two-fingered peace sign, while knelt in the sand, was an image I would send back home to my kids.

Aware some kids had missed out, Saeed braved my fate. A further glimpse of wallet instantly turned empty-handed disappointment to a fury of excitement, once again. With one arm outstretched high in the air, clutching his wallet, he pointed into the distance like a referee sending off a footballer for dirty play, Saeed quickly brought the situation under control, furnishing the remainder with cash, as the time came to make our way back.

"I think we did our little bit to redress the balance, don't you?" Saeed agreed as we retraced our steps. Such an obvious imbalance between these coexisting cultures didn't seem to be sustainable indefinitely, especially when you saw the new stilts poking from the sea in readiness for expanding the bungalow complex. It's not difficult to imagine that before too long the Gypsies would be displaced by the commercial might of this expanding lucrative business powerhouse that may already have the resources to influence government policy as their business and profits continue to grow.

Back at the rendezvous, we sat and waited for the Chinese guy to return from his first dive of the day. Other boats from similar diving companies also moored up here, as did the police in their slick black craft. Theirs was the only boat I have come across with three engines. I wouldn't be surprised to hear other boats are not allowed such power. With limited moorings, boats stack up here. It's quite normal to climb across boats at busy times and with nothing better to do with my time at present, observing the boat hoppers became a source of amusement, that along with the tourists' reaction to pestering gypsies paddling up alongside the dive boats to sell the odd coconut or hold a crying baby in your face in hope it will convince you to part with some money.

Neither our boat or Saeed were anywhere be seen by this time so I called for a quick pint. Up a couple of timber steps brought me onto the dining room complete with central water feature and carefully manicured floral displays. The waitress spotted me and made her way over.

"Can I help you, sir?" she enquired.

"Could I get a beer please?"

"Yes of course, sir. Please take a seat sir and I will bring it over." It was pretty clear this was not going to be a cheap beer, bearing in mind the amount of times she called me 'sir'. I walked through to the open area at the other side of the room and took a seat overlooking the water.

The sea was perfectly clear and shallow enough to clearly observe the local inhabitants. One fish in particular caught my eye. At around 20 cm long with plain brown scales, it had a den under a rock and would loiter around outside, chasing off trespassers every time they came too close, shooting straight back to its post after each pursuit in an amusing fashion. Nothing out of the ordinary there you might think but a further pattern of behaviour was also being employed here. Said fish would often go in and check under the rock, but only as long as the coast was clear long enough to get in and back out without giving away the location of the den.

"Your beer, sir," the waitress informed me pouring half the bottle into my glass. Now £6 in England would be expected if there was such a location like this but, although that's how much it was here, relatively it felt much more. I sipped my beer as a lionfish approached the restricted area. I was interested to see how the guard would react to the venomous spikes, if it was allowed to pass freely. Like a post-Brexit, soft-Irish border, there were no restrictions to the lionfish's travel plans here: unlike others, it passed unchallenged.

My phone rings. It was Saeed. "The boat is coming. Where are you?"
The dickhead's wife continued to avoid eye contact as she waited silently in her sycophant bubble for her master to return along with a couple of others as I reached the rendezvous once more. My attention was drawn to a handmade, dug-out, log canoe making its way over as our boat parallel parked alongside another moored against the tiny jetty. Dark brush stroke blue with a squalid yellow upper panel to the outside and pale blue inside, the three-metre gypsy craft then pulled alongside our boat.

A young girl around six years old wearing pale blue pyjamas with orange-coloured bows on the shoulders paddled from the front, while her younger brother of around 3 years old with long, dark, dusty brown, fluff knot hair, naked apart from a short-armed, blue, woollen jumper, stood and held out his hand at the back of the boat. Without invitation, I clambered across the first boat to ours just in time to catch a shot of them at work. Our skipper gave them a bottle of water and they moved on, as did we, leaving behind a world where money can buy you as many dives as you like in any one day.

The begging children soon became specks in the distance as we moved onto the next dive site. The sun beamed down and the white propeller foam was close behind as we followed the shoreline around to the other side of the island. We dropped anchor 50 metres off coast and the Chinese guy prepared for his next dive.

"You want lunch now?" the round-faced Chinese boat owner asked. By now we knew the drill for lunch. The large plastic box with lid was slid from under the seats at the back containing the meals. I lifted the lid on my container. The ubiquitous rice in one section, crispy chicken in another, prawns in another and vegetables in the last.

"Better than yesterday's food," Saeed commented. I didn't mind the food the day before but he did have a point. The large white urn of green tea, decorated with flowers, was provided again with a dispenser tap on the side. We placed it on the rear bench and, using the plastic beakers provided, pushed the plunger and helped ourselves.

I pretended not to be interested in the Chinese guy's preparations to enter the water again so I only watched when he had his back was turned. I'd heard the dive crew talking about him doing his first 27-metre depth dive today. I was fascinated to learn the difference between my dives at five metres and his. I expect at a further 18 metres down the atmosphere is noticeably different. How much darker must it be? Maybe the sealife is less used to human interaction down there; maybe you see less by way of creatures.

From around his neck, he pulled his yellow patterned snood up over his head, then put on his mask. Lifting himself and his gear off the bench, he made his final prep on the edge of the boat, putting on his fins with his back to the water. Eyes to the skies, both men submitted to gravity, blindly rolling back, tank first into the abyss.

Although just off the coast of Mabul, you'd be forgiven for thinking this was a completely different location. No stilted bungalows or shanty town round this side: just a couple of other dive boats moored up nearby. Although rain isn't so off putting when it's 33 degrees, it's not conducive to day trips out on speed boats. Thankfully it continued to be kind to those of us who like a bit of a tan as I donned my mask and fins once more. Snorkelling here is secondary though. The main attraction of these islands is to divers, due to an ideal topography for life to flourish as the depth of water increases beyond the scope of a snorkel. Sipadan, by far the best island locally to here, is what's known as an oceanic island meaning it was created by a volcano on the seabed building up lava to sea level. The resulting slopes that drop down to the alien world below provide a diving experience said to be amongst the top three in the world. Luckily this time no one followed as I bobbed about in search of marine encounters. More out of boredom than a desire to get closer to the action, I would dip my head, tuck and paddle down to the ocean bed for a closer look every few minutes. It turned out to be a bit less exciting than I'd hoped today so before too long diving off the roof of the boat seemed like the sort of fun I was about to have next.

Back at the stainless-steel ladder, I needed to lose my fins. One hand holding on and the other removing one fin at a time isn't easy when you're the ice cube in a sea cocktail. As I threw each fin on deck, the crew were scanning for signs of the divers resurfacing. The owner of the boat and the dickhead were again diving together and their time must have been about done. Saeed had beaten me back and was drinking tea.

"Want some?" he said, as he gestured to me with his plastic beaker.

"Yeah, thanks, I will," I replied while drying off. Saeed tilted the urn to dispense the last half a cup.

The autocratic guy's wife was laid silently along the bench seat, completely covered head to toe from the sun, with a towel across her legs and a wide-brimmed, weaved straw hat laid over her head providing both shade and a social distance, thus reducing the chance of being drawn into an unsanctioned conversation. Saeed passed my tea while making his way through to sit in the shade of the roofed cabin. "Thank you."

I joined the search and soon spotted an intermittent carbonated water fizz break the surface close by. A muffled shoal of jostling spheres fought their way to freedom, like eager pupils through a half-term school gate. I quickly realised it wasn't our guys. Another team from one of the other boats turned out to be the source of the disturbance, as the crew continued to squint at the horizon. Lost in the moment, it's easy to drift off and lose track of your boat when diving, so well-equipped divers keep an inflatable plastic tube to indicate their position, if they find themselves too far away by the time they require picking up. At around a metre long and usually some shade of luminous orange, the marker is inflated using the air from the scuba tank and allows them to be spotted from further afield as it sticks up out of the water.

After exchanging a few words in Malaysian, one of the crew started the engine while the other pulled up the ladders. They'd ended up 150 metres off coast but we were soon alongside them and their inflatable sausage, gently caressed by a transparent turquoise infinity.

Overwhelmed with exhilaration, the Chinese guy seemed to return a different person with a youthful excitement and playful mannerisms. But, as I was about to find out, his animated chatter was reserved exclusively for the dive master: the one granted the privilege of trying to keep up with his high horse along the twisted path of bigots.

Kneeling on the bench, I leaned over. "Did you see many fish?" I asked the Chinese guy.

"Oh no, no," he replied and turned his back on me once more.

In my head he had just said, "Anyone can look at fish! I'm here for more important things that you will never understand or be able to afford. Do not speak to me again." I was that hot milk on a stove and he just turned up the flame. Back on board, once again he became chairman of the board.

The man with the punch bag face spoke briefly to his wife, devout in his new-found enthusiasm, before sitting with his new buddy. The excitement continued between the two divers as we cut a swathe through wind and water towards dry land.

Sat quietly with her eyes closed she listened on, "We had a drink of Coke at 27 metres down," the owner explained to one of his crew. Then the Chinese chatter continued between the two, while everyone else fell silent.

After a few minutes the woman stood up and pointed out to sea saying something in Chinese. I both hated and pitied this woman. We all looked out to sea. Her husband, after doing the same, quickly turned his attention back to his chat. No one seemed to see anything until she pointed once again. Just as I heard the word 'fish', I spotted a smattering of objects breaking the surface 20 metres out. She'd pointed out a shoal of flying fish, driven out of the water by some latent predator.

Flying fish have been known to glide 100 metres on a good wind, using the updraft against their wing-like, outstretched fins to evade death on a daily, sometimes hourly, basis. But not all their airborne acrobatics lead to a positive outcome. Like the saying 'Out of the frying pan, into the fire', some have been known to be plucked from the sky by random frigate birds. Literally caught between the devil and the deep blue sea.

This flock managed about five metres out of water before gravity pulled them back under the danger zone. A flock of around 40 would rise up every few seconds. The odd flying fish had used the same technique to avoid the boat's propeller a couple of times on other journeys but this was a proper spectacle. Like raised arms in a sports stadium, the shoal created a Mexican wave effect as in turn they frantically flapped a tail fin to propel them from danger, following each other out of the water, adding to the flock at one end and dropping at the other.

After our brief encounter, I sat camera in hand the rest of the way back in hope of catching a shot of some of the less conventional craft you could randomly come across out here. Most common would be a canoe sat in the middle of nowhere with a solitary guy and his nets. Although an unusual sight for a tourist, it didn't make the best image for a social media post. What I was looking for was another chance to come across something like the vastly top-heavy looking fishing vessel I saw the previous day. Distinctly oriental with bright wooden paintwork, it evoked historical images of wizened old men with whispy moustaches wearing flat-cone, weaved straw, wide-brimmed hats with knotted chin straps, casting their nets off gangplanks alongside herons, serenaded by springy metallic, almost anarchic warblings from traditional Chinese ruan guitars.

We passed by a couple of islands, a handful of boats and, as we neared the coast, lines of stilted slums. Scores of homes followed the shoreline of the nearest island to the mainland, hovering above the sea, tightly packed in what seemed like No Man's Land. Just far enough off the mainland not to be deported, but close enough to eke out an existence. Often when I spoke to Malaysians about their history, Filipinos were mentioned in a bad light, either gypsies, illegal workers or illegal migrants, so I wondered if these were Filipinos too.

Our flight back to Kota Kinabulu was later tonight and, with an hour's drive from Semporna to the airport at Tawau, it didn't leave much time for anything other than a quick shower, pack and an early dinner. Because my budget flight ticket didn't allow me the luxury of a big bag, I'd had to be a little more thoughtful with the choice of items I managed to bring as hand luggage. For instance, I didn't bring any footwear other than the flip flops on my feet. Today I missed my trainers for their robust protection but I think the comforting feeling of soft, dry natural fibres against my skin was the main reason. No rubber flip flop soles slipping from under you when they are wet causing the toe lug to cut into the web of my big toe would be great.

"Are you hungry?" I asked Saeed.

"Maybe we should eat before we leave?"

"Yeah I think so too. I wonder if we could find that restaurant that we ate at on our way here, the one with the rotis. They were the best roti I've had," I explained.

"I think we will not pass this place. It was when we went to nature park," he continued.

"Ah yes. It's the other side of the airport," I agreed.

"Yes. We can get roti at place we went before. I think I will go there," he said.

"Yeah, that is fine."

I talked more slowly when talking to non-English speaking people. I realised I was also emulating the broken English I heard from others. I would leave out less necessary words when communicating, such as asking a question in a shop, and found myself saying things like, "You have beer?"

Showered, changed, packed and loaded, we drove back to the jetty one last time. From our back street location, we had eventually found an alternative route that didn't involve the bottleneck on the main street. It also cut the journey time by a third. It involved driving to the opposite end of the street, swinging a left onto the other main road leading to the roundabout, then straight across, missing out the barrow boys' patch.

One of the main reasons, in my opinion, Saeed liked the idea of returning to the same dive shop for two days running was the fit girl in the office with the bath bomb personality. Her youthful peach plump cheeks, poised in tight denim, were built to bounce and with a smile as bright as diamonds, any single guy would have struggled to ignore her seemingly innocent allure. I noticed it but the urge to impress felt wrong so I sat back and watched from the periphery of the flirting in my old man bubble. The same could be said of Saeed's desire to visit the Muslim cafe that served the roti. Here the rotis were good but not as good as the place near the nature park and a little more expensive too, but Saeed believe this bread to be better. The four girls, excited about the fact he was Muslim, may have clouded his judgement somewhat.

As we approached the outdoor tables, I noticed the young Chinese guy from Coral Home sat with this friend. I said, "Hello," as we passed and found a seat nearby. Three of the girls who worked here were sat together at a table chatting. 'The wages must be so cheap here to afford seemingly too many waiting staff,' I thought to myself as we waited to be served. One of the other girls came over to take our order, while her colleagues kept a sneaky eye on Saeed.

A couple to my left in my periphery came towards us and, as they reached our table, I looked up. It was the Chinese dickhead and his wife walking through the tables. My eyes locked on target and he gave me a reluctant nod. That single gesture of weakness was enough to reap my revenge as my projected hatred diverted his eye to the floor. One awkward moment later, they were gone and, although it was literally a moment, it was enough for me to feel like I'd settled the score.

Half a tank of fuel on return of the vehicle was required by the hire company so a degree of guess work was required when calling at the filling station on our way back to the airport. The tank was showing around a quarter so we needed to bring it back up past halfway to take into account the fuel usage by the time the one-hour trip was over.

"What do you reckon?" I asked Saeed, as we pulled in.

"Maybe ten," he said. Ten ringgit seemed too much but at a cost of £1 each it wasn't worth any more consideration. The filling station reminded me of the ones back home, modern and bright with a large block-paved forecourt. On close inspection there were subtle differences: the language the signs were printed in for instance. "Do you want from shop?" Saeed asked as I studied the pump, trying to work out which fuel to use.

"No thanks. I'm ok," I replied. "Which one do you think is unleaded?" I continued.

Saeed turned back toward the pump and inspected the wording on the nozzles. "Is it this one?" Without asking someone, who could actually read Malay, we couldn't be sure.

"I know: I will smell it. I can tell from the smell," I explained. I opened the vehicle's filler cap and filled my nostrils then I sniffed the first pump, the second and back again to the first to double check. Heavy oil-based 'dirty diesel' has a distinctive smell; yet its lighter, cleaner cousin has a pleasing aroma, making them easy to distinguish. "This one," I reassured myself, while squeezing the trigger with 80% confidence.

I almost drove directly through the roundabout the first time we took this route due to a combination of tiredness and lack of road signs. This time tiredness wasn't an issue and the previous close shave intensified my concentration, which resulted in an incident free trip; that was until we neared the airport. Family bag of barbeque crisps and chocolate biscuits gone, Saeed tried the phone number of the car hire desk for instructions on where to leave the vehicle.

"Hello."

"We have car here to drop off," Saeed explained.

"Oh I am going home at five," the voice on the other end of the line explained.

"But you knew we were coming at this time as you charged us extra to be able to keep it till this time."

"Yes but it is Saturday. I go home early on Saturday," he explained.

The conversation continued in vain as I reached a row of road cones between the left-hand side of the kerb and the locked car hire kiosk at the airport. I waited while Saeed made his way over to the kiosk, while still on the phone. It was now the start of check-in and, as Saeed scoured the adjoining kiosks to no avail, the option to wait for the guy to turn back up looked less likely each passing minute. It didn't look like time would allow, even if it was suggested, so I looked for an alternative plan. If I removed a few cones, I could drive the car over and straddle the curb near the kiosk, replacing the cones after.

"We can leave the keys at the taxi kiosk," Saeed explained as he returned.

"We paid cash for the car hire, didn't we?" I asked.

"Yes."

"Ok let's leave it here. They cannot charge us any more than we have already paid," I said.

"There is no person at the taxi place," Saeed explained.

"We will have to post the keys through the door then!" I exclaimed. Surprisingly nothing further ever came of dumping the car in front of the departure lounge.

Tonight's destination was back at Zoku in KK and, with a one-hour flight followed by a ten-minute Grab ride, supper wasn't far off. Three days ago on leaving, we intended to let the staff at Zoku know our intentions to return tonight but there was no staff coverage as we left. We relied on a handwritten note and a couple of missed call voicemail messages to re-reserve our beds. Our calls had not been returned so no confirmation was received by either of us before returning.

"I hope they got our messages," I put to Saeed.

"We have the door code, so we can sleep on floor if no bed."

Just what we would have actually done had the place been full could have been an issue but luckily, as we entered through the door, the young Chinese lad was on the desk. "Welcome back, Ian. You have the same room and the same bed," he explained.

"Oh great thank you!"

A clutch of new faces were grouped at the sitting area at the far end of the open plan space. I walked over.

Chapter 7
Sepilok

The place was quite busy. A guy sat in a bean bag and a girl sat in the chair opposite him were chatting, while another pair of new faces sat at the dining table along with Spence, the Indian guy who had been staying there for a few weeks due to his work. I walked across to the kitchen area and said, "Hi," while putting on the kettle. I offered my hand to the twenty odd year-old guy sat at the bench seat. "Hi, I'm Ian."

"Hi – Tom!" he exclaimed with an Aussie twang.

I repeated the words, "Hi – Ian!" to the older woman with almost shoulder-length blonde hair. We shook hands.

"Hello, I'm Claire," she proclaimed, trying to act like she wasn't single.

"Hi, Spence. How are you?"

"I am fine, thank you. How are you? Did you have a good trip?"

"Good thanks, yes we've just arrived back from diving in Semporna," I explained.

The introductions stopped there for a while. Saeed was flying to Bali early the next morning and wanted to use the washing machine then the drier before leaving so that was keeping him busy.

"So have you just arrived?" I asked the guys at the table.

"I got here yesterday," said Claire, pushing her hair behind her ear with her finger. She was most definitely single.

Then I turned to Tom, "And you?"

"I just arrived today. So you have stayed here before then Ian?" Tom asked.

"Yeah me and the guy through there, Saeed, left a couple of days ago to go diving," I explained.

"That sounds awesome. Did you have a good time?" Tom continued.

"Yeah great thanks. So what have you guys been up to?"

"Well I've not done anything yet, apart from get here, but Claire has been travelling for ages."

158

"Yeah I've been away for three months so far. Bali, Indonesia, Cambodia and Thailand up to now," she explained.

"That sounds great. Do you have long left?" I asked.

"I took a year out of my job. I work as a police officer at Heathrow Airport normally so I have 9 months left."

"Wow you are so lucky!" I continued. Claire came across as one of the lads and, although attractive, slightly butch, which all tied in with the police officer role. My eyes followed as she passed me by in her faded and frayed daisy duke denim shorts and sweeping open-backed top. On display from behind, her exposed coffee-cream tanned spinal gully flowed down intriguingly, uninterrupted from her neckline to a low swag of pale yellow cotton, hovering just above her waistband, sandwiched by a camber of tactile silky toned flesh.

"Fancy going out for a beer tonight Claire?" I asked.

"Yeah why not? I have a bottle of wine that I treated myself to yesterday but it's been a while since I had a beer. That sounds good."

"Tom? Are you up for a beer, or is that a daft question to ask an Aussie?"

"A beer? Why not?! Super, count me in."

I grabbed myself a coffee, moved over to the lounge area and plonked down in the beanbag, between the other two new faces. They were discussing flights and sharing travel tips. I turned and caught the girl's eye with a smile.

"Hi, I'm Ian."

"Hi, I am Olivia and this is Kurt." She explained. The guy looked up from his phone and smiled.

One consequence of the backpacker lifestyle is to dedicate plenty of WiFi time to keep in touch with friends and family or, in my case at the minute, to look for my next destination. Things fell silent for a short while as we each zoned into our smart screens. Almost unnoticed, another new face came out from the dorm and joined us in the lounge. It was a slight-framed pretty girl in her early twenties with long light brown hair and variegated sun-bleached blonde tips. Comfortable in her surroundings, she crouched down beside her friend, chatting quietly in her ear.

I looked up and said, "Hello."

"Hi," she replied, quickly turning back to her chat.

159

Tom walked over. "What time are you thinking of going out?" he asked.

"I'm easy. Any time for me – I just need to get a quick shower but I can be ready in 20 minutes if that's ok?"

"Excellent. Claire, is that ok? 20 minutes?" Tom said.

"Yeah I can be ready by then," she explained.

Gusto thrust me from the chill out end of the bloated corridor. I grabbed my toiletry bag from the locker near the opposite side, passed the central kitchen, dining and reception areas, en-route to the shower block around the corner. I took the far cubicle, as I could leave my clothes outside to keep dry without doing the discourtesy of blocking anyone's path. As I turned on my shower, the sound of a cubicle door closing nearby instantly took me back to the vision of those tanned legs and toned back. I imagined Claire's arse cheeks wiggling out of tight faded denim and her top slowly slipping off her silky shoulders. The sound of shower water beginning to flow nearby triggered a gush of masculinity through my tingling veins. Soapy hands sliding seductively over firm silky dunes, momentarily disappearing down between secret feminine valleys, felt almost as real as if my eyes, rather than my head, had told the story.

Whoever it was was still in there as I walked around the corner to the sink. Still overexcited by thoughts brought on by the chemistry between us, I stood proud, fully aware of the bulge in my pants, brushing my teeth waiting for the mystery person to come out of the cubicle. 'Click.' I flexed my muscles slightly while staring into the mirror practicing a slightly surprised expression. Claire, adorned with white towel around her torso, barely large enough to cover both her boobs and bum cheeks, came around the corner.

"It won't take me long to be ready," she explained while drying her hair beside me. Through the thickness of the towel, her visibly pert nipples, suggested a mutual chemistry that increased the bulge in my pants to a point beyond safety. I watched as she sauntered off with pronounced steps to her room with her towel just short of her arse cheeks and a clear view of her moist golden tanned legs. All that was needed now was a few beers, followed by a bit of cheeky flirting and I might just get lucky for the first time since the split with the gorgeously complicated mother of my two youngest children, many months ago.

160

A quick rub with the towel followed by a comb through with gel-impregnated fingers and my time in the mirror was done just in time for the swelling to have dissipated.

"What are your plans then, Ian?" Tom asked as we waited for Claire.

"I'm not sure yet, Tom. I may go to do a bit of jungle stuff. There is a river cruise you can do that sounds interesting," I explained.

"Awesome! Is it the Kinabatangan River?"

"I'm not sure."

"Yeah it probably is. I'm doing that tomorrow," he explained.

Spence appeared from his room wearing smart trousers, smart belt and a smart shirt. "Who would like grilled aubergine?" he enquired, over pronouncing the end of the sentence, in typical Indian fashion.

"Oh I was thinking of going round the corner to the Chinese restaurant that does a large bottle of beer for 14 ringgit," I replied.

By this time Claire and Tom had moved within earshot and we were poised to leave. As usual, Spence was determined to get his way. He ignored my remark and repeated the question, adding, "It is the best; I guarantee you will like it." Out of Spence's field of vision, Claire's eyes widened under the pressure; she looked to Tom for direction. He responded quickly, looking down at her feet.

"You're wearing thongs?" he innocently questioned. Made all the more amusing by the fact we all knew enough about Tom by now to know, had he known the English call them flip flops, he would never in a million years have made the comment.

I responded, "That's a bit personal, Tom! Do you normally ask such questions of a lady?"

Through a burst of laughter, Claire added fuel to the fire, "Straight to the point then?"

"Hmm hm-hm, ok let's go," said Spence. We left with playful understanding.

He led us out to the right in the opposite direction to the place I was hoping to start the night but then, at the end of the block, we swung a left and then another left, drawing closer to the cheap beer restaurant. Spence stopped outside.

"Is this the place you were talking about?" I asked.

"Yes. This is it."

I smiled. "This is the place I was talking about. That's weird. You could have just come around this corner," I exclaimed, pointing. Spence ignored my comments. He wasn't the type to admit he was wrong. It was much closer if we had walked the other way but all's well that ends well. We all got what we wanted in the end.

Having sex with someone new was the obvious tonic my ego needed to help to push the staggering process of splitting up forward. I knew it was a good thing but the more I tried to convince myself, the less I wanted it. She simply wasn't Kay.

There was a slightly better promotion of three large bottles for 35 ringgit, which we duly took advantage of – twice. They came with oversized whiskey glasses emblazoned with the Heineken logo, just enough for one good mouthful. Two plates of slightly boring grilled aubergine and 20 shots of beer later, we were drawn to town in search of excitement and more beer.

The promenade, a wooden structure sitting on columns rising from a swaying saltwater basement, home to a row of around ten seafront bars, was our next destination. The ubiquitous Irish bar in the middle tended to be the busiest, although next door, with an eye-catching row of giant shisha pipes ready to load and premier league football showing on high level multi screens, was also an attractive option.

Things were not turning out as my alter ego had hoped with Claire. Less flirting and more lad chat was the direction things were going. I felt a weird combination of relief and disappointment.

We sat around a tall bistro table outside on the decking overlooking the sea. "Are you travelling alone tomorrow, Tom?" I asked.

"Yes. I fly out to Sandakan in the morning."

"Do you have a local SIM card?"

"No but I've paid to use my Oz number for a week out here."

"I'll have to get your number and see if I can catch up with you later tomorrow," I told Tom.

"Yeah, no problem. I've booked to stay at a place called Sepilok Nature Resort. See if you can get in there."

The premium price tag on drinks here didn't seem to put anyone off. Even the odd stench of shitty sewers didn't dampen the party mood, as groups of drunken men with arms around each other's shoulders laughed loudly in the doorway over the top of the house band, killing covers of popular western hits inside, while the occasional jet noisily shrank into the abyss overhead.

After taking my fill, I returned alone to Zoku to check out the cheapest carrier to get me to Sandakan the next day. Once again, AirAsia just pipped Malingo and Malaysia Airlines to the post on price so now, well past my bedtime, I booked the flight and got my head down. I was to arrive around teatime the next day so I told Tom the next morning over breakfast.

"That's awesome," said Tom. "I am going to the memorial park when I arrive, then on to the accommodation, so I will give you a call when I know what time I will get to the digs," he continued.

"Yeah thanks that's great. What tour operator did you book with for the river cruise?" I enquired.

"It's a two-day, one-night tour, with two boat trips and a night walk through the jungle, but I'm not sure of their name," he told me.

"Cool, I will see what I can find and hopefully we can go along together."

"I booked mine through Sepilok Nature Lodge so maybe you could talk to them about it?"

"OK I will that thanks."

The vision through the window of grid lines slowly expanding into blocks of streets, as we descended into Sandakan, no longer resulted in anxiety's fat fingers gradually wrenching tightly at my gut. Many years have passed since the prospect of putting my life into a pilot's hands created such irrational discomfort. Now, after achieving ambivalence, I hurtled, like the trees outside, towards the ridiculous, finding myself daydreaming about the prospect of experiencing a minor touchdown incident as we hurtled towards solid ground. 'A skid off the runway might be exciting perhaps,' I foolishly dared to imagine, as the screech of rubber on tarmac momentarily resonated from the underbelly of the beast. 'A pretty cool story to tell the lads down the pub,' I thought.

Outside arrivals, I attempted to call Tom repeatedly to no avail. Then a call from Tom. After a few seconds of silence, I could hear Tom's voice: "So I will.................. a few minutes I guess."

"Hello, Tom can you hear me?" After breaking up a number of times, the call dropped out.

"Hello, yes that's better I can hear you now."

"I'm in a Grab car on my way to the accommodation now," said Tom.

"OK I'll do the same and see you there in a few minutes," I replied.

The route from the airport to Sepilok avoids the town of Sandakan. It does, however, pass the Duchess of Cambridge Hospital on the main road, an indication of the ongoing colonial influence.

Invaded by the Japanese during the Second World War, Sandakan was the location of a prison of war camp set up to detain Australian and British troops captured during the conflict. Their purpose was to build a runway to further advance the Japanese war effort. Tom had just called me from the memorial park that now sits on the former site, just a few minutes' drive from the hospital.

The taxi dropped me on the drive of the complex where I was to stay that night. There was a car park to the right with a long building made up of an office, shop and restaurant to the left. I made my way up the wooden steps onto a raised veranda, along the frontage, under the cover of an extended roof and pushed open the door of the shop.

"Do you know where I check in?" I enquired.

"Do you have a reservation?" a local middle-aged guy asked.

"No not yet but my friend has checked in here and I am hoping to stay with him," I explained.

"Ok you need to go up there," he pointed across a sloping lawn with a long row of steps leading to another building up the hill. As with all buildings on this complex, it was wooden. The dark clouds which had been edging ever closer for the last few minutes opened up just as I set foot out towards the lawn and this was no shower. I ran up the steps in an attempt to avoid the deluge. At the top I turned right around the side of the path then left, more steps leading up to a seating area with a desk opposite brought me to a receptionist sat behind it.

"Hello can I help you?"

"Hi. Yes, my friend is staying here tonight and I would like a bed in the dorm please," I explained, while haplessly shaking my arms in an attempt to be less wet.

Four dormitory buildings lay at the other side of the reception. The nearest one, along a tarmac path that splits off and connects to other dorms, was where I would find Tom, I was informed. 'Please take off shoes' a hand painted sign read at the bottom of the steps up to another covered walkway, almost identical to other buildings, except this time a little 40-centimetre double gate at the bottom of the stairs needed to be opened to gain access. Quite a simple task for me but maybe not so easy for the creatures it was presumably meant to keep out. Other than well-kempt manicured lawns, colourful flowerbed borders, neatly trimmed dwarf box hedges and a high level of cleanliness, this place was quite basic and almost empty.

Tom was laid on the bed alone in an eight-bed dorm on the phone to his girlfriend, as I walked in. "Australian and English guys," I overheard him say. "It took about two hours altogether but really interesting," he continued. "Ian has just arrived... Yeah." I picked the low bunk opposite him, dropping down my bag, unzipping the side pocket and pulling out my phone charger. "Okm see you later. Bye," he told his girlfriend.

"Hi. Just us then?" I asked.

"Hi yes, it's very quiet around here. You found it ok then?"

"Yes no problem. I asked the woman on reception for the same price you had been charged but she was having none of it. She said yours was an internet price so she could not match it but it wasn't that much of a difference," I explained.

"I've not been back long myself," Tom explained.

"Oh yeah? How was the memorial park?" I asked.

"Good thanks. The audio tour takes quite a long time though – around two hours," he explained.

"I downloaded the app you told me about before I left Zoku."

"Oh right. Awesome!" Tom used the word 'awesome' more often than he probably realised. He was a doctor back home in Oz, enthusiastic and compassionate, with an enduring personality that often found him being somewhat overly interested in other people's stories to the point it felt slightly contrived. As if to make others feel at ease with his superiority, he would tend to over emphasise their qualities. It was clear from speaking to him previously that he had a passion for the Second World War. The camp at Sandakan was the reason he was here, probably due to the staggering amount of Aussies and a quite a few English soldiers too who died there.

After a long, slow time effort by the allied captives to drag out the construction of an airstrip they were being forced to build at the camp in Sandakan, it became increasingly likely the Japanese were about to lose the war, along with their German and Russian comrades. Rather than dealing with the aftermath of mass grave, a decision was made to force the prisoners on a march that resulted in 2,345 men's deaths. Just six Australian troops survived by escaping, the rest of the 1,700 Aussies, along with all 600 British troops, died at the hands of the Japanese before reaching their intended destination of Kota Kinbalu.

We decided to take a walk as dusk fell, attempting to get our bearings and find the entrance to the orangutan rehabilitation centre. With the exception of the frogs and insects, all was quiet as we walked along the verge of a surprisingly well-maintained tarmac road, lined by trees.

"Apparently we are really close to the orangutan place. It's just down here," Tom revealed.

It was a sleepy tree-lined, semi-rural side street, with no street lighting. Around a sweeping bend half a mile from our base revealed a large brick archway and a pair of steel gates blocking the road. There was a light in the compound, just inside the gates in front of us. It was coming from the gatehouse building to the left of the road that continued beyond the obstruction. A big sign above the gates read 'Sepilok Orangutan Rehabilitation Centre' stretching the width of the road.

Gates slightly ajar, I walked through and up to the lit room. A man was sitting at a desk. He sat up sharp with a surprised look as he spotted me approaching.

"We are closed. Can I help you?" the middle-aged local guy asked through the open window. The place was obviously closed but I hoped to clarify the information gleaned by various chats about the day to day running of the centre.

"Yes hi, what time do you open in the morning?" I enquired.

"We open at 10."

"Ah ok thanks and the first feeding is at 10.30?"

"Yes and the last is 3.30pm," he continued.

"Terima Kasih," I told him, as I walked back to Tom on the other side of the gates.

"Maybe I should have come here today," Tom explained as he was returning back to KK straight from our jungle river cruise in two days' time. I had allowed myself one more day than Tom before flying back to KK.

There was a T-junction in the road, halfway back from the entrance to the complex, with a couple of rustic signs directing you along its route advertising 'The Banana Cafe' and 'Sepilok Jungle resort' lit by dim yellow light in recycled tin can shades. Continuing its perpetual journey, the Earth's back was now fully turned on the light of another day but tonight the sky was naked, laid bare by an absence of cotton candy cloud cover, allowing a celestial spectacle worthy of a two-minute gaze. Overhead, a looming ebony depth, peppered with an infinite periphery of minute jewels of light, cast a warm glow over gently swaying palms.

We started back and immediately noticed another complex. I'd spotted the entrance on our way in but not the peppering of serene soft lighting peering through the trees that had us like a moth to a flame. We walked up the drive past a tiny gatehouse tucked away in the bushes. The barrier lifted, allowing us to take the curved drive around to the right, revealing easily the most inviting structure so far seen in this area. We climbed a brace of timber steps leading to the foyer. The building's opulence, complemented by manicured shrubs and hanging floral displays, began to show through the reception.

Magnetised towards lines of delicately swaying reflections of coloured light on still water, we walked in past the front desk, into a long open-roofed veranda with three wide terraced steps graduating down towards the water's edge where sofas, tables and chairs further contributed to the relaxing atmosphere. Beyond the waist-high, rustic, wooden pole repeating cross brace fence along the edge of a small manmade lake, bushes and trees on the far bank were tastefully illuminated, enough to create the sort of ambience you don't mind paying five quid for a bottle of beer for.

The central section of the building was a bar area where a couple of waitresses were chatting and, apart from a retired couple lounging on a settee on the next level up from our waterfront table, the place was empty. Rows of clear glass jars containing trailing plants suspended from strings, petitioned off sections of the seating areas and a couple of suspended weaved rattan hammock chairs gently spun in the breeze, as one of the waitresses made their way to our table.

"Two beers please," I requested as she arrived.

"Anything else?"

"Not for me," Tom replied.

"No thanks," I continued. "Well this'll do!" I said with a surprised tone, raising my eyebrows.

"Yeah great. Pretty cool," Tom replied. Then a short silence was broken by further chat. "What is it you do, Ian, for a living?"

"I'm a builder."

"Do you work for yourself or?"

"Yeah I work for myself," I replied with a nonchalant twang. "I build loft conversions, extensions, that sort of thing," I explained, as our beer arrived.

Two glasses and two bottles were set out in front of us. "Thank you," we both declared simultaneously, as she turned around and left.

"And you are a doctor, I hear?"

"Yeah, I work in Sydney, very busy for the most part," he explained.

"Have you been doing it long?" I asked.

"Around four years now."

"I bet it's not as busy as when you were a junior doctor though, is it?"

Tom thought for a second and then said, "No, It's pretty full on at the minute."

"Oh? In England we are always hearing of junior doctors doing ridiculously long hours – sometimes 18 hours a day!" I exclaimed.

168

"We don't really have to put that many hours in luckily. I think the UK recently reduced the working week for junior doctors from a maximum of 91 down to around 72 I think," he explained. Sensing I didn't know that much about the subject, he moved on. "How about the trip tomorrow, Ian – are you up for it?"

"Yeah definitely. It's just if I have time to book on in the morning at short notice for that day."

"Well I get picked up around 11 from the digs," he explained.

"And you booked it through the nature lodge?" I asked.

"Yeah. Maybe you can talk to them first thing and see what they can do."

"Yes I'll do that. Hopefully if they are picking you up already it shouldn't be a problem," I told him.

"Do you want to head back?" Tom said as he placed his empty glass carefully down. My love of booze and this jungle paradise location compelled me to stay.

"I think I'm going to stay for one more," I explained.

"Do you want me to order one for you on my way out?" Tom offered.

"Yes, please, that would be great. I'll see you back at the room in a bit."

"Cool."

I kicked back and allowed my eyes the freedom to disconnect somewhat from my thoughts, both of which drifted separately out across the water. The familiar, yet unbelievably impressive noise, of crickets rubbing a scraper built into their leg against a serrated file under their wing, was just one of the tens if not hundreds of competing noises, projecting from the shadows. Male crickets use this process called stridulation to attract females. The louder the chirp, the better their chances but, still, frogs for the most part were the ones to beat. Silence is of a premium around here, especially at night; in fact the more you take time to notice, the more you realize there is no silence: just a constant battle to fill the air with clucks, grunts, chirps, whistles, ribbits, peeps – oh and, of course, croaks. A more familiar noise jolted me back to reality.

"Beer, sir?"

"Thank you." The sands of time, along with the contents of the bottle, drained and headed back amongst the shadows.

I'd become well practiced at filtering out white noise over the years. It was a trait I developed as a young parent. Now luckily, with nothing more important to do with my time, I allowed myself to notice the beauty of it.

Above the competition, I recognised a noise that I first heard in the nature park a few days prior. At the time, I though it to be an electric drill or distant chain saw but, as the location of the source of the noise moved around me quickly as I moved forward, I realised whatever was making the sound of a far-off speeding electric motor about to explode was much closer than I first thought. Here the same sound was coming from the trees at the side of the road a couple of metres away. Within the time it took to walk two steps, the screech had amplified then returned to its former level. I turned back to investigate this weird phenomenon and, at the exact spot as before, the noise increased once more. Whatever creature this was had the ability to concentrate its call, magnifying it into one location. I checked back and positioned myself in that exact spot again, finding amusement in altering the volume by swaying from side to side. That and the frog that starts his call with a low beep that repeats, increasing in pitch and frequency, like a bomb reaching the point when it explodes, were my highlights of the evening.

The next morning was fine and dry and, after securing a place on the river cruise, I made my way around the decking past the office and the shop, around the corner to the restaurant at the rear, where one young frumpy English girl sat alone.

"Good morning," I said as I passed her table.

She took one look at me and instantly looked away muttering, "Good morning," under her breath.

Breakfast was included in the price of the accommodation, which was partly self-service. A young local guy came to my table to take my order but his words made no sense.

"Sorry what was that you said?" I asked.

"You af breakfast. Prease elp yoursef to cafffe ow tea. Wan scamble or omelette?" he repeated.

"Scrambled, please," I replied after a quick decipher. I put down my camera, making my way to the table behind that ran along the whole of the back wall. Tea and coffee urns, a platter of sliced watermelon, bread, toaster and a selection of individually wrapped biscuits were set out on a white tablecloth with cups, sugar and milk. As I filled my first coffee cup of the morning, another person walked in.

A woman of around thirty-five years, possibly European, with a blonde bob and pretty face, wearing a pale blue Berghaus jacket and walking boots, sat down at the table next to me. Any woman alone and vaguely my age was of interest to me at the minute. I craved just a little bit of attention post break up and, although my heart wasn't really in it, I felt I should be trying, if only to help draw a line. I looked her way as I returned with my coffee but her inactivity was enough of a sign to divert my eye.

Time then to free up storage on the memory card by deleting all but the best recent photos. 'Tom must have woke up pretty early this morning,' I thought, as I reviewed the snaps. He was nowhere to be seen. I'd not seen him since last night so he must have gone walkabout pretty early. I watched as the cook handed the waiter a plate. He walked my way and spoke.

"Scramble?" as he placed the food in front of me.

"Yes, thank you." It was a fair attempt at a full English breakfast: sausage, scrambled egg, grilled tomato and almost typically English tinned beans in tomato sauce, apart from the weirdly oversized beans.

The office round the front looked out onto a twin terrace of lawns that ran into a gravel car park beyond the lower elevation where the coach had already pulled up. It still wasn't clear if Tom was on the same trip until I heard his name called out after taking my seat. The miserable girl from breakfast climbed aboard and walked straight past me as if I wasn't there, and still no sign of Tom. A smattering of further likeminded travellers were already on the coach and, after a further futile call for my temporary travel companion, we headed off to pick up further guests. 'I can't believe he's missed the coach,' I thought to myself, as we trundled along to our next stop. Just around the corner, another three people joined us.

"Ok, ladies and gentlemen, my name is Ahmad. I am your driver. Welcome aboard our tour bus. We are about to set off to Kinabatangan, which will take around two and a half hours so please sit back, relax and enjoy the ride."

Luckily for Tom, I'd parked myself on the front seat nearest the door to check out the scenery en-route and for a little extra leg room. I spotted him walking along the road ahead, on his way back to the accommodation as we passed back along the road towards the lodge. "There's Tom! The missing guy!" I exclaimed as we approached. The driver pulled over and opened the door.

Imagine a stereotypical Australian outfit straight out of the film 'Crocodile Dundee' and you have the image of Tom's attire as he climbed aboard. He was clothed in light khaki trousers with zip off legs, a matching shirt, wide-brimmed hat with chin strap, high laced army boots, long socks over his trousers and rucksack. He stopped short of dangling corks.

"What happened?" I asked as he took his seat, completely unfazed.

"Sorry, guys, I lost track of time," he explained as he parked his bum three seats up from me. Tom seemed like the last person you might expect to allow himself to be so absentminded.

The best thing to come out of the first two hours of the journey was an amusing dummy at the start of some road works, dressed in a hard hat and high visibility clothing, waving a warning flag from side to side at approaching motorists. I imagine its last job involved wearing a Santa Claus suit, waving at window shoppers beside giant hanging baubles from behind the festive glass of a city department store.

A gradual feeling of isolation developed the further we continued on the last leg of the journey. Buildings became less frequent and perfectly straight parallel rows of palms, like a giant hair transplant stretching as far as the eye could see, began to dominate the landscape. My initial thoughts as an explanation for this manmade phenomenon was that it was possibly a government initiative to re-plant trees after logging but it turned out to be slightly more controversial.

The palm oil industry has started to gather increasing criticism on social media sites such as Facebook over the last few months, being blamed for the mass destruction of the natural habitat of many well-known animal species in Borneo. Only 50% of the rainforest still remains today, down from 75% in 1985. With those statistics in mind, obvious connotations for the indigenous wildlife on the world's third largest island don't need to be spelled out. Apart from loss of habitat, the growth of the trade in wildlife, as remote areas become more accessible, is also a big concern for environmentalists, reinforcing concerns for the long-term survival of the primates who live amongst the branches and the elephants who wonder under its leafy shade. Between 1985 and 2001 over 50% of protected forest was felled in Indonesian Borneo, an area roughly the size of Belgium. A sad fact but who can blame people for doing whatever was necessary to feed their children.

The coach turned into a narrow, potholed, dirt track lane, running parallel to a large river. Branches swept across the windows as we squeezed against trees along the riverbank on the left, avoiding a number of residential properties to the right. Swaying in our seats, we crawled in and out of each crater, towards a handcrafted hardwood jetty, where rails of luminous orange life jackets waited patiently to do their job on either one of the two speed boats about to run the gauntlet across an intimidatingly wide, determined, scruffy swirling soup. The odd speeding log not only shone a different light on the relatively calm looking stretch, but demanded to be recognised as an obstacle of considerable danger. The wildlife lodge was on the far bank of a river less visually exciting than other more exuberant water courses, yet its gentle persona couldn't fully hide a depth and power to induce fear in whoever first crosses it.

I remembered seeing a large crocodile swimming downstream a river similar to this, previously in Malawi, so I asked one of the guides handing out the vests, "Do you have crocodiles here?"

"Yes there are crocodiles here, but you are safe, they will not come," he explained.

A woman stood next to me turned her head slowly towards her partner. "Did he say crocodiles?" she asked with wide eyes. The vulnerability that comes from putting yourself within chomping distance of a creature capable of twisting off your arm, like a child ripping apart a French stick, tends to make you more determined to stay dry.

We fought our way gradually upstream, across the 100 metre width of the second largest river in Borneo, with engines racing. Four guides wearing army combats and boots chaperoned us across the water, two in each boat. One older black guy around 35 years old and three apprentices made up the team bringing us over to the opposite jetty. It was a similar set up on the opposite side of the river and, as we handed back our vests, the team leader grabbed our attention. He was of medium build and height, with short hair and a constantly serious expression.

"OK, please, welcome to Kinabatangan Wildlife Reserve. My name is Tandy. Please make your way down the path to your left and take a seat in the reception area where we will give you a briefing shortly."

At the end of the jetty, beyond the life vest rails, a red brick herringbone path led into the complex, splitting off in two directions. A row of trees along the riverbank to the left screened off the water from a row of hammocks on a grassed area overlooked by two dormitories beyond the reception building.

We made our way quietly together along the path, slipped off our shoes as per the notice and climbed the three wooden steps up to an area furnished with tables, chairs and a kiosk in the corner. Gradually all twelve of us filtered in: some seated, others standing. This was the first time we had come together as a full party. I looked around at the random faces sitting in silence, staring at the ceiling. It felt like the beginning of one of those horror films where a group of strangers are forced to work together instinctively in an attempt to survive being picked off one by one by some illusive danger in the middle of nowhere, and the instant bonds created through desperate necessity. I thought I'd break the ice and share my observations with the group.

"Is it just me, or does it feel like the beginning of a horror film?" I asked.

Encouraged by the little titter that rippled through the crowd, the big American guy responded as Tandy reappeared. "Yeah but who's the killer?"

"Maybe him," I suggested, looking towards the team leader as he found his spot.

"Ok, can I have your attention please? We will soon be making our way back out for tonight's river cruise where we hope to find some creatures you will find interesting. Obviously we cannot guarantee anything and you might not see anything but we will be out approximately two hours. Then dinner will be served at 8 pm in the dining room, down that way," he said, pointing back towards the jetty. Tandy spoke quietly and quickly with a slightly broken vocabulary and local twang. It was obvious this was a speech he had made

174

many times and, after a further ten minutes of information on the location of our accommodation and our itinerary, he finished by telling us, "So if you don't have flip flops, please come down to the jetty in half an hour with bare feet."

I linked back up with Tom as everyone filtered off in different directions. "Do you have flip flops?" I asked. We made our way to our dorm, past scores of upturned, scruffy, bright yellow wellington boots sat in a long rack, between the reception and the first dorm down a separate path, running at right angles to ours, leading to the shower block.

"I'm going to keep these on I reckon," he replied, looking down at his boots.

"I didn't bring mine," I explained over the clatter of tiny wheels struggling to keep up, as my case rattled over block paving. Tom's booking included a night trek through the jungle and, up to our briefing, I wasn't sure if my package included the same. The wellies were obviously to squelch through the mud without ruining your footwear and to help keep leeches at bay while tracking through the jungle paths.

They don't do buildings without steps leading up onto balconies in Borneo. A good guess why is it's probably a design feature to combat the rainy season floods. At the top of the ones leading to our room was a veranda with coffee table and a couple of rattan sofas. From here, rooms to the left and right ran parallel to each other at right angles to the river. Our room was on the left side, first door to the right. It was unlocked when I tried it so I walked in. Inside three bunk beds almost filled the space.

"Once again, just you and me," I pointed out to Tom.

"Yeah it's becoming a habit. At least you don't snore."

"Don't say that! That's the kiss of death to your quiet night's sleep tonight now," I replied with a cheeky tone.

"Did you see the girl from the nature lodge?" he asked.

"Yeah she's a right miserable cow. Did she speak to you?"

"Not really."

"No, me neither."

The room was sparse as you might expect from a budget-priced jungle lodge. Handmade, rustic, wooden bunk beds with a plywood base, hard mattresses,

175

near threadbare sheets and pillowcases, two double sockets and a clothes hook on the back of the door made for a barely adequate stay.

"I have some mosquito coils back at Zuko. I should have brought them." I paused, then continued, "And my flip flops. Or should I say thongs?" I said with a sideward comedy glance.

"Oh yeah, hmm hmm, I don't think I'll make that mistake again."

Tom was hanging back so I told him I'd see him outside. "Yeah ok I'm just going to make a call," he explained.

I walked out with my camera bag over my shoulder but we weren't alone as I opened the door. A little, vivid, light green lizard scampered off quicker than a clockwork toy to hide from the giant creature that suddenly appeared without warning.

The meeting point for tonight's journey was the second jetty, which apparently was along the path I had yet to explore, straight on past the dining area and, as I got closer, I recognised a couple of bearded guys from the coach journey sat at one of the tables near several shiny steel bain-maries. Having not yet had a chance to introduce myself, I walked over and sat down.

"Hi guys. Are you ok? My name's Ian," I told them, simultaneously offering my hand.

"Terry! Aright?" said the first guy.

"And Rob!" said the other. We exchanged handshakes. Both guys seemed sound, unmistakably Welsh and old friends, as it turned out.

A small crowd donning life vests had gathered at the far jetty ahead of me and my two new pals. Behind them the two speed boats, used to bring us across the river earlier, were moored against the stilted timber structure. Each open-topped craft had four rows of moulded twin fibreglass seats and an outboard motor controlled from the back. Along with the driver, each boat also had a spotter.

Again Tandy took the lead. "Ok so here we are. We will be out for around two hours then back for dinner. Hopefully we will see some proboscis monkey, orang-utan, macaque, or maybe we will not see anything because this a natural environment so you just never know. Finally, please remain seated at all times. OK let's go."

176

"Hang on – Tom is not here," I exclaimed as the boat slipped away from the jetty.

"Someone is missing?" Tandy asked.

"Yes, Tom. I just left him back at the room. He is supposed to be coming along." By now we'd drifted five metres away from the jetty so, with a quick burst of the throttle, we pulled back alongside the jetty just as Tom appeared. "Here he is," I announced as he stomped across the hardwood decking. "There's a pattern forming here, Tom. You're getting good at being late pal," I said, this time slightly more irate.

Once again Tom was completely unfazed by his lack of punctuality. "Sorry guys, I was on the phone." The boat listed slightly for a second, along with my heart, as he climbed aboard.

As expected, Tandy was skippering the lead boat and we were following up behind. A sweeping U-turn had us following the direction of flow, with the near bank side to our right. A few metres in front, Tandy decided to negotiate his way around a number of drifting logs as he switched to the other bank in search of socialising simians. We followed but soon a dull thud brought our engine to an abrupt halt. The young skipper leaned over the back of the boat and, at full stretch, lifted one end of a two-metre tree trunk out of the water, as the flow began to take us. It was dug in solid to one of the propeller fins and the inexperienced lad could not pull it free. Tandy's boat raced back on noticing us joining the conveyor of speeding junk heading downstream with increasing determination.

Heading out on this river without apprehension is tough enough, like complying with the local rule to dispose of used toilet paper in the bin, as opposed to the 'foreigners' way, which runs the risk of blocking the inadequate sewers. The term 'sitting ducks' never felt more appropriate, as eyes scanned in all directions and thoughts turned to the ease the local inhabitants could use the dark brown watery haze to mask their approach.

Arms outstretched, the guy couldn't get enough leverage to prize away the obstruction but the other boat would soon be alongside to deal with the task. Tandy killed the throttle at the perfect moment and drifted in his craft. "Logodile!" Tandy exclaimed loudly. A quick nervous titter rippled through the

177

boat as he lifted the log. After a little tug in the right direction, it was detached, free to continue its journey. "Logodile! We have many logodiles around here," Tandy reiterated. If he wasn't sure of getting a guaranteed laugh, he might not have told this joke every time this happened. Even with that assurance, you could tell he still found it somewhat awkward. Being humorous just didn't suit him.

Five minutes steadily downstream through an almost drizzle-like damp mist held by the foliage of the jungle canopy under a steel grey sky, our guides continued to scan the trees to no avail, then, around the next corner, another boat sat holding its ground near the bank side had obviously spotted something. A rusty brown fluffy mass became visible around ten metres back from the edge of the water. I readied my camera and pointed it roughly in the general direction, as did the group of Chinese guys on the other boat.

"An orang-utan?" one of the girls asked.

"Up there to the left of that big branch. To the left!" Tandy informed us as he also joined the flotilla. I could see the dark patch but every time I aimed my camera – nothing.

"See him there?" pointed our skipper but, apart from a quick glimpse of what I think may have been its his arm as he swung off into hiding on the next branch, the man of the forest was gone.

We followed as Tandy swopped banks once again, continuing downstream. Terry and Rob were sat two seats behind and chatted to each other continually. I overheard about their friend who had been here and saw a troop of elephants swimming across the river nearby. "He was probably making it up," Rob told Terry.

"There are no elephants here at the minute," our spotter informed us. "They are moving down towards the coast at the minute. They were here a couple weeks ago," he continued.

"Maybe he did see 'em," said Terry with a rising then dipping tone, in a typical Welsh twang.

At last: a result. We made a beeline for a tall straggly tree populated with a number of what turned out to be long tailed macaque. A troop of around 20 had spread themselves evenly throughout the branches.

Fully grown males stand around 50 cm tall and weigh around six kilos, with furry sideburns and swept-back fur on their foreheads. Otherwise known as crab-eating macaques, these guys prefer to be close to civilisation in order to pilfer the easy pickings that crops provide. The conflict between pilfering primates and smallholders is understandable and can often result in deaths amongst the troop, especially if they break in locals' homes to steal food. Pythons, feral dogs, large cats and even monitor lizards will take these fluffy little fellas, so it's just as well they are great swimmers.

I snapped away with my SLR but the lens wasn't quite long enough for a decent shot and the dampness in the air didn't help. "These monkey like to sleep over the water on the end of branches facing away from the water," our skipper told us. "They are safer from predators there because they can jump off into the river," he continued.

Pythons, feral dogs, large cats and even monitor lizards will take these fluffy little fellas, so it's just as well they are great swimmers. My attention turned to the Welsh guys once again, as they gave out a burst of laughter. I turned and laughed along. "Go on, what?" I ask.

"Well, we speak a bit of Welsh like and talked about how fit one of the girls in the group was and what we would do to her right. It turns out she's Welsh. Let's just hope she doesn't understand what we were saying," said Terry with another burst of laughter.

This is the time of day primates turn their attention to finding a suitable spot to bunk down for the night, which tends to be almost as high as possible so not to attract attention from eagles on the prowl and by the river. Their choice of location is thought to give consideration to their proximity to a food source and the avoidance of mosquitos. The simian diet here comprises mostly of fruit during the plentiful rainy season, if not leaves or grubs, but at other times of year things have been known to become much more desperate. Its not unheard of for hunger to force them into eating clay or breaking into buildings.

Most importantly though is the ability to escape predators by positioning themselves within jumping distance of the river.

The simian diet here comprises mostly of fruit during the plentiful rainy

179

season, if not leaves or grubs, but at other times of year things have been known to become much more desperate. Its not unheard of for hunger to force them into eating clay or breaking into buildings.

Other than the odd skirmish between playful adolescents, the troop sat spread out through the branches, chilling as a large bird crossed the river overhead.

"Here! Look! Hornbill! Hornbill!" the guide pointed out loudly as it disappeared over the trees.

We moved on – this time at quite a pace. The skipper pointed out the odd macaque on the way as he followed. His ability to spot wildlife was impressive at this speed, especially while constantly keeping one eye out for floating obstacles. Suddenly the lead boat did a U-turn and, as we followed suit, I saw Tandy pointing up at the trees. We slipped up alongside them, across from a tree heavy with leaves, branches twitching. There was movement and it wasn't the wind: then my first view of one of the most revered and weird looking creatures, due to its unfeasibly large nose – the proboscis monkey.

Bigger than a macaque, with males weighing around 20 kg, this is the only place in the world you will see proboscis monkeys in the wild and, like the macaque, they like to be close to water for safety. They are particularly good divers and swimmers, using their aquatic abilities to avoid becoming a python or leopard's supper. They can swim up to 20 metres underwater, helped by their partially webbed digits.

A decent-sized male looked down at us from between the branches. His smokey orange face gave the impression of being almost out of focus, like a serene, orange, glowing mask. Even the penis stuck in the middle of his face dangling down over his mouth wasn't quite as weird. As he turned to move away, the dark brown mane on his back became visible but, like most things with this species, it too was a strange sight. Imagine a small, rectangular, dark brown sheepskin rug had been stuck to his back and it might give you some idea. It was difficult to tell as they were quite active but there seemed to be around four or five of these guys in the tree, each intermittently visible through the branches in random locations. Armed with the knowledge this is the only area on earth anyone can catch a glimpse of a creature that looks more fictional in real life than on TV, I looked on with giddy enthusiasm. The others in the group were smaller with no manes or penis noses; they were the females of his harem, won over by his dominance over other males, as is the way of the jungle.

Tandy spoke from the other boat close by, "Ok it will be dark in a few minutes so we will now make our way slowly back up river to the camp."

Back on not so dry land was an opportunity to review the contents of my memory card but first: a shower. I remembered from our welcome meeting, there was only one heated shower so, with shampoo in hand, I set off in search of the furthest cubicle in the block. At the end of the path, just beyond the yellow welly racks, was a row of sinks set out along a white emulsioned block wall under corrugated tin roof panels. This was the front of the shower block where a row of men's showers to the left and women's to the right lay beyond. The miserable girl from Sepilok was at a sink, quietly brushing her teeth. She spotted me through the mirror but kept her head down as I walked past tight-lipped across shabby red painted concrete in the men's side. A scruffy plastic shower curtain attached to rings on a rusty pole hung in each opening. The last of five cubicles had the only electric shower. I turned it on, taking care not to touch the lose wire looping down from rustic timber roof joists, into an open hole in the side of the casing. Each cubicle was built from construction blocks, once again painted white, up to a height of around seven feet where it became open to the underside of the pitched roof.

I lathered up my hair as the shower in the opposite cubicle was turned on in the female side of the building and, from over the wall, I could hear every noise. I heard the naked woman behind the 10 cm blockwork wall, rubbing shower gel all over her soft flesh. My mind flashed back to Claire at Zoku and my squandered opportunity. I imagined the woman behind the wall was her, her large, moist, squelching, soapy breasts slipping around uncontrollably in her hands. A rush of warmth pumped down through my veins towards to my groin. Otherwise silent, the concentrated sound of water flowing over her silken skin, like the sound of a mountain spring washing over voluptuous boulders, gushing down between her glistening curves, caused a pounding of testosterone through my veins, my balls to tighten and my pulse to race. What

181

if she heard me right here literally 30 cm away from her naked body? With tightly clenched arse cheeks, I tried to keep to a minimum the noise of quickly repeating splashes, while imagining her soapy wet fingers sliding effortlessly between the cheeks of her goose-pimpled buttocks. Slowly I came down from my pirouette, the pressure melting away like ice in a fire. I would never know the identity of the mystery lady behind that wall, or if she sensed the energy from hormones with the power to create metamorphic changes in men's anatomies.

I'd not noticed Tom was on the phone again as I walked back in the room. "Aright pal?" He looked up from his bed, then back down again while holding up his hand in acknowledgement, as he continued his conversation. This wasn't the sort of room you would want to spend much time in other than sleeping or for the privacy to speak candidly on the phone so I wasted no time in leaving him for dinner. I left him private 20 minutes before dinner.

I sauntered over to the dining area and found a good smattering of people already there. The miserable girl had found a group of girls of a similar age and was suddenly the life and soul of the party, which compounded my dislike for her even more. "Why not speak to me?" I said to myself. "Oh, you think every man who says hello wants to get in your knickers? Look in the mirror, love." The girls filled a table for four and, sat opposite, the Welsh guys. An American woman with her gentle giant boyfriend had also found a table, as had a couple of others. I sat back with the Welsh lads and, a few minutes later, so did Tom.

"So are you guys on holiday?" Tom asked.

"Well, Rob lives in Bangkok and I came to visit him," said Terry as the waiting staff began filling servers with food.

"Ahh, cool. How long have you lived there Rob?" Tom continued.

"Err, around five years," he replied.

"You still living in Wales, Terry?" I asked.

"No, I live in Manchester now."

"I have a few friends in Manchester, nice place," I continued.

"So when you were you last back home, Rob?" Tom asked.

"Every couple of years I go home for Christmas but I've not lived there for 15 years," he explained.

"You got stuck in Australia for a while, didn't you Rob?" Terry revealed. The two friends giggled.

"I was thrown out of Oz for overstaying my visa," he told us.

"Really? What happened?" Tom quizzed.

"Couldn't afford a ticket, stuck there, fucking skint pal."

"Weren't you living in a barn for a while pal?" his friend enquired, pretending he didn't know the story that well.

"Eventually yes, but most of the time I was travelling around doing bits of work, like. I ended up knocking around with some right idiots who would always be out on the piss not giving a fuck about anything. The worst one was a cockney guy, Vince. He would wake me up in the middle of the night and say, 'Right, come on! We're going out!' He was a fucking nutcase man so you couldn't really say no. We had some laughs like, but I was glad to get away from them in the end."

"So how did you end up getting kicked out?" Tom quizzed.

"Well, my visa ran out, like, but I didn't have enough money for a ticket home, so I just hung around. I ended up staying in the barn of this farm earning shit money, but it was cash. I told the farmer I would work as many hours as he wanted if I could doss down in the barn so I did that for about three months until I had enough money to get a ticket home like. The problem was, when I got to airport, they pulled me in asking me, 'Why are you a year over your visa?' Getting arsy, like. They started saying they would kick me out of the country, but that didn't bother me so I said, 'Ok then just do it.' They didn't know what to fucking do then. In the end they let me use the ticket I bought to get home and that was that."

"That's awesome man. Great story!" Tom added.

Five minutes before official dinner time, I walked over to the central table just behind us to inspect the contents of the bain-maries. A young staff member was stood by the table waiting to oversee proceedings and, when he saw me taking an interest in the freshly prepared cuisine, he said, "Please help yourself, sir. Here we have fish and here is vegetables, also here rice and chicken in that one," as he pointed to the last platter.

"Thank you," I grabbed a plate.

"Drinks over there," he explained, pointing over to the table to the left. Soon a small queue of hungry wildlife lovers formed.

"Are you guys going on the night walk?" I asked the Welsh lads as Tom was off filling his plate.

"No we are going back tonight. We only booked for the one river trip today as we have got to be back."

"So how are you getting back?" I asked.

"I think we are going in a car, like, but I'm not sure. We have to be at the jetty in half an hour."

"Oh well have a safe journey and that. It's been good to meet you," I told the lads. The food was almost as good as the conversation thanks to the bearded buddies, but before too long we were two men down.

"Ok, everybody, please listen. We are meeting outside reception in 15 minutes for the night walk," Tandy explained, as he stood in the centre of the food hall. "You will need some boots so please find the boots for your size on the racks, ok?" A ripple of acknowledgment came back from the tables as he disappeared down the front steps.

At the boot rack, I wasn't the only one confused by the European sizes moulded into the soles. "Anyone know what the equivalent of size nine is?" No one answered. "Good leech protection, if nothing else," I continued not wanting to be ignored, but still nothing. "I feel like a fisherman with these on," I exclaimed as I looked down at my exaggerated stomp.

We followed Tandy single file into the darkness. I was back marker, behind the American woman and her bloke. "Best not to keep your head torch on your head because of the bugs," the American woman advised, as we followed a squelchy path, slaloming between trees on the forest fringe.

"Of course they're attracted to the light, yes. Thanks," I replied removing the strap from my head. The faint mumble of a message being relayed from the front filtered back.

"Elephant tracks," the American woman said, shining her torch over a spot to the left of the path, just ten metres from the camp buildings. There was no mistaking the soggy dinner-plate-sized indentations, grouped around a small clearing in the trees. We moved slowly along the winding sludge track, torchlight searching the branches.

"Anyone spotted any leeches yet?" I quizzed while inspecting the back of my legs with the torch, then a shriek from one of the girls up front. The path was too narrow to get a better view of the ensuing commotion but I wouldn't have bet against it being a clever little blood sucking parasites.

Moving on, the path opened up, allowing us to bunch as a group. Tandy pointed out the bright blue head of a sleeping kingfisher in the trees with his torch, while his colleague offered out his hand for a closer inspection of the small leech he had just removed from the girl's arm. It had attached itself between his fingers, waving around like a miniature elephant trunk sniffing out a sticky bun. "Flick it," he said to one of the girls, but after three attempts she gave in. "Here. Flick it," he said to me. With one swift man flick, it was gone. If only it would be that easy to rid myself of the dampness inside my wellies. Ten more minutes, two more sleeping birds and a centipede later, we were back at the boot rack.

"No snakes then?" I exclaimed to Tom as he made his way over.

"No snakes," he replied leaning down to remove his wellies. "Although I do have a leech attached to my groin," he explained while rummaging in his pants.

"Oh god! I hate them things. I got away lightly this time," I explained.

"Yeah there're pretty horrible. I'm just going to the shower to remove it," he stated calmly.

"Errr! Oh my god. He has a leech attached to his groin," I explained to Tandy.

"Yes they like to find the warm place. I have many times removed them from private places for people," he said screwing up his face.

"How do they manage to get there?" I asked.

"They are clever," he explained abruptly as Tom reappeared from the shower block.

"Did you get it off?" I asked.

"Yeah, super easy. I used insect repellent and it came straight off. I feel a bit sorry for it really," he explained.

185

"Insect repellent? I didn't know that worked! There's one to remember."

"Yeah, someone told me a while ago. It works really well."

One by one our fellow explorers drifted off for the night, in readiness for the early start. Our coach was due to leave at 10.30 am in the morning to take us back to Sepilok after our final river cruise at first light.

"Did you sleep ok?" Tom asked the next morning.

"Like a logodile," I replied.

Back out at the jetty, the ubiquitous Tandy spoke, "OK we are about to go back out to find wildlife that is hopefully still near the water's edge, before they move inland to eat breakfast. We will be out for around two hours and on our return we will also have breakfast," he explained.

Brush strokes of layered grey and orange moisture, shrouded in silent sprawling ribbons of pink mist, attached to distant leafy canopies downstream, was an oil painting waiting to be captured, as we turned to make our way upstream once again. Other than an amazing spot by Tandy to notice the motionless glassy stare of a baby crocodile, semi-submerged under bushes on the water's edge, nothing happened for the first 90 minutes until, that is, a truly amazing close encounter with a troupe of long-tailed macaques.

Sat in the lowest branches of a tree overhanging the water, we drifted in to a gradual stop, almost within touching distance of a big male with a segment of jack fruit hanging from the side of his mouth. With no more than a metre between us, he sat motionless, allowing a great opportunity to snap some once in a lifetime close-ups.

Seemingly unfazed by the disruption of his breakfast by a floating gang of giant shaved monkeys, he stared straight through us as if we weren't there, out over the water with glistening dark brown eyes, under a prominent monobrow lined with long furry lashes. A scuff of dark brown fur, darker than his tan-coloured body, running down between his eyes, formed a continuation of the bridge of his almost non-existent nose and all the time his nonchalant expression remained throughout his pose through a window framed by a garland of lush greenery.

Others in the troupe were also close by, moving around behind the intermittent leafy curtain. A female, with infant clinging instinctively around

186

her chest, broke cover and sat posing for the camera for a few precious moments, while her innocent offspring stared continuously, mesmerised by the big, strange, floating creatures. She pursed her lips then, with swinging baby, strolled back under cover on all fours, before becoming hidden once more behind the glossy green screen. This final encounter of our floating adventure turned out to be the most memorable. A sighting of a crocodile's knobbly back gliding across the river, amongst its logodile friends, would have been the perfect end to a great trip as we made our way to the opposite bank, bags in hand, to the waiting coach but it wasn't to be. Sleeping the two-hour return journey was the preferred option for me but it wasn't till the driver announced we were back that I realised that's exactly what had just happened.

Chapter 8
Rehab'

It was 12.30 pm, two hours before feeding time at the Orang-utan Rehabilitation Centre: the ideal amount of time to find some better accommodation for my last night at Sepilok. I dragged my cabin bag along the tarmac towards two other complexes down the side street near the entrance to my final attraction before my flight back to Kota Kinbalu the next day. One of the signs on the junction advertising the 'Jungle Resort Lodge' had images of an idyllic labyrinth of footbridges over a lake and boasted a swimming pool. That had to be better than the empty lodge up the road and, if too expensive, there was always the 'Banana Cafe', which, according to the sign, also looked pretty good. My intention was to check out both establishments then make a decision before the mid-afternoon photo shoot.

I turned up the drive to Banana Cafe, following the road up to a covered turning circle then up steps leading to a circular reception. "Hi, do you have dormitory rooms here?" I asked the local woman behind the curved reception desk.

She passed me a laminated price list. "Yes, we do. Here are prices, sir, but I need check if we have room available for you. When you want to stay?" she asked.

"Tonight for one night please," I replied.

"Ok I will check, please wait." She picked up the phone. I scanned the tariffs as she talked over the phone in Malaysian. 50 ringgit per night was the rate. "Yes we have," she explained on putting down the phone.

"Ok thank you I will think about it and let you know."

Not more than 20 metres further along the road, another drive leading to Jungle Resort Lodge also turned in to the right. I followed the drive towards buildings up ahead. Stairs to the left led to an open restaurant. Beyond the rows of chunky, solid, wooden dining tables, made from sliced rustic logs, a spindled handrail protected guests from dropping down the two metres into the pond below. Meandering banks on the far side of the water marked the

188

start of a wooded area. A clutch of trees on an island in the centre of the pond was enough to seal the deal on a room here for the night regardless of the potential difference in cost.

There was a small office behind a counter in the far left of the restaurant. There a local woman was sitting at a desk. "Hello. Do you have a dormitory here?" I asked as she got up out of her seat.

She looked around, slightly confused. "Excuse me. I am new today," she explained.

An older Chinese woman came over from the table where she had been sitting with a group of others. She spoke abruptly to the receptionist in Malay, turned around, smiled and walked back to her table. Now armed with a laminated room tariff, the new girl offered it over the counter.

"Yes we have dormitories, sir. Here are the prices."

According to the list, it was the same price as next door so, wasting no more time, I said, "I would like to stay one night please." I took my pick of bed in the empty dorm, bottom bunk far corner, with time still for a quick dip in the pool before my close encounter with the hairy gingers up the road.

I was told to follow the walkway through the restaurant and keep going to the far end of the complex to find the swimming pool so I grabbed my trunks. The pond overlooking the restaurant continued through the complex, as did the footbridge. Deeper into this landscaped oasis, now benefitting from the time nature had been allowed to work its magic, the murky pond opened out either side of the walkway to a crescent of trees and exotic foliage lining the far bank some 20 metres away. Further still, in the centre of what was now more like a cloudy emerald lake, a square wooden seating pergola draped in glossy leaf and brightly-coloured blooms stood over the water on stilts. From here further footbridges set off in opposite directions. A sign to the swimming pool pointed left so, after a brief photographic interlude, I followed the sign to a second pergola and a further footbridge to a building that looked rather familiar. This was the back of the reception of what I mistakenly took for another complex when I walked up the drive a few minutes ago. The Jungle Resort and the Banana Cafe were one and the same!

Because of its impressive attempt at natural beauty, albeit contrived, it didn't have the feel of place a tourist could lay drinking beers on loungers, topping up their tan beside a pool side bar, so, as I made my way down the steps tucked away on the far side, I was pleasantly surprised to see just that. An attendant leaning back onto two legs of a chair behind the bar was snoozing as I walked past towards a clutch of wooden sun loungers. The ones around the far side weren't shaded by the forest fringe. I dropped my towel and placed my camera bag under the lounger then dived in the empty kidney-shaped pool.

Opposite the pool bar, a fibre glass cliff with prehistoric looking boulders sat on the water's edge with a natural backdrop of huge trees on the fringe of the jungle beyond. A perpetual flow of water cascaded down to the pool by means of a hidden pumping mechanism, creating a synthetic waterfall reminiscent of a budget all-inclusive resort.

On hearing me enter the water, the bar man opened his eyes and dropped his chair back onto four legs. My reward for three lengths of the pool was, yes you've guessed it, a beer. I pushed myself up onto one bent leg from in the water then onto two feet, leading a dripping trail to the bar.

"Beer please," I asked the guy. He unlocked the padlock on the glass-fronted fridge and passed me a cold one.

"Room number sir?"

"215," I replied.

Realising the close proximity to the Orang-utan Rehabilitation Centre, I asked the guy, "Do you see many orang-utan here at the pool?"

"Yes, sometimes they come if there is no one around but they break the seats so we do this," he explained waving both arms up and down in unison.

"Do they ever go down the slide?" I asked, but he looked back at me with a blank expression. I pointed over to another fibreglass creation on the water's edge. Steps leading up to the top of a water slide in the shape of a grey shark which spews you out of its mouth into the pool. "Orang-utan go here?"

"Baby one, yes."

"Oh my god! That is so cool! I would love to see that!" I explained excitedly as I signed my tab.

Every couple of minutes, an odd stray cloud would block the sun for long enough to make you realise how much you need the warmth when you're wet and half naked in the breeze. Luckily for me, each time I looked skyward from my lounger, further clear skies were soon to return. Three more lengths and one more beer saw me head back to the room for a quick change of clothes, ready for feeding time.

As advertised by the Jungle Lodge, the Rehab Centre was literally a five-minute walk. Back up to the T-junction, turn left and you are outside the gates. I walked under the archway with the words 'Selamat Datang' in large letters emblazoned around it. I'm pretty sure it doesn't translate to 'Work sets you free' in German but it did look very reminiscent of the gates at Auschwitz. I mistakenly thought this was the main entrance but it turned out to be the outer gate leading into the car park. The increased footfall up ahead led me to the entrance at the other end of the car park. A bus saying 'Airport' was parked up near the entrance.

"What times are the buses?" I asked a guy sat on the kerb opposite the open door, smoking a cigarette.

"It is 11 o'clock here," he replied. I didn't notice him place the fag in the corner of his mouth, between thumb and index finger, to take his last long drag, while I considered if it was a daily service.

"So here at 11 tomorrow?" He nodded in agreement with closed eyes and screwed up face, before tossing what was left of the hastily smoked cigarette.

If I asked you to guess what nationality was most prevalent at this attraction today, you might say Chinese and you would be right, although not so many of the gorgeous ladies in designer jeans and Gucci handbags here like in Singapore. Here it was more family-orientated, couples with kids and cameras.

I approached the counter. "One ticket please," I requested.

The assistant noticed my camera bag and asked, "You want to take camera also?"

"Yes," I replied. "Ok, 30 ringgit and ten for camera," she explained. I handed over the equivalent of £8.30. "You must leave your bag in the locker," she explained.

"But this has my camera lenses in it."

"You have to leave your bag because the orang-utan will steal it," she continued.

"But I have paid to take my camera inside and this bag has my camera and accessories in it," I argued.

"Sorry, sir, you have to leave it," she insisted. Begrudgingly I took the padlock that was offered and complied with the annoying rule.

Armed with my tickets rather than spare lenses, I was now allowed to exit the ticket office through the far door. Still chuntering under my breath, I stepped out onto the jungle fringe. A man with a loudspeaker dangling from his shoulder ushered me to another one of those raised wooden walkways leading into the forest. As I approached the second bend in the path, another guy also armed with loudspeaker, wearing khaki green shirt, trousers and black army boots, gave me the stop sign by holding up his palm in my direction. I obliged curiously but it quickly became clear.

Slow and steady, with a swaying gate, an adolescent orang-utan slipped out from behind a tree onto the handrail, around five metres in front. This placid primate, with his disproportionately long limbs and sweeping quiffs of long ginger fur running down the back of his arms, dropped down to the floor and sauntered along in the same direction as me, flanked by his chaperone. I soon got within two metres but it was just as the path forked off in different directions.

"First you go there," the man said, while pointing to the left path, in a different direction to them. "To the nursery," he continued.

"Ok thank you," was my reply as I stood and watched the orang-utan slowly disappear out of sight.

At the end of the path, I entered through a door leading into a building with a sign above the door saying 'NURSERY'. Inside, tiered seating stepped down to a floor-to-ceiling glass viewing wall where groups of wide-eyed visitors sat pointing and giggling at the joyful innocence of around 30 boisterous baby orang-utan playing together on a large wooden aerial playground equipped with horizontal swag ropes, high platforms and swinging tyres. The twinkle of excitement in their eyes was a joy to witness as a room half-full of smiling

faces were gifted with a chaotic display of slapstick acrobatics littered with hilarious infantile calamities.

I found a spot to sit, one row up from the bottom tier and out came the Nikon again. It was a mixed crowd of Chinese, locals and westerners, whose sporadic outbursts of appreciation were testament to a level of cuteness far beyond the likes of puppies in the snow. It was like break time at primate primary school and the crowd revelled in it.

Sporadic bursts of adorable exuberance made my attempts at capturing the moment on film as difficult they found it to sit still for more than a moment at a time. The reflection from the glass didn't help either so before too long I gave up on the task and moved back outside towards the viewing platform as feeding time approached.

There was no sign of the orang-utan or the guard as I retraced my steps back to the junction in the walkway. It led to a clearing with steps up to a two-tiered timber viewing area, three metres high, overlooking a raised circular platform clamped around a tree approximately ten metres away with ropes leading in from numerous directions. A large male and a youngster sat side by side on the platform under a bright blue sky, while a mother and her adolescent offspring dangled from a rope close by.

After a minute or two, others joined the party as the keeper threw the first bunch of bananas up onto their platform. All the other orang-utan kept their distance, except one baby, while the dominant male tucked into the free lunch. One banana dropped from the bunch as the big male steadily consumed the handout and the baby picked it up. Not satisfied with all but one of the donation to himself, the male slowly swung around to relieve the baby of his prize but the baby wasn't giving it up easily and turned his back on the big alpha. He stretched out an arm, reaching around the gritty little ginger mite, prizing the banana from his dark brown digits until he, like everyone else, had to sit and wait for the next course to arrive. A main course of – yes you've got it – more bananas soon found its way onto the platform. This time four or five bunches landed on the wooden structure. Their understanding of the hierarchy of the group was clear as the feeding progressed. Only after giving the male a good chance of taking his fill did the others attempt to move in and share the remaining food.

By now though, something much more intriguing than the pecking order had caught the attention of the crowd. Something that, had it been humans, would have been hugely shocking. A mother and adolescent child were hanging on a rope stretched horizontally between the main platform and a nearby tree, around five metres from the alpha male. Mum was hanging by her arms and one leg with her other leg dangling, while her young daughter took advantage of the opportunity to investigate the inside of her mum's vagina. Mum just calmly looked on as she received her examination, while the little one hung there on the rope by one arm, the full length of her fingers lost inside her mother. For orang-utan, this is obviously not a taboo, no matter how disturbing we humans may find it. None of the troop was distressed by their actions. Whether or not the mother gained any pleasure from the experience I could not say but, from what I saw, I got the impression the youngster wasn't intending to pleasure her mother rather just being inquisitive.

Generally orang-utan are known to be incestuous and it's not unheard of for a brother to be the father of his sister. Females have evolved to become highly promiscuous as this reduces the occurrences of infanticide. Only the dominant males get to mate with the females and there's always a new alpha waiting to take their crown. This creates an urgency to procreate in the male that historically has led to him killing babies in order to incite the female to mate. Research shows the more promiscuous she becomes, the less infants he kills.

Slowly, as the bananas ran out so did the audience's interest and we began to disperse. I made my way back to the entrance to collect my camera bag, reviewing some interesting niche images of incestuous hairy ginger primate porn on my way. It softened the blow of being hit with a fee for taking photos but that 'camera ticket' also added to a feeling of exploitation. I pondered further on the issue of exploitation versus rehabilitation. There was definitely a bit of both here but to what extent? Enticing fully grown orang-utan in from the jungle to eat free grub, while being observed by paying tourists cannot be totally without some degree of exploitation, but if this pays for the care of orphaned youngsters, who's to know where you cross the line? The amenities for humans created here vastly outweigh the structures built for the benefit of

194

the creatures they are here to see, yet there is obviously some benefit to the youngsters having access to the playground they clearly love.

There was just time left in the day, to have another quick dip in the pool before dark. The weather was still typical for the time of year, around 30 degrees, very humid, with the occasional heavy shower. The weather continued to be kind today: the sun warming my neck, as I drew ever closer to that early evening poolside beer. Other than the posh place with the lake across the road, this was the only choice for dinner tonight so that's where I ended up later.

Out of around 20 tables, only two were taken up. One with a Scandinavian family of four and the other, a corpulent lady of retirement age was sat alone. I parked down two tables away from the woman, who was just ordering food.

"And could I have a bottle of the sauvignon please?" she asked the waitress bent over her table. On finishing her order and noticing me, she turned and spoke, "I thought I would treat myself," she explained.

"And why not?" I replied.

"I can save it for tomorrow – it works out more reasonable then," she continued. Instantly likeable, the woman gave the impression of not caring too much about what others might think and was very approachable. She wore a short flowery patterned cotton dress, much younger than her years.

By now, the light had faded and the frogs were in good voice. "Are you travelling alone?" I enquired.

"For the past six weeks, yes. My husband is going to join me next week and hopefully bring along a few more items of clothing," she laughed, then continued. "I have been travelling with hand luggage all this time." She was at an age where the fear of giving the wrong impression was no longer relevant: that and her obvious continuing lust for life made for an easy conversation.

"Any travel tips?" I asked.

"Yes, don't talk to strangers in restaurants!" she said, with a cheeky smile.

"I wish you'd have told me that five minutes ago," we laughed as the waitress came for my order.

Jungle Lodge menus were starting to look quite similar. Fried noodles, boiled rice, chicken. I was hoping for more local delicacies to brag about on

Facebook, but I suppose this is a tourist area and they need to be catered for. Most tourists tend to steer clear of frog porridge or boiled mouse.

"Are you ready to order?" the waitress asked. She was a teenager, dressed in dark clothes, one of a handful who sat around with nothing to do most of the time while the place was quiet.

"Can I get the fried chicken noodles and a beer please?"

"Yes sir," she replied, turning back towards the kitchen.

"So are you a photographer?" the Englishwoman asked.

"No, but I enjoy taking photos. I don't usually have the time so I'm making the most if it, and there is some great subject matter here too. What about you? What do you do for a living?"

"I'm a retired teacher and you?"

"A builder."

"Oh so is my husband," she revealed, with a surprised tone. "Would you like a glass of wine?" she asked.

"No thanks, I have a beer on its way." To be honest, I would have loved a glass of wine but I knew how much she had paid for it and, around £25 for the bottle, I couldn't accept her offer. Now 25 quid for a bottle of wine in a restaurant isn't that bad when you are at home but, bearing in mind the food may be no more than the equivalent of £2 here, it's a luxury I didn't want to spend my own money on so accepting her offer would have been wrong. Her food arrived so I left her to it, turning my attention back to reviewing the day's orang-utan images.

Before long, one of the male staff came over. "You take photos of wildlife?" he asked.

"Yes. I have some photos of my visit to the Orang-utan Rehabilitation Centre today. Here look." I'd already found a few decent shots, so I passed over the camera.

"Very nice. If you want, I can show you some of the wildlife here at night. Can you hear the frogs?" he asked.

"Yes I can," I explained.

"I can show you if want me to?" he continued.

"I have ordered food, but afterwards that would be great."

"Of course. I will come back later," he said kindly.

My food arrived promptly and, just as I was finishing, the lady got up to leave. "Well, have a lovely trip if I don't see you again. I'm off to bed," she explained gripping the wine bottle by the neck.

"I leave late tomorrow morning so, yes if I don't see you by the pool first thing, I hope you have a great trip. Goodnight."

Around here when darkness falls, the decibels rise; the difficulty is finding the source of the noise – that is if you want to. Luckily for me, the guy made good on his offer to show me the wildlife hidden under the cover of darkness; he and his friend proved to be dab hands at spotting all number of little creatures.

First, they pointed out a kingfisher sleeping on a low branch over the water below the wooden walkway leading around the lake. Although well out of the reach of us humans, I was surprised to see how exposed he had allowed himself to be while waiting for daybreak. Perched on a branch out in the open, one of the guys illuminated the flamboyant fellow with a torch. With surprising lack of foliage to hide his presence, his deep electric blue head plumage glistened and, although you would think the light would have caused him some disturbance, he seemed not at all startled by the glare. I attempted to capture an image on my camera for the benefit of my hosts but my lack of understanding of the best function to use under these situations made for another batch of deleting next time I had the chance.

"Did you get a good picture?" the taller of the two, who first came to my table asked.

"Yes, thank you," I lied.

"Do you like frogs?" he enquired.

"Yeah, I like frogs," I lied again.

"We can find them up here."

We walked the ten metres back to the restaurant then continued out through the other side, up the path towards my dorm. Halfway up the path running along the side of the building was a small pond with bushes around a metre high growing around it. The noise was enough to convince me: it would be easy to spot where it was coming from, but I was wrong. Even the experts took a while to pin down the source of the din.

"Here, look," the smaller, lower-ranked staff member pointed. "You see?" he continued. But no matter how close I seemed to get to the spot, I didn't see a thing.

"Ok here," the taller guy instructed from the other side of the bush. I moved around and at last caught a glimpse. A tiny dwarf of an amphibian was clung to a branch croaking his little head off, trying to attract a mate. Loud and proud, easily hidden in a crowd, this guy was around two centimetres long. Tiny indeed, although not the smallest around here. A 'pea-sized' frog was first discovered in Sarawak just as recently as 15 years ago, at half the size. The sound of at least half a dozen frogs rang out around the metre wide circle of shallow water, yet only one could be found, which is more than could be said about the toad they found next.

In contrast, he stood out like a Tourette's sufferer in a library. This knobbly scrotum-skinned lump was stood bold as brass, practicing the world's longest burp on the open ground two metres from the pond, with no apparent interest in hiding away from us giants. The stereotypical wart-covered creature, any self-respecting witch would throw straight in her cauldron, was on the pull too and nothing was about to stop him. After a number of twists and turns of the dials, I managed to get a few decent images of the toad and the frog.

"That is ok for you?" the tall guy asked.

"Great, yes thanks. I have some good photos. I will show you in the morning," I replied.

"Yes ok. Thank you," he concluded.

Mentioning 'the morning' seemed to do the trick of not having to tell them I had had enough of their hospitality. "Goodnight," I said in raised voice, as I turned to my room.

Known by some as the barometers of the forest due to their acute sense of climate change, frogs are excellent indicators for assessing forest condition. There are said to be 100 species of frog in Borneo but only one third of that number are found here in Sabah. The more southerly province of Sarawak boasts two thirds, all of which are to be found in the Gunung Mulu National Park. It would be interesting to hear what level of noise would be generated by double the amount of species on their nocturnal courting rituals.

198

Back in my dorm room, the egg box internal door with its green crudely hand-painted finish closed behind me. Still just me occupying one of the six beds made up of three handmade bunks squeezed into a small double room, I put my phone on charge and slipped into my bottom bunk. The last night in Sabah soon became the next morning.

It was no surprise to find myself wide awake at 7 am. My body clock always has me up at the crack of dawn these days, which is usually annoying, but not today because now I had a chance for a last quick dip in the pool before checkout. Unlike yesterday the pool was not exclusively mine today. An older gentleman, around retirement age, was lounging on the terrace with long, striped, cotton swim trunks but he didn't speak, which felt a bit awkward. Six lengths were enough to see me heading back to the room for my bags.

I wanted to be at the Orang-utan Rehabilitation Centre by 10.45 am to make sure I didn't miss the bus. I was to be reunited with my big rucksack back at Zoku later that day, which left me to wheel my hand luggage-size bag up the street, the five-minute walk to the car park, with my camera bag slung across my shoulder. I reached the car park in good time and contemplated taking off my shirt to catch a bit of sun. It was moderately busy as people arrived for the morning feeding session but no sign yet of my cheap return transport to the airport. To kill a little time, I decided to copy a couple of the Chinese tourists who I'd spotted coming out of a nearby door and purchase an ice cream from the onsite cafeteria. Mindful of the problems that missing the bus would cause, I hurriedly returned back outside, Cornetto in hand, as it was now 11 am and time for the bus.

Ten minutes later, a slight sense of anxiety and sunburn started to become noticeable. I put on my shirt and walked back through the car park to make sure I hadn't missed the bus pulling up in a different location to yesterday but there was no sign of it as yet, as I reconsidered my options. I could order a taxi from the accommodation but it would be expensive in comparison to a Grab car for instance, but I had not had much luck in using the app on my smartphone to order an Uber-style lift up to now.

A car park attendant was walking in my direction so I asked, "Excuse me. Have you seen the bus that goes to Sandakan?"

"No it doesn't come until around 2.30 pm," he explained.

"But I saw the driver here yesterday and he told me he would be here at 11 am."

"Oh, maybe he is late, but if people don't come here from Sandakan, they do not come," he continued.

"Okay thank you," I replied. The airport was on the way to Sandakan, the main town around here. The journey to town takes around 45 minutes by bus or around 20 minutes by car, if you can find one to take you that is, which preferably would be a Grab car, as they are around one third of the cost of a taxi. As time passed, it was looking more and more likely the bus wasn't going to turn up and, to make matters worse, the Grab app on my smartphone wasn't playing ball again.

I started to retrace my tracks back to the Jungle Lodge to order a taxi. As I reached the junction, I decided to call in the little food shack on the corner just outside the centre to see if they could order me a Grab car. There were two tables outside and a board with hand-written dishes fixed to a wooden column. As I approached, a smart looking four-wheel drive pickup pulled up. A local man got out and walked my way. I followed him towards the outdoor tables but he continued through, climbing over the fenced-off barrier of chicken wire penning in a puppy in the back kitchen area.

"Hi, I don't suppose you know if I could get a Grab around here, do you?" I asked the guy as he disappeared into the back.

"Where you want to go?" he asked.

"I need to get to the airport," I proclaimed.

"What time is your flight?"

"7 pm but I was also hoping to see the town before I leave as well."

"Why? There is nothing there," he explained.

"It's just that I have come a long way and it would be a shame not to see what is there, as I am so close." Now by my reckoning the Grab should cost around seven ringgit from here to the airport so, when the guy offered to take me to the airport via Sandakan town for 20 ringgit, I knew he was trying it on, but it would get me out of a tight spot. "OK 20 ringgit, but can you drop me at Sandakan Memorial Park, then a quick tour of Sandakan town on our way to the airport?"

200

"OK 25 and I will take you now," he offered.

"OK let's go."

After a few words in Malay to the old lady in the back, he opened the boot. "OK put your bag here." It was pretty clear he wasn't a registered Grab driver but he obviously knew what they charged and took the opportunity to make a little cash on the side. Had he been registered, he would have used his smartphone app to record the journey and the cost would be worked out according to the app. "How long you stop for looking at the memorial park?" he asked.

"There is a tour that you can do that takes one hour," I explained to him.

"One hour is too long for here. You will be finished in maybe 20 minutes I think. Ok you ring me when you are finished and I will come back for you," he explained.

"Yes that sounds like a good idea. I will ring." I had no idea what to expect as the guy pulled up outside the park.

Visible through the other side of tastefully ornate high metal railings was a new log cabin-style reception centre, leading to an ornamental concrete path winding its way around grassy knolls and undulating woodland. A stark contrast to the view on the opposite side of the main road. There stood a row of grotty looking flats, a dusty path and two canvas-roofed stalls selling snacks and drinks run by a bunch of children on the corner.

Entry to the park was free and, as I walked through the gates, the only giveaway to the history of the place was a small khaki green digger with rusty caterpillar tracks on a landscaped banking, across the other side of a long ornamental kidney-shaped pond. I followed the path down and back around towards the rusty lump, while starting the audio tour on the Sandakan Memorial Park app on my smartphone. The audio tour starts with a dramatic drum roll and then an Australian narrator starts telling the story of the camp and the plight of 1,793 Australian and 641 British soldiers that were still there as the surrender of the Japanese army became imminent sometime in 1944.

The camp was created in 1942, with the purpose of building an airstrip for the Japanese air force. Prisoners of war, captured by the Japanese in and around Singapore, were shipped in for the task. They did a great job of slow timing their captures; most notable was the sabotage of the digger I had now just passed on the path back down the hill. Someone put sand in the engine on the second day it was in service and, although the prisoners gave the impression they were constantly attempting to repair it, it never worked again. The airstrip that was eventually created was repeatedly bombed by the allied forces, rendering it useless before it ever became fully operational. As the net closed in on the Japanese towards the end of the war, they decided to abandon the camp and eradicate the remaining POWs by forcing them on an impossible 226 km march inland towards the town of Ranau. Not one of the 641 British POWs and only six escapees out of the 1,793 Australians survived at the hands of the Japanese. Now known as the death marches, it is the largest single atrocity to have been inflicted on the Australians throughout the Second World War. Almost 70 years later, the former camp is a symbol of peace and tranquillity, having been lovingly transformed into a beauty spot in remembrance to those poor souls who gave their lives for our freedom.

The driver was right: 20 minutes passed and I had finished my tour of the park.

"Hi it's Ian, the guy who you are taking to the airport."

"Hello. Are you ready?"

"Yes. I am making my way out of the park now. I will meet you at the food stall across the road if you want?"

"Ok no problem; see you soon."

I walked across to the stall on the corner. Three clear plastic urns stood side by side on the stall filled with ice and different coloured refreshments. Green, yellow and orange were on offer. As the youngsters noticed me approaching, they started to look busy. "

Hi, what is this one? Lemon?" I asked while pointing at the yellow cylinder.

"Ok," said the oldest girl. She lifted the lid and gave the liquid a stir with a ladle before filling a large flimsy plastic cup with the icy refreshment.

To the left was a large wok filled with crackling hot oil. One of the other younger girls held up a wooden skewer with something pre-attached. One long twist of some sort of vegetable spiralled along the majority of the stick. "You want?" she asked.

202

"Ok yes," I replied. Little experiences like these are what turn trips into adventures. I didn't care what it was on that stick: I was having it. She dropped it in the hot oil with a smile.

"You want spicy?"

"Yes please."

Within seconds the snack was back out of the pan, dipped in a red powder, striped in mayonnaise and passed to me. "Thank you," I said, as I took it and paid. The food was nice – not amazing but nice. Nor was it that adventurous. One continual potato crisp with paprika but enjoyable all the same. The drink on the other hand was divine. The Malaysians have a special gift of creating some gorgeously refreshing drinks. From iced juices to hot lime tea, I just couldn't get enough, especially on a stiflingly hot day like today.

My car was soon back on the scene and we headed into town. After a few minutes, the driver said, "This building here is the Princess Diana Hospital." As we passed, I saw the sign saying the Duchess of Cambridge hospital, so he was on the right track I suppose. "How did you like the memorial park?" he asked.

"It was ok."

We approached a roundabout. "Up there is the airport." A sign to the left confirmed it.

"Is it far?" I enquired.

"From here only five minutes, but we go into town first."

He headed straight across at the roundabout, to allow me to see for myself just how insignificant a place for tourists Sandakan really was. One road led through into town with bus stops and a row of shops. It was one-way and continued to the right at the end of the street, down to the waterfront, where it turned once again to come back on itself. Other than the shopping centre, an indoor market and selection of shops, none of which looked in any way exciting, that was about it. It was the sort of place you could get a new tyre for your motorbike or get your TV repaired, but if you were looking for a live gig, or an art gallery, you would probably be as well heading to the airport, just as we were now about to do.

"I see what you mean. It doesn't look that interesting," I explained.

203

"Yes I know, like I said to you."

"At least I got to see it for myself, thanks."

We carried on straight back out of town, back towards the airport, up the roundabout. A right turn and five more minutes driving and we were there.

As long as you tick all the right boxes online, AirAsia usually turn out to be the cheapest carrier for most flights around these parts and today was no different. For around 30 quid, they'll get you from A to B with no frills. You get a seat, room to store one piece of hand luggage and the use of the in-flight magazine. I slipped it out of the pouch in the back of the seat in front. Covering the outer rear page was an image of a local-looking young man with black, shoulder-length, wavy hair stood stern-faced staring at the camera with his arms folded across his chest, holding a foot-long stick in each hand. Intriguingly, each stick had a needle sticking out of the end at right angles, giving the appearance of a choreographed ritual battle pose, weapons in hand. I was directed to an article inside to find this guy was actually a tattooist in KK who specialised in hand-tap body art creations.

Tattoos have long been a thing of mine. I got my first one at 15 years old from a man's house in Crookes, Sheffield, sat at his kitchen table at the side of a monkey in a cage, while listening to the newly released 'Rapper's Delight' by the Sugar Hill Gang, but that's a whole different story altogether. None of the many tattoos on my body mean anything: it's more like a historical mismatched tapestry that started off as a deterrent, a visual warning to wannabe bad boys, that evolved over time into a collection of indelible images. Having already experienced a similar non-machine method of application from a monk in a temple in Thailand who used an ornate silver spear, the feeling of fate hit me, compounded by the weird coincidence of having researched Borneo tattoos prior to leaving for this trip.

Back home after a number of internet searches, I found a design and saved it on my smartphone to show whichever tattooist I might find. It was an Iban tribal tattoo, called a Bunga Terung, that I intended to get done while on this trip. It's a stylised circular flower to signify a young man has left their village for the first time to travel. It is always positioned on the front of the shoulder, where the strap of his bag would have been.

The magazine feature told the story of a guy called Lim, who uses an ancient tribal technique of tattooing called hand tapping, in which a needle attached to a stick is tapped into the skin repeatedly with another stick to create a lasting image, at his studio on a back street in central Kota Kinbalu. Monochrome tribal sleeve tattoos made up of triangular symmetrical shapes, creating a modernist twist on a traditional style, was his thing. Suddenly the Bunga Terung was less interesting, with or without its gruesome history. I needed to get inked by the man in the picture, so quite fortunate then that I was en-route to the city where his shop was located, with lots of time on my hands. An announcement came over the loudspeaker in Malay, then repeated in English, "Lady an' gentlemen, please return to your seat an fasten your see bel. We are abow to make our final approach to Kota Kinbalu."

Chapter 9
The Headhunters

Even though I had only spent a handful of days at Zoku Lifestyle, it was comforting to think I was returning. It was a modern, homely place that instantly felt nice from the outset, now familiar as well. Maybe it says something about my attitude to life that, as much as I get bored with perpetual things, there's only so much unknown, exciting and adventurous stuff I can take.

The lift door opened on the second floor. Walking out I turned right, up to the anthracite aluminium-framed glass door, with the now familiar words Zoku Lifestyle etched in the glass. The door was locked, as was the norm at night. I tapped in the key code and walked in. A good smattering of new faces were dotted around and a couple of familiar ones too. On spotting Tom sat on a chair, I walked through the galley kitchen to the lounge area.

"Hi Tom!"

"Hey Ian! How was the rest of your trip?"

"Great thanks. I got some really great shots of the orang-utan. How about you? What have you been up to?"

"I've just got back from Mount Kinabalu, so I'm pretty knackered."

"Oh yes, of course. I'd forgotten about that. How was it?"

"Pretty amazing really. A two-day, one-night trip."

"Was it tough going?" I asked.

"Not too bad. You wouldn't have a problem. It's 4,000 metres above sea level, but you can trek most of it. You do the first 3,000 metres to a stopover camp in about six hours on the first day, then a very early night's sleep, because you are up at 1 am ready to set off for the last leg at two. The sun comes up around 5 am. Awesome."

"Sounds amazing. I would have loved to have done it."

"How long do you have left? You could book it," he said in his typical Australian resonance.

"Two days left before my flight back to Kuala Lumpur, so I won't have time.

Did you suffer from altitude sickness at all?"

"No, I got away with it pretty much. Some of the others did, a little bit."

Two others were sat in the lounge area: pretty Caucasian girls in their early twenties with long blonde hair, each sat in a beanbag. Subtle differences in their appearance gave me an inkling they were German or Austrian perhaps. I caught their attention to say hello.

"Hi, my name's Ian. New arrivals I see?" Hand outstretched, I bent down towards the first girl.

"Hello," she replied, taking my hand. "I'm Helmi and this is my sister Sofia."

I turned to Sofia and shook her hand too. "Hi Sofia. I'm Ian." 'Yep, they could be German,' I thought. Although they both spoke it fluently, it was clear English wasn't their first language.

"You are from England, right?" Helmi said. Helmi was the slightly older and less reserved one, it turned out later.

"Yes Sheffield."

"Shefild?" Helmi questioned.

"Yeah, Sheffield. It's near Manchester."

"Ah OK, Manchester." Wherever you find yourself in the world, people know of Manchester or, to be more precise, they know of the football team.

Usually at this time of night, you would find me searching the internet for the cheapest flights, digs or places of interest but, having already booked all the flights and accommodation for the rest of my journey, I was free to join the guys for dinner and drinks downtown again. Tom was up for going out despite his weary legs so at around 10.30 pm we headed for the door. Stood on the landing, the lift doors parted to reveal Claire's face.

"Hey, where are you lot going?" she asked as she stepped out.

I tried not to act too interested but the truth is I was. "Ohh? Hi Claire, I thought you had left? We are going for food. Want to come along?" I asked.

"Errr? Okay why not, you only live once."

So tonight's team of Spence, Claire, Tom, Helmi and Sofia headed towards the harbour. I suspected Spence used the promise of further custom to get himself discount wherever he could, anytime he managed to bring along a party of guests while eating out, so tonight we were going to a seafood cafe on the quayside on his recommendation. Even though it didn't feel quite right, I still had visions of Claire's nipples in my mind and, while she stayed out tonight, there was still a chance I could make a move.

Market stall by day and restaurant by night, we sat and waited on plastic patio chairs under a patchwork of tarpaulin sheets, surrounded by other similar establishments, after selecting from a trolley of fresh fish and seafood on a bed of ice. Amongst the usual offerings, I spotted a fish I recognised. It reminded me of my time on Perhentian Island and what the Irish girl told me. A dead parrotfish no longer gleams with vivid colour, like it does while being followed through forests of coral by eager snorkel-faced humans, but it does taste good apparently. Had she not furnished me with such culinary advice, I might not have bought it.

"I hear the parrotfish is delicious. Yes, I'll have the parrotfish please," I explained to the waiter. Either she was wrong or I had been served food past its sell by date but, disappointingly, it was nothing like as good as I expected. It arrived open mouthed, butterflied and milky-eyed but the meat was translucent and tasteless.

After food we moved on back to the moderately exciting quayside bar area and, as bedtime drew closer, our group dwindled. By the time Tom disappeared along with the two sisters, who turned out to be from Finland by the way, Claire and I were alone at last. It was my ideal opportunity but I bottled it. Now slightly drunk, I realised I wasn't really ready and lost interest. This turned out to be the last time I would see her.

The self-service breakfast here consisted of toast with either jam or peanut butter, two possible types of cereal and either tea or coffee. I usually avoid coffee away from home if it's not freshly brewed as I'm a self-confessed coffee diva but here at Zoku was a new one to me. They had coffee bags. "Why had I never thought of that myself?" I wondered. Although it may seem slightly gimmicky, it was actually an easy way to make a decent quality freshly brewed cup of coffee by using exactly the same principle as with a tea bag, albeit a bigger bag. Why I have never seen such a product at home is strange: I reckon they'd be popular.

Today was the day I would get my tattoo so, toast and two coffees later, I set off walking the 30 minute stroll to the Orang-utan Tattoo Studio, wishing I'd got a parasol. Up to now all excursions into town had been along the sea front, whereas today my journey was taking me inland into unchartered territory to the outskirts of town. I followed the river against its flow, as per the instructions from Google Maps and something unusual caught my eye.

Around 100 metres upriver from the sea, a frail looking, skinny old man around 70 years old, wearing a wide-brimmed rattan hat and dark sarong, was sat looking down at his lap. It wasn't possible to see what it was that kept his attention: maybe he was untangling or repairing his nets while sat in his small hand-carved log canoe, casting a solitary figure in an otherwise clear stretch of the estuary. I watched as he got out of the boat, then disappeared under the dirty brown swell for few seconds at a time. I didn't get close enough to see exactly what he was doing so I can only presume he was checking lobster pots. Nevertheless, it was an impressive display of agility from a man of an age you might expect to see being helped across the road in England.

According to their website, Lim's studio opened at 11 am, which gave me ten minutes to arrive as it opened. Deeper into the centre of town, the roads increased in size. Without the benefit of pedestrian crossings, negotiating the triple-lane inner city roads, through to the backstreets at the far end of town, would be practically impossible. On the corner adjacent to an open-air market, through a car park selling second hand clothes and footwear in piles stacked on tarpaulin sheets, was a row of chairs. Here you could sit and receive a 30 minute foot massage for around £3.50, while observing the exuberance of city life trundling along past your aching feet.

Nearing my destination, the footfall increased dramatically as I passed through a pedestrian precinct lined with temporary market stalls. The tailgate of a car hung open. Its contents, a litter of mongrel puppies yapped by the side of a stall selling snide Bangladeshi backpacks, while close by I spotted what resembled crispy battered sycamore leaves, sealed in clear plastic bags on a well-stocked dried food stall.

At the far end of the street, things calmed down somewhat and, after crossing a further busy road, I could practically smell the ink. A clutch of hostels, a flashy fruit smoothie bar and two tattooists nestled themselves in this quiet enclave on the outer fringe of the city. Unfortunately for me, neither of the tattoo studios were open. The Orang-utan studio should have been open by now and the other across the road and around the corner didn't open for an hour so, when I spotted a sign saying 'Jungle trek to Signal Hill Observatory Tower', I followed it.

15 minutes of step aerobics and a pair of damp armpit shirt patches later, I reached the top. Meandering between adolescent palms under the shadow of the odd forest giant, hundreds of wooden steps brought me to a cafe overlooking the lower level of the city. I rewarded myself with a Diet Coke, sat on a high stool at a bistro table and took in the view. Two circular open concrete platforms with circular flat roofs, each held up by its own single central column, poked out between the trees on the top of the hill. The vista between a couple of multi-storey hotels on the coast below offered a view of Manukan, the second largest island in the Tunku Abdul Rahman National Park, off the coast of the South China Sea nearby, where scores of daily tourist boats ferry punters to and from nearby Jeselton Point.

An hour later an A-frame sign outside the other place, with the words 'Deadlights Tattoo' had turned up. I passed it on my way back to Lim's place hoping he would now also be there but the shutters were still down. I carried on over just in case but no joy. 'Fuck it,' I thought as I doubled back to Deadlights. I walked in to find a weird-looking, beautiful, petite, oriental girl with half a basin fringe, flesh tunnel and heart tattoo on the side of her neck setting up.

"Hi, I'm looking to get this done," I said, handing her my phone.

"Ok yes I can do that but you will need to wait a while for me to draw it out for you."

"That's ok. Maybe I could come back. How much will it be?" I asked.

"Erm, it will be 150 to 200 ringgit."

"Oh ok," I said with a deliberately disappointed tone.

"What about we say 150?" I bargained.

"Yes ok."

"Great. How long shall I wait before I come back?" I asked.

"About 40 minutes. Is that ok?"

"Yeah, that's fine. See you in a bit."

Some say the symbolism and tradition behind tribal tattoos is often made up these days in order to give the client what they want and this seems to hold weight if you listen to what tribal village elders have to say in our world today. Great grandfathers talk of never knowing a time other than when tattoos only made you look more masculine, affluent or important in their culture. As far back as they can remember, they've regarded tattoos as a symbol of strength in the tribe. A sign of higher status, rather than ritual markings, to give you long life, ward off evil spirits or give good luck in battle for instance. Maybe these were the beliefs hundreds of years ago but, if so, they're not any longer and haven't been since the days tattoos were produced using carbon scraped from the bottom of a cooking pan and mixed with sugar cane water.

In 1928 Christians from Australia began missions in Borneo and proved to be quite successful. One of the things that was frowned upon as a convert was tattoos. As a consequence, many traditional tribal tattoos disappeared from society. That was until the world seemed to go tattoo crazy ten years ago. Now a new wave of Borneo youth are getting back to their roots and Iban tribal tattoos, such as my Bunga Terung, are on the rise once more.

After killing time back at the market stalls, seeking out exotic bargains, I walked back over faced with the dilemma of what to do if Lim had turned up. Knowing the stencil would now have been drawn by the rock chick, yet still desperately wanting the hand tap tattoo, I was relieved to find Lim was still nowhere to be seen as I walked back past his shop. The goth chick jumped up off the stool behind the counter as I walked back in, picking up the bespoke image she'd been working on for the last few minutes.

"OK it is ready," she explained as she ushered me through the empty waiting room, while donning her black latex gloves.

"Shall I take my shirt off?" I asked.

"Shirt off," she repeated.

First she smeared on petroleum jelly, then transferred the design to my shoulder by pressing the paper template onto the area. "Please look," she asked, while gesturing to the mirror on the wall through in the business end of the room, where a vinyl-covered stretcher and pillow covered in cling film laid in wait. The ink from the pen she used to draw out the design was now visible on my shoulder.

"Yes that looks fine thanks," I explained, after checking it was in the right spot.

"Ok please lay down," she asked. Rock music played in the background as I reclined back onto the bench, in anticipation of the inevitable puncture punishment. "Ok it should not take too long," she explained as the electric ink wasp buzzed into life.

Not until the numbness overtook the pain, did I fully notice the beauty of the silky female leftfield vocal resonating around the room. That melancholy tone of alternative rock emanating from reception created the perfect mood, amongst collections of macabre stickers fighting for space around the outer edge of the full-length mirror with images of skulls, scrolls and sinister sirens, closing in on the reflection. There was a constant stop-start, as she repeatedly swivelled round on her stool to reload the ink, by dipping the gun in a tiny plastic pot of black goo. I had absolutely no idea why but I felt confident in her ability to make a good job of my most recent permanent decorative statement and, after 20 stinging minutes, my instincts were correct. A full black circular flower with a spiral in its centre, around five centimetres in diameter, was exactly what I had wanted and, as expected, was a perfectly executed job, serving as a lifelong reminder of an amazing trip.

If you have time and you look hard enough, downtown KK has some great images to point a lens at and, with the rest of the day free, I spent it looking for some good photo opportunities. Chinese signs advertising weird and wonderful drinks and foodstuffs are one of my favourite subjects. Many things caught my eye, as I happily wondered the streets alone. A tea stall with fungus, sea coconut and Chrysanthemum favours and the nearby 'Yu Kee' restaurant gave me good material and the odd chuckle. Grannies wrapped in brightly coloured fabrics sat barefoot at plastic tables shaded in the doorway of a lottery ticket shop, threading garlands of fresh flowers, and the guy sat in front of his impressive stock of hundreds of packets of dried foodstuffs at a huge corner stall in the market.

Another hot day meant I could walk around bare chested again and the dried food stall guy gestured to his friend, as he noticed my revolver tattoo poking out from the top of my waistline. I looked over with a smile. He nodded in appreciation while pointing two gun fingers and holding his wrist.

"I had this one today, Borneo tribal tattoo," I said, pointing at my shoulder, as I walked over.

"Arrhh good. Sarawak," one guy replied.

"Thank you," I said, as we exchanged smiles.

There are two provinces in Borneo: Sabah, where I was now, and Sarawak, further south. As I walked off, the guys laughed amongst themselves but this wasn't a two-faced macho putdown, like I might expect at home, just a continuation of a happy encounter.

I love traditional local markets and yet again I was drawn to the prospect of finding something a bit more exotic than roast beef, mashed potatoes and Yorkshire pudding, like the two innocent looking baby reef sharks laid side by side amongst mounds of clams, on a stall five metres back from the shoreline. After recording the image, I turned to find an even more upsetting sight. A man on the quayside was bent over a large white carcass of some sort. As I approached, I noticed it was a manta ray being dissected with a knife. Manta rays have been known to grown to seven metres in width so this was just a child in comparison, at around two metres, but still worthy of a photograph. "OK?" I asked the guy, holding up my camera. He nodded in agreement then turned his head back and continued gutting the fish. His knife had opened up the underside of the creature below its mouth to reveal a series of five or six blood red pockets, which I presume must have been its gills, in a seemingly gruesome act, made all the more so by its sheer size.

This was the fish market that transforms into a cluster of seafood restaurants on an evening and it was approaching that time of day when the vendors were starting to prepare their pitches. A display comprising of a bed of ice is placed outside each establishment, where the day's catch is set out to entice hungry punters. A middle-aged couple, who by their clothing were obviously tourists, were given a close, up and personal introduction to a pair of lobster by the teenager, whose job it was to put bums on seats. The crustaceans flapped their tails like a pair of seafood castanets in desperation as he held them up in the faces of the unsuspecting passers-by. What better way to prove the freshness of their catch but, for all his efforts, the lad did not manage to seal the deal, turning around in search of his next victims.

I sat and ordered a lime tea as the sun went down on another stiflingly hot day at one of the quayside seafood cafes as they started to fill up. Suddenly three young guys in their late teens darted past my table, scattering chairs and jumping over boxes, as uniformed officers gave chase. In a desperate attempt to evade capture, two jumped directly into the sea, fully clothed, between two fishing vessels moored up against the concrete jetty, while the other ran up a plank leading onto one of the decks. 'That's their phones knackered,' I thought to myself, as two armed police offers and a soldier stopped short and gave up the chase. Luckily for the lads, the sea was calmer than their nerves must have been as the sound of a distant high power speed boat grew louder. As suspected, it was a police boat. They trawled the back of the bobbing row of vessels for a while then also gave up. The authorities didn't go as far as to board the stowaway's vessel either, just looked out over the edge of the water for a couple of minutes, afraid of messing up their uniforms, until walking back the way they'd just ran. The dust settled quickly. Neither the youngsters or their hunters were anywhere to be seen after a couple of minutes and normality returned. I followed suit shortly after.

I made my way back towards the digs and, as I headed on through the fringe of the night market, I noticed pockets of officials stood around killing time, some wearing berets, others with blue and yellow high-vis vests emblazoned with the word 'POLIS'. This was some sort of multi-authority night operation. The further I walked, the extent of the operation began to be apparent.

At the opening on a corner of some boarding around a building site, the authorities were dragging out workers from a partially constructed multi-storey building. While here, I had noticed a sense of uneasiness from locals with regard to the Filipino population; they were viewed as a problem and I suspected they were the targets of this operation. The streets didn't feel safe right now. Cage vans and uniformed officers dotted the streets looking for people who could potentially do desperate things to evade the law if confronted, but curiosity had got the better of me and I approached the scuffling crowd.

214

"Filipino?" I asked one of the officers.

"Illegals yes," he replied, as his colleagues bundled another two prisoners in the back of one of the black cage vans dotted around the side streets. Medium-sized pickups had been converted to carry around 20 people at a time on bench seats running parallel down each side of the rear, with a curved tin roof and enclosed in steel mesh. The prisoners were led up two steps at the rear and through a mesh door. Surprisingly to me, many of the captives were women and they all looked quite calm given their plight, whatever that was. To be deported back to the Philippines and having to find their way back again, or back to Gaya maybe?

Gaya is ten minutes off the coast of Kota Kinbalu, the biggest island in the Tunka Abdul Rahman National Park, and home to an offshore community of 6,000 displaced Filipinos. Amongst other things, they provide a source of cheap labour to Malaysian entrepreneurs to the dismay of the authorities. They began to arrive as they fled the Moro conflict in the Mindano region, southern Philippines, between 1969 to 2019. A battle between President Marcos's government forces and Maoist rebels, comprising of the communist New People's Army. For decades now, this island has been their home, a Filipino enclave in Malaysian waters with makeshift homes stretching out from the beach in an ever-expanding band of stilted shacks. This island with the reputation of having become a criminal and pirates' haven may be where the prison vans got emptied later.

After taking the last opportunity to use the washing machine before tomorrow's flight, I slumped in a bean bag with a coffee for a ten-minute Facebook browse, while pondering the enlightening events of the evening. I took a sip of my drink and I thought to myself, 'If these operations to capture illegal aliens happened on a regular basis, maybe some Filipinos allow themselves to be captured as it suits them, as a free ticket home.' These outsiders, who are probably unduly blamed for many illegal acts, are obviously a resourceful bunch and may be adding to the figures used by the Malaysian government when deciding how often to send out the capture squads. The more often the operations take place, the more frequent the service becomes and potentially the more popular. Food for thought as I climbed into my bunk, considering how to best use my time on the last day here. I drifted off considering retracing my steps back across town for a final attempt at the hand tap tattoo I longed for.

The next morning the decision had been made. If things panned out as hoped, my idea was to add to the underside of the Sak-Yant tattoo on the top of my back. Sak translates to jab and Yant means blessed in Buddhism. The only way to get such a tattoo is to travel to a temple, like the one I visited outside Bangkok where a shaved-headed monk wrapped in saffron robes did mine many years ago for an offering of 20 Marlboro light and a bunch of flowers. He used a silver spear, around half a metre long, with an ornately detailed bulbous knob on one end and a tiny razor-sharp knife on the other, creating an image that loosely resembles a temple. They are said to be ancient designs of Buddhist prayers. This, by far the most interesting tattoo I've had to date, starts around armpit level. The Borneo hand tap design, although a standalone piece in its own right, would form part of a larger collage, continuing down my back where the Sak-Yant left off, with the idea of further additions designed around it at a later date.

I'd timed the start of my walk back to Lim's studio to coincide with opening time again to give me the maximum chance of being fitted in today. Past the now familiar roads en-route, I turned the last corner, the shutters were up and so were my hopes. I walked in to an empty room, dimly lit and stinking of stale cigarettes. I looked around for someone to give me the bad news. Feathered tribal spears and pigmy sculls hung on the wall behind a glass counter filled with a collection of macabre stickers produced by rival artists. Three sofa chairs facing a coffee table with cups, pots and an overflowing ashtray told a story of killing time.

"Hello, anyone there?" I said in a raised voice.

A door swung open from behind the counter and a guy with long dark wavy hair and olive skin walked out. It was Lim – the guy in the magazine. "Hi. Can I help you?"

"I'm hoping to get a hand tap tattoo but I fly back to KL later today. Is there any chance you can fit me in?" I asked.

"How big you want?" he continued.

216

"I suppose that depends on cost really," I explained.

"How much do you want to spend?" he quizzed.

"Yeah, my budget is around 300 ringgit."

"Arr ok, quite small. What are you thinking of?"

I pulled off my T-shirt and explained my idea to extend the Buddhist hand tap creation, while looking back at him over my shoulder. He pondered the job for a while, then explained, "I can make this, but it will be hand poke not hand tap. You know hand poke?"

"No I have never heard of hand poke. What is this?"

"No sticks just hand, with a needle," he explained.

"Okay, how much?"

"About 450."

Years of being self-employed had honed my negotiating skills and, although I would have easily paid the 75 quid he was asking, I gave out a meek, "Oh!" then with a pondering expression. "Mmmm, I can't really afford that much. How about 400?"

"OK," he agreed.

"And you can do it today?"

"Yes but you need to wait for me to draw design. Every one is different, all original. Come back in one hour."

"Yes," I excitedly agreed, as I struggled to put my T-shirt back over my clammy skin. 'This is really happening!' I thought, as I skipped down the steps onto the street and back around the corner.

With no market stalls to help kill time today, I followed the sound of an English-speaking voice coming from a TV on the wall of a Chinese buffet, on the corner of a nearby street overlooking a crossroads. I could see a few empty tables over the railings around the open sides of the restaurant so I walked in and took a seat, looking around trying to work out how to feed myself. Eventually, after watching a couple of hungry locals fill their plates, I followed suit. Guessing the contents of each of the 20 odd pots laid out, I helped myself. Large grotty open fans, heavily covered in a combination of years of grease and dust, swaying in and out of sync high on the ceiling, kept my interest for a while, until the narrator mentioned, "Catfish! River

217

monsters taking pigeons from the bank side," in an attempt to build tension on a Discovery Channel documentary.

As in many basic restaurants and street food stalls around the world, drinking water is complementary. It's the norm to find jugs and plastic beakers on tables but very few Westerners take up the offer. I occasionally take the risk of catching Dehli belly but, having never had a problem drinking un-bottled water while eating out previously, I decided to be brave once more and washed down my pork with spicy noodles with a couple of glasses of council wine, as it was known round our end, back in the day.

Back at Orang-utan Studio, Lim was ready as I walked in. He picked up a piece of paper from the counter and held it up. "OK here it is. I made it little bit bigger because it did not look right." There was a pattern drawn in black pen of interconnected triangles with an overall shape, loosely resembling some sort of futuristic face mask. "I made the same size as the other tattoo across here," he explained while pointing out the width.

"That is amazing. Thank you!"

"Good and it will be the same price OK?"

"Yes of course, that's great," I explained.

He led me through the door he'd appeared from the first time I saw him into his studio. After a number of attempts at transferring the image to my back while standing, he led me to a tilted bench. It resembled a cross between a massage bench and a posture chair, those chairs that make you look silly, that doctors might sit at in a semi-kneeling position while writing out your prescription for haemorrhoid cream.

"OK lay here please," he instructed.

"So how did you come to be on the cover of the AirAsia flight magazine?" I asked.

"My friend asked me if I would do the story for her. She works for AirAsia. So it is in the magazine?" he asked.

"Yes you are famous. Your picture is on the cover."

"Oh no, not famous! I don't like to be famous," he explained.

"You should get lots of work from the publicity, don't forget," I explained.

"Yes that is good, but not famous." He looked genuinely embarrassed at the

218

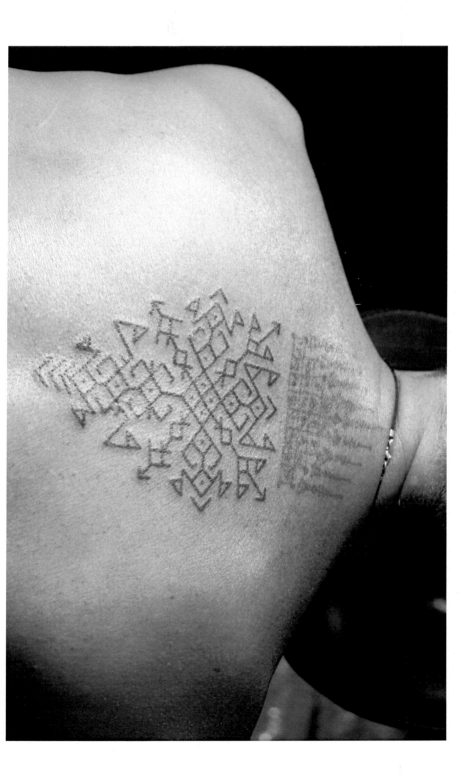

thought of my suggestion, as he got his shit together. I positioned myself on the bench, chest down with my chin hung over the curved top edge and arms by my side.

I immediately noticed, unlike the Buddhist Sak-Yant tattoo, the hand poke technique he was employing was more painful. In comparison to machine tattoos, initially the level of pain involved was less but I find some degree of numbness masks the pain of machine tattoos after a little while, whereas the slower application by hand poke didn't create numbness. Each jab was like the first: a tactile raw pain from start to finish. The importance of managing the pain, while having an everlasting image applied to your body, is obvious. To move is to mess up and the profoundly intimate discomfort produced by a needle being pushed through the skin by hand was a struggle to ignore. The distraction of his questions relating to my trip helped to suppress the instinct to bolt, as the odd muscle spasm searing through my back was becoming increasingly tough to overlook. The usual small talk ensued: how long was I here for and where had I been.

"So you leave today?" Lim continued.

"Yeah my flight back to KL is in a few hours, then two days after that I fly home."

"Will you come back?" he asked.

"Yes I would, but also I like to travel to new places and there are lots of places I have not been to yet, so maybe but I don't know. What about you? Have you travelled much?"

"I have not even been to the places you have been to while you are here, but next month I am going to England, to visit my friend in Manchester."

"Oh great, I hope you have a good trip," I told him as he pushed back on his chair, rolling away across the floor.

"Okay all done. You can look in that mirror," he explained, flicking his head up in its direction. As much as I could make out over my shoulder, it looked amazing.

"I love it. Thank you," was my reaction as a vivid black symmetry of straight lines on a canvas of temporarily puce skin revealed itself.

I arrived back at Zoku with a couple of hours to kill, as Tom and the two sisters stood around the dinner table.

219

"We are just heading out to the museum. Do you want to come along?" Tom asked.

Most of my packing was done. Just a couple of items of clothing that needed a little extra time to dry needed to be loaded into my rucksack, so "Yeah why not? I don't have a lot of time. I need to leave in a couple of hours for the airport, but I could come back for my bags in a Grab on my own if you are not finished by the time I need to leave."

"Awesome, shall we go down and get a Grab?" he asked.

"Let's do it."

Helmi and Sofia enjoyed making fun of each other. They bounced insults back and forth, in a way that only best friends, or sisters, can do. If ever one of them pronounced a word wrong, which can happen quite often if English isn't your first language, the other would pounce on the mistake. Involving others in belittling their sibling was fun for all of us when it happened but only because it was obviously water off a duck's back to these two. They loved it and it showed a level of friendship and confidence that few can achieve. Tom in the front and the rest of us in the back, Helmi asked, "Did you ever play the game, Ian, where you think of a question to ask everyone, then everyone have to pick a person who they think is most like in the question?"

"No, I don't think so. It sounds quite complicated."

This conversation was about to continue heading in a direction that Sofia at least knew as she began to giggle along with her sister. "Ok, so I might say who here is most likely to save someone's life and you might answer Tom, as he is a doctor."

"OK," I replied in a drawn-out intrigued manner.

"Or you could ask who is most likely to commit genocide," Sofia blurted out loudly. The two girls exploded into laughter. "Oh my god it was so funny," Sofia started to explain.

"Yeah we played this game the other night and this Aussie guy whispered something to his mate, who burst out laughing," Helmi explained.

"You see there was this German girl there and she was not happy when she hear what they said," Sofia continued.

The laughter infected us all as we pulled up at the museum. With smiles still

220

emblazoned on our faces, we made our way to the pay desk under a canopy connected to the main entrance. A notice on the window read 'Locals 15r Tourist 30r'. The best thing about this place wasn't the boxy 1970s building, or the poor exhibits ranging from cooking pots and traditional robes to ancient artworks. For me, only one thing stood out. It was the tribal history exhibit.

The infamous headhunter tribesmen of Borneo are well documented and, bearing in mind the practice didn't mostly cease till around 100 years ago, well remembered too. Enemies' heads were a symbol of masculinity and were taken home as proof of success in battle, becoming trophies to be displayed back in their village. Variations of the barbaric act evolved amongst rival tribes in different ways. The Iban tribe made it a requirement for the hand in marriage of a prospective bride for their partner to have taken at least one head, while the Kadazan-Dusun believed their victim must be alive as they are decapitated, in order to gain the power from their spirit. The Murut, however, took this murderous tradition to a whole new level. With brutal disregard to age or gender, the young males of the village had to prove their masculinity or face being ostracised. Little respect was given to any man who had not brought home the skulls of at least two people, children or otherwise. Although banned around a century ago, headhunting still happens to this day, between tribes deep in the jungle. In the odd isolated community, a handful of murderous wrinkly elders still bare the mark that signifies their involvement by way of a zig zag tattoo on the back of their hand and many of the communities they are part of still display the trophies, hanging the skulls from the roofs of their long houses.

Overall this historical display was pretty poor but one aspect set it apart. The unconvincing, dark skinned, crusty mannequins with wild mains and scabby loin cloths had seen better days. Their shabbiness seemed to trivialise and somehow camouflage the endemic historical evidence of extreme brutality, sitting in slings made of Silad reeds hanging from above. Before my eyes were numerous real human skulls, lined up along a pole, with nothing but clear glass separating us. A spectacle, that could have easily been overlooked while strolling around the exhibits, was suddenly staring me in the face. To imagine what the eyes that once sat in these empty sockets witnessed a hundred years ago is enough to make you blow out a cold breath and shake your shoulders.

Looking at my phone for the time made me anxious to leave, so I looked around for one of the guys. Everyone had split up, dotted around the place doing their own thing. I spotted Helmi up ahead and walked across.

"How's it going?"

"Hi. Yeah good, and you?" she replied.

"I'm starting to feel a little nervous to leave. My flight is soon and I think I am going to get to the airport so I can relax."

"OK no problem. Did you enjoy the museum?" she enquired.

"Mmmmm I've seen better, although did you see the headhunter exhibit? It was worth it just for that."

"Yes I did," she continued, just as Tom sauntered over.

"Hey Tom, I'm going to get off now, to make sure I don't miss my flight."

"No worries, Ian. It's been awesome. Have a safe journey and enjoy the rest of your trip."

"Yeah thank you and you too," I replied while coming in for a hug. We wrapped our arms around each other briefly, with a little pat on the back. "Take care Tom," I said, turning to Helmi. "Goodbye Helmi. Would you mind telling your sister I said goodbye?" I asked while bringing it in for a hug with her.

"Yes I will tell her. Goodbye, Ian." I smiled and turned for the door.

Down the long-terraced steps, I emerged from under the cover of the car port canopy, heading for the car park. I pulled out my phone, turned to shade the sun from my screen, opened the Grab app and through squinting eyes attempted to order a ride, while the midday sun made me want to remove my shirt. Throughout the trip, the app had been temperamental, which was the main reason for leaving in plenty of time today. I looked up from my phone to witness a Grab car driving away, after dropping off a couple of tourists. "Shit." I was down to ten minutes leeway and a mild panic was looming. Next I tried the phone I brought from home, rather than the local phone purchased at the beginning of the trip that allowed me to use cheap local credit. I tried my smartphone along with the roaming charges as a last resort to no avail. I bead of sweat ran down my chest, as I convinced myself I could hail a car

222

from here. 'This is a tourist attraction. Lots of Grab cars will come through here every day,' I thought, as a stared over at the entrance to the car park. Five minutes later, after constantly attempting to hail an internet ride and with no sign of a Grab car pulling in, I needed to find Tom back inside. He didn't seem to have the same issues with his smartphone when using the Grab app, so finding him was my best bet of resolving the soon-to-be crisis.

Two minutes later, after pressing a few buttons, Tom had saved the day. "Ok. All done. Five minutes," Tom explained.

When travelling alone, some things are much more critical, especially forward planning, which I am shit at. Thankfully this part of my trip involved other backpackers, who almost always help one another. You quickly create a bond of trust while living in each other's pockets, even going as far as lending money to be paid back after parting ways. Thanks to Tom, I wasn't about to miss my flight back to the mainland and the knock-on effect of the cost and inconvenience that comes with it.

A young round-faced guy, in a small bright red car pulled up and wound down the window. "Grab?" I enquired.

"Yes. You are going to airport?"

"Yes but I need to call at the hostel for my bag first, if that is ok?" I explained.

"That is ok. Where is hostel?"

"Times Square. It's only five minutes," I continued.

I left my camera bag with him as proof I would to return, as he waited down on the street for me to run up for my bags. He came around and opened the boot as he noticed me, my rucksack and cabin bag approaching. One by one he took my bags and loaded them in. "Thank you," I explained as I riddled out of my straps.

As an Englishman, it's weird to think you don't open the car window when you are hot, but air-con is a necessity around here and open windows defeat the object, so enclosed in our personal fridge on wheels, we chatted while en-route. We broached all the usual subjects: cars, religion, the government and England.

"So how long did you come?" he quizzed.

"One month," I explained.

"One day I will go to England. How much did you pay for flight?"

"I got a real bargain. I paid £430," I told him.

"Mmmmm, 430," he repeated with a ponderous tone. "How many ringgit?" he asked.

"I'll check my phone." I brought up the currency converter and tapped in the figures. "It's around 2400 ringgit but that's cheap. It is normally around 3,000," I continued. I could practically hear the cogs turning, as he went quiet on me.

"That's a lot of money," he dejectedly replied.

Chapter 10
Back to KL

My last leg on my way back to the capital and this time round I'd plumped for the more vibrant area of Bukit Bintang for my last few days – known for its bright lights, bustling markets and cheap counterfeit goods. I'd enjoyed staying in Brickfields for the first leg of the trip, with its traditional Indian buffets and transport links, but it was time for a change. I'd booked a single room at the posh sounding Royal Palm Lodge, with air-con and fridge, for 100 ringgit per night. It was slightly more expensive than my usual preference of a dorm room but I thought I would treat myself for the last couple of days. No more flights to organise, rooms or trips to deal with – just food to eat, booze to drink, sights to behold and of course the odd photo.

This time I used the KLIA Express to get to Sentral Station: it's an abbreviation of Kuala Lumpur International Airport. As you might expect, it connects to the city and, for me, is slightly more entertaining than a taxi. From the terminus, as the lights dimmed on a long day of travel, I transferred to the monorail for the last leg to a stop at busy junction where bright lights attracted flocks of people like moths to a bulb. Giant futuristic video screens, flashing billboards and the illuminated windows of passing overhead trains threw a warm cascade of colour over colonies of bodies, marching in worker ant formations, in opposing lines of direction.

It was as dark as a betrayed mistress's mind as I reached the steps to street level. A young Australian couple with dreadlocks, flowing hemp pants and soothing smiles were on the corner selling handmade jewellery from a trolley with the words 'please help us to raise money for the next step of our journey' written on cardboard, as intermittent streams of potential customers herded back and forth under the monorail and across the busy carriageway each time the traffic lights allowed it.

"Royal Palm Lodge?" I asked a third passing stranger to no avail. I took a seat on the steps in front of a shop on a fulcrum corner, amongst crowds of punters, eating, drinking and soaking up the atmosphere created by breakdance troupes and cheesy buskers. With bags close, I rang the hotel.

"Royal Palm!" a woman with an Indian accent answered.

"Hi, I have a reservation but I cannot find you," I explained.

"Where are you?" she asked.

"I'm near the monorail stop at the crossroads."

"Okay can you see the KFC?" I looked around.

"No."

"We are next to the pharmacy across from the KFC," she explained.

Sharpening the senses, pushing the boundaries, whatever you care to call it, it's anxious moments like these that gives backpacking its appeal to me. I'd now learned the general direction of the KFC from another helpful passer-by so it was all just a matter of time now before I found my comfort zone, a feeling I might otherwise have overlooked, if not for the shot of adrenaline uncertainty had administered. I headed down the street past an escalator and an underground station enclosed by a glass structure at ground level, presumably to keep out the heat.

A band busking outside KFC across the road had drawn a large crowd five deep in a circle around the lead singer who wore a sinister, white, full-face mask incorporating a bright red punk wig and white gloves. He shook his hands in the air while stomping and singing covers of Foo Fighters classics with a pop twist. Any purist fan of real music would have hated it but this crowd obviously weren't.

Then over a sea of bobbing heads and the odd burst of appreciation from the crowd, I spotted something across the road. A green flashing neon cross above a doorway: the universal pharmacy symbol had come to my rescue. I closed in on the flashing beacon, spotting a tiny sign poking out over the footpath with the words 'Royal Palm Lodge' over an open doorway leading up a flight of concrete stairs.

At the top, through a floor to ceiling glass door with an intercom and electromagnetic lock, I could see the black hair on top of someone's head move from behind the counter as I pressed the bell. A voice came over the speaker. "Hello?" It was the woman from the phone call. The door clicked open. Her smile permeated a glow of warmth through her dark brown, acne-scarred complexion but there was a sadness in her bloodshot eyes that she struggled to hide. After the usual check-in ritual, the 30-year-old, slightly overweight, frumpy lady dressed in dark slacks and baggy T-shirt showed me to my room.

It was a good-sized hovel, with a long window with sliding openers, whose view was obscured by the rear of an illuminated box sign, lightly peppering the room with a sequence of flashing light designed to catch the eye of passing pedestrians on the noisy street below. Metal brackets holding the sign, with cables swinging down close enough for a team of burglars to reach was another drawback, especially given the window had no lock. A double bed, under-counter fridge and a doorway leading to the en-suite was the extent of the amenity this room offered. I could have lived with the bare minimum as far as decor and furniture were concerned but the noise and vulnerability I couldn't.

"Sorry but this room is not suitable," I explained back at reception. "It is too near the street and the windows do not lock. Can I get a different room?" I asked.

"I can put you in this room until another is ready," she said, handing me the key. "You can look, to the left," she pointed.

Apart from being much more safe, this room was worse in lots of ways. Stinking of cigarettes, no fridge, no natural light, dimly lit, a decade overdue for decorating and the size of a cell in Marsh Gate but, despite all that, I decided to swap, regardless of what her majesty's inspectorate of prisons might have had to say about the cleanliness.

I draped two T-shirts on a couple of unused hangers and placed them outside through the open window at the end of the corridor alongside someone else's laundry items then, after spreading out my pants on the windowsill, I went back down to the other end of the hallway for the fridge. I carried it covertly from the penthouse to the panic room, stashed some valuables above the suspended ceiling panel, grabbed my camera and headed out on the town.

I stood and pondered my route at the bottom of the steps, sandwiched between tiny kiosk shops packed in along the underside of the hotel, with glass display counters facing the road crammed with selfie-sticks, cameras, night vision goggles and drones with coloured lights that the Bangladeshi vendors wearing smart dress shirts flew up and down the street over the heads of passing pedestrians. I was drawn to what looked like a tiny indoor market on the corner, just across the road opposite the KFC. Scores of T-shirts, floor to ceiling, filled the walls on one stall facing the road, rucksacks and trainers on another. Across the busy one-way street, I walked in. Instantly like a wasp in a beehive, I was swarmed by over friendly salesmen.

"Hello sir, how are you today? Where you from?"

"Please, please sir," said another while pointing the flat of his hand in the direction of his stall further inside.

Every stall seemed to have a couple of young Bangladeshi men, all competing for commission on goods sold. If situations like this bother you, the worst thing to do is to show an interest. Luckily for me, the pressure I was about to endure wasn't unexpected. A deliberate ploy is not to display any prices, allowing the most gullible of us to be royally stitched up.

"How much for this?" I asked, unhooking a hanger from the rail.

"This one, sir, is best quality. Feel it. How many you want?"

"I don't know how many, until I know how much."

"Please look. Take as many as you want and I will give you the price," he continued. Unlike me, he didn't know what to expect from the negotiations and it was time for me to step up.

"How much for this one?" I asked holding up a red T-shirt with the 'Champion' logo in white lettering emblazoned across the chest and a label stitched into the back with the words 'Hoque fashion'.

"For this 80 ringgit, very good quality."

"No, no. You think I don't know how much these are?"

"Okay how much?" he enquired.

"I give you 20," I told him in some weird broken English, for some reason.

"Oh no, I cannot," he laughed.

"Do you have this one in small for my little boy? He is ten," I explained.

He slid out a large cardboard box, from under the rails and sifted through the clear plastic packages. "How about this one? This is a good size," showing me a completely different style.

228

"No, I want this one," I confirmed. Delving deeper in, he announced.

"Yes, here I have," passing me a black T-shirt with a Captain America shield on the front.

"Okay, I give you 40 for these two."

"No, I cannot."

"Okay 50 and that is it. That is my final price," I explained.

"I will try for you. I must ring my boss."

I looked on as he pretended to call his boss, talking to himself for a few moments, before turning back to me in an attempt to squeeze the last bit of profit. "Okay 60," he exclaimed, returning the phone to his pocket.

"I told you final price 50. No more," I explained again with determination.

Silently scowling, he stuffed my goods in a carrier bag and stretched out his arm in my direction. I swapped the cash for the bag and checked the contents, then battled my way back through the labyrinth of stalls to the outside through a different exit, further round the corner, randomly edging ever closer to the best attraction yet to be discovered in Bukit Bintang.

On another corner, next door to the market stalls, was a Chinese restaurant, whose tables spilled out over the pavement. It marked the beginning of a mecca to lovers of street food and the start of a tapestry of aromas that drift through the nostrils into the heart. Crowds had begun to gather as the sun went down, to trawl the sea of nocturnal stainless-steel street food stalls that lined the street, each displaying images of food or descriptions of their particular speciality on illuminated signs fixed on poles above their heads.

Purely by chance, I was approaching the top of Jalan Alor. Once a notorious red-light area, now famous for its loud street food scene and vigorous night restaurants. Hidden from view from my hotel by the row of buildings that lined the opposite side of the street, Food Street, as it is more commonly known as by tourists, runs parallel. By night this public highway transforms into a magnet for hungry fun-seeking pedestrians and I was just about to learn of its existence, an area I'd travelled thousands of miles to discover without knowing it.

Scores of plastic patio sets were set out on the pavement in all but the centre of the road, leaving a path down the middle of the street. Be it steaming street food stall, restaurant table or drinks stalls, there was no wasted space here. You know the times you go for food with that fussy friend who can't find anything to eat off the menu, ordering plain chicken without the sauce. Imagine their face when they see these menu options. Dried meat and floss bun, moon cake, oyster cake, golden coin dried meat, golden floss pillow, crispy floss, sharks fin and prawn soup, fresh cockles, steamed frog with essence, chilli crab, sea cucumber, pork balls, meat floss, birds nest, fresh oyster, cendol, oyster omelette, BBQ stingray, sour egg, bamboo clams, snails, snow peas, baby kalian, lemon steamed squid, pineapple fried rice, red tilapia, scallops, seaweed dumplings, fish balls – oh! and my personal favourite! – naaaart: fried pig's intestine. I was travelling a path through a culinary wet dream, spoilt for choice in a harem of calorific temptation, amongst exotic virgin foodstuffs that I longed for beyond reason of simple sustenance. Deep fried crispy squid kebabs became the essence of my desire and I took great pleasure in tasting that young moist flesh.

I was due to return to the UK in three days so back in my cell I cracked open a beer, grabbed my smartphone, laid in my pit and researched KL tourist attractions. I decided to sleep on three choices. Either the piercing retro curves of the former king of the skyline, the KL Tower, resembling a spaceship from a black and white film, impaled on an obese vertical javelin, or the gleaming metallic conjoined twins that picked up the architectural baton from its aging iconic uncle, the Petronas Twin Towers. After my first attempt at setting eyes on the inside of the Grand Mosque didn't go to plan, a second attempt at that was my third and final option.

My digs were never going to feel what you might call homely, so the next morning I left bright and early. I'd decided on the Petronas Twin Towers for today's activity but, first, a ridiculously cheap breakfast of pancake and curry sauce, washed down with a steaming cup of gorgeously frothy, sweet, milky chai, round the corner at the cafe on the side street was in order, then back up the road to the MRT station.

The machine grabbed my ticket like an impatient parent, then spat it back out of another slot in the blink of an eye, while simultaneously flinging open its flaps. Herded along by the crowd, I descended yet more moving metal stairs to the platform. You'd be unlucky to find yourself waiting five minutes for a train down here. I was picked up in half the time.

Apart from the blatantly obvious towering structure, the area around the Twin Towers looked different from when I took photos at dusk three weeks prior and at first I couldn't put my finger on it. Then I realised, 'I must have been at the opposite side of the building.' There was no main road nearby last time so it must have been around the other side that boasted the tranquillity of fountains and back-lit bushes in manicured gardens. There was an air of urgency around this side. Like bees around a hive, gangs of smoking office workers and the odd security guard, cluttered the footpath around the entrance, behind maze of cordons, poised in readiness for the swell in visitor numbers later in the day.

It was around 10 am when I walked in. I was one of the first handful to be processed that day. After an airport-style bag check and x-ray, we were led through by security officers wearing black uniforms with bright metal buttons and gold police-style badges to watch an induction video projected onto a curtain of mist spraying out from the wall. It was an attempt to look like a hologram and, although impressive, it didn't convince everyone.

"First you will be taken to the sky-bridge which is situated at level 41," a man wearing a smart blazer and name badge informed us. "Please follow me," he asked, as he led our group of around 20 people to the lift.

On our way up, we were reminded of the time restrictions at each stage of the tour, while video footage of surrounding buildings was projected from floor to ceiling screens built into the sides of the lift, giving the impression of ascending in a glass elevator. We were the purple group. It consisted of three young tall Italian men around 20 years old, a few middle-aged European couples, a German family and the ubiquitous Chinese tourists.

"Here you have ten minutes. Please listen out for my call when it is time," the guide informed us as the lift doors opened onto the sky bridge concourse. It's a glass corridor flanked by a crisscross of metal braces, connecting the Twins at around their halfway point. I spent the next underwhelming ten minutes with my camera, seeking out artistic camera angles to no avail. Next stop: the top – well not quite the full 452 metres but it's high enough for pedestrians to resemble ants as you rest your forehead on the glass.

This was the world's tallest building for six years up to 2004, until Taiwan topped it with their Taipei 101 building at just over 500 metres. Now of course the Burj Khalifa in the UAE dwarfs them all at 828m and has done so for 11 years but not for much longer. 2020 was the original completion date for the acrophobe's worst nightmare: the Jeddah Tower. At a staggering one kilometre tall, it hopes to put Saudi Arabia firmly on the map but the project that would make possible the vision of two sunsets in one day by means of riding a lift fast enough to outrun the sun over the horizon was put on hold in 2018 less than a third of the way through the project. Issues with contractors was the official explanation, although the lack of clarity on this matter makes me think there's more to it than that. I wonder if they will allow women up it...

As the main lift reached its highest point, we transferred to another smaller lift for the last few floors. A corridor connecting the two lifts, with screens displaying scale drawings of the world's tallest skyscrapers as neon outlines, added an interesting touch to the short walk.

The doors opened on the observation deck and we filtered out into a glass-enclosed space with the feel of a modern museum. Shiny and sleek with a shop, cafe, interactive displays and an impressive scale model of the structure. I wondered around looking out over the city, for a photo worthy of the occasion, ever conscious that our allocated window of time was ticking. Distance had transformed the city into a stylised vision of flowing components, following meandering lines that negotiate their way around differing sized obstacles, like staring through a magnifying glass into a minute mechanical mechanism.

Prior to this impressive addition to the landscape, the KL Tower was the main architectural feature of the city's skyline, which you can see in the distance from behind the second tower, around a kilometre away. Leaning against the glass, I snapped a few selfies then wondered around the other side into the shop area. In the centre of the gift shop, a post box offers an opportunity to send home a postcard from an altitude that would make a sparrow's bum twitch: the dizzy heights of the 86th floor. At a reasonable cost from the shop, you can buy a post card and a stamp, borrow a pen, scribble a message and drop it in to one of the most novel post boxes in the world. You'd be forgiven for thinking it was the highest location for depositing your correspondence in Malaysia but you'd be wrong. Mount Kinbalu boasts this accolade as 3,289 metres above sea level at Pendant Hut there's a post box three quarters of the way up the highest peak in the country. There are other novelty post boxes too, such as the underwater one in Sabah, 40 metres down on the seabed at Swallow Reef.

I scribbled quickly and finished just in time to be summoned to leave: 'Dear Bailey and Isabella, I am writing this card from up the top of the Petronas Twin Towers. It's the one on the picture over the other side of this postcard. I love you very much and miss you loads. Can't wait till I get back to give you lots of little presents I've picked up along my travels. See you soon and love you loads, Dad x.'

"Purple group please... Purple group! Please make you way to the elevator," a raised voice announced. I shuffled into the lift with the others as the ascent began on a rushed visit, somewhat spoiling the overall experience.

A couple of hours later, I was back at Bukit Bintang with a few more plastic carrier bags containing cheap goods to add to my collection. I dropped them off and headed back out after a quick shower, to hunt down more bargains before dark. In front of me, on the concrete stairs making his way out was an Arab guy I had noticed begging yesterday a few streets away. He was a big, tall man, with full length white robes and long plain white keffiyeh scarf tied around his head, around 60 years old, with big black shoes and a club foot. I hung back as he struggled to make his way down the stairs with his disability. I found it strange to see a guy wearing clothes I associate with rich people, begging in the street, but even more so was the fact he seemed to live in the building a was staying in.

Past clothes stores, perfume shops, a 7-Eleven and a smattering of restaurants, I was approached at the end of the street by a guy who was on the lookout for single male tourists. "You want girl?" he quizzed. Knowing he'd caught my attention, he continued. "Look here," he explained, holding up his phone, scrolling through pictures of the girls on offer.

"How much?" I enquired.

"250. How far is your hotel? Not too far?"

"It's just up the street, you can just about see it from here, but I don't want girl now. Maybe later," I explained. "Are you going to be here later?" I asked.

He looked and laughed. "I am always here."

"Okay I'll come and find you later." I could tell he knew I wasn't going to come back as I walked back towards my room. I grabbed a can of anchor beer from the fridge in the 7-Eleven and opened it outside while leaving it hidden in the tiny white plastic bag it came in. Past a side street, a guy laid in the shade, sleeping barefoot on a bed of cardboard on the footpath. Another man across the street stood at the side of his motorbike selling single cigarettes to passers-by across from the cafe I used for breakfast. I intended to make my way back to Chinatown, with its labyrinths of stalls selling cheap manufactured goods. It was close by, just a couple of stops away on the MRT, so I headed for the escalators back underground.

I stood behind a middle-aged couple on the descent and overheard their English accent.

"Hi. You're English, aren't you?" I asked. They looked round.

"Yeah, hi," the guy replied.

"Are you on holiday?" I quizzed.

"Yeah we are travelling around for a while. We fly to Bali tomorrow."

"Have you been here long?" I continued. They looked at each other for clarification.

"A week?" she asked her partner.

"Yeah, about a week," he confirmed.

"Do you have any recommendations?"

"Have you been to Chinatown?" she asked.

"I'm on my way there now," I explained.

"You should try the hawker's area in Chinatown," she told me.

"The food is amazing," he said. "You should look for a queue at one of the food stalls and stand in it. It doesn't matter if you don't know what they are selling, you know it will be great due to the amount of people waiting."

"I like the sound of that, thank you," I told them.

"Did you go to the Batu caves yet?"

"No what is it?" I enquired.

"That's pretty good, isn't it?" the guy asked his partner.

"Yeah you should go if you haven't seen it. It's a big cave on a hill that has a temple inside," she explained.

"Interesting," I replied as we reached the subterranean platform. "How about Singapore? Have you been there yet?" I asked.

"Yes we went a couple of years ago. It's amazing, isn't it?" they replied.

I looked up at the electronic noticeboard as the conversation dried up to check I was on the right side of the platform. After a couple of stops, I came back up at Pasar Seni station in the direction of the markets.

Although I had been here three weeks ago, I had only scratched the surface the first time around. This place blew Bukit Bintang out of the water for choice but to me that was secondary. An aura of vibrancy permeates the air here. An infectious life force lifting the spirit had put a bounce in my step and I headed along a labyrinth of tight paths and interconnected streets full of intriguing items, prices, noises and aromas condensed into the available space; abundantly stocked sectional steel tubular market stalls drew me ever deeper towards the epicentre of this retail maze.

On a block paved intersection where you could just about swing a cat, an unusual looking heated mechanical device caught my eye on the corner. It was a modified steel oil drum with an electric motor attached to the outside near its base used to drive a central vertical shaft visible from the open circular aperture at the top. I looked inside as a cross bar attached to the shaft with metal prongs hanging down into a pit of smoking black gravel perpetually raked around tiny rocks as it revolved slowly. I struggled to work out the possible reason why someone would want to sell what looked to me like deconstructed tarmac, as Muslim families wondered past followed by Chinese shoppers and the odd tourist. This strange, mesmerizing contraption sat under strings of red and gold Chinese lanterns dangling from the clear open-sided glass canopy high above. The intrigue continued until later in the day when I happened across another identical rotating device, this time

235

containing a second ingredient – chestnuts! It turned out to be a device to produce an even roast. Once cooked amongst the stones, the chestnuts are separated by means of a wire-framed straining ladle, allowing the stones to fall through holes too small for chestnuts to fit.

This is the place you can buy slippers made up of Adidas-embossed rubber soles with black faux-leather, Louis Vuitton-patterned straps embroidered with a white Nike logo, but much more abundant are the quality counterfeit sports or designer brands, bags, trainers, baseball caps, T-shirts and tracksuits. If all that shopping makes you thirsty, how about a visit to a soya milk stall like the one I queued up at behind a couple of thirsty Chinese shoppers, even though I had no idea what I was buying. The vendor, also Chinese, was filling plastic bottles from a large clear vat, while on the stall next door a display of mechanical toys kept me entertained as I waited my turn. A dancing Minion penned into a low-sided box showed off his moves, while a cute blonde-haired dolly with pig tails and frilly dress laid on a bed in the background tipping her head from side to side, while swinging her legs in a scissor fashion behind her.

"Yes?" the stall holder asked urgently.

Realising I was at the front of the queue, I turned and replied, "A small bottle please."

"One?"

"Yes." It seemed reassuringly expensive for such a small bottle. He tightened the lid and dropped into a small carrier bag.

"Five ringgit," he demanded abruptly. He got the money but he didn't get a thank you and just as well because, apart from his rudeness which isn't unheard of from some Chinese, I learned that I don't like soya milk, no matter how fresh it is.

An hour later, clutching enough plastic carrier bags to pollute a seahorse sanctuary, it was time to eat.

I found a roadside restaurant with individual stallholders each paying rent for a space, cooking different specialities from their own workstations surrounding the dining area. The owner employs a waiter who serves drinks and cleans tables and the stallholders share the custom and the amenity. A huge black woman of around my age got up to leave just as I ordered.

"Seafood noodles please," I told the old Chinese guy behind the wok.

"Tell them to leave out the shellfish," she said in a southern English voice as she passed by. "They don't cook them enough and you might get cholera. My friend had it," she continued before waddling out through the door.

The waiter was a skinny, old, nimble guy with plastic sports sandals, brown nylon trousers, a white vest and a cloth permanently in his hand. He came over in haste. "You want drink?" he asked while giving my table the once over.

"Lime tea please."

He spun round quickly and scurried off for my order. Like me, if you're the sort of person who would eat intestines or insects, a warning from a stranger against risking the chance of catching cholera from seafood isn't going to put you off. I let the food come as it was, clams and all.

A western-looking couple stopped and hovered around for a while on the path outside, looking in. The sight of another Westerner sat inside may have swayed their decision as they made their way to the table next to me.

"Thank you," I told the cook as he plonked down my plate. I could understand the cockney lady's concerns, as I made my way through the plate of food. Albeit tasty, the clams were snotty and seemed as if they could have done with a bit more time in the pan. Still undeterred, eventually I placed down my chopsticks on the empty plate and pushed it away. 20 seconds later the plate was gone and I was soon to follow. I slid back the chair, stood up and finished the last of my tea.

"Been doing anything exciting today?" I asked the couple, as I grabbed my bags.

"Just shopping. How about you?" the guy asked.

I held up my bags and smiled. "Yeah, I've done a bit of that too," I explained. "I'm just thinking what to do tonight now," I continued.

"Have you tried the helipad bar?" the woman enquired.

"No," I replied with an intrigued tone.

"It's a bit expensive but worth a look. It's a helipad by day and at night they transform it into an outdoor bar on the top of a skyscraper. We went there yesterday," she told me.

237

"Mmmmm. Sounds like a plan. I'll look it up on my phone. Thank you. Well, I hope you have a good trip. Goodbye," I said with a smile. It was time for a siesta before the evening excursion so I headed for the MRT.

I didn't have any spare luggage allowance as I left home so the growing collection of shopping bags back at my room was becoming worryingly excessive. I was told I could move to a better room after one night in my cell but, now the smell of stale cigarette smoke had almost gone, this was my little shithole and I couldn't be bothered to move again. I pushed some carrier bags to one side to clear some space on my bed and lay down to rest my throbbing feet and scrolled through my social media account. After 15 minutes, I jumped in the shower, placed my passport in my camera bag, stashed all other valuables above the ceiling tiles again and set off out. Whatever time, day or night the Indian woman was always on reception, lifting her head over the counter with a quick smile each time I passed.

"Hi, is it okay to leave this bag with you for a while behind the counter?" I enquired.

"Yes, you can leave here. I am here all night," she explained.

"Thanks that's great."

I pressed the door release button and made my way back down to the street past the counters selling zoom lenses that clip onto your mobile phone and Bose Bluetooth speakers, that look identical to the real thing till you hold it in your hand and realise it weighs half that of its hefty original. Past the Thai lady constantly stood in the doorway of a foot massage parlour, waving a price list in your face every time you pass and past the scary looking Turkish guys in the kebab house.

I was heading for the roof of the 34-storey Menara KH building in Jalan Sultan Ismail, to see the transformation from daytime helipad to terrace bar in the sky of night that had been recommended earlier, known as the Heli Lounge Bar. A poor signal on my smartphone meant Google Maps wasn't much help as I struggled to find the elusive bar, walking backward and forward, quizzing passing pedestrians. I spotted a concierge in the foyer of an upmarket building on the main street so I walked up the steps to the door.

"Hi, sorry to bother you but do you know where the Helipad Bar is?" He looked confused. "It's a bar on top of a skyscraper somewhere near here, but I can't find it," I explained.

He pointed directly across the road at a building I had passed a few minutes before. "It is here. Go to the front inside, just there," he explained.

"Thank you." I walked under the monorail track, running down the middle of the dual carriageway, back to the opposite side of the road. The longer route was the safest, up the steps and over the pedestrian footbridge but the evening traffic wasn't as busy as in the daytime so I dodged the odd car to save time.

With no clue of its existence until you enter the lift, this is not an easy place to find if you don't know where you are going. That must be how the owners of this exclusive hidden gem wanted to keep it. Still confused, I pressed the button for the lift, all the time checking around for something I might have missed. The sight of two girls, entering through a pair of clear glass swinging doors and up five steps into what was a typical office block lobby, dressed in sequin mini dresses and heels, made me feel more at ease, even with the confused looks on their faces. Up to then, the place had been deserted and silent.

"Are you looking for the Heli Bar?" I asked, as the lift door opened.

"Yes, have you been before?"

"No, someone told me about it earlier but I'm not sure where it is."

"We were told you had to go straight to the top," the girls explained.

"Ahhh here! Look," I pointed to the tag beside the top button saying 'Heli Pad' on the lift wall.

After trying to find a level of chat somewhere between awkward silence or seeming like I was trying to chat them up, the sound of funky house came to my rescue and added another piece to the jigsaw puzzle. The lift doors parted to reveal a tall gloss black alter in the centre of an open plan entrance to the left of the communal landing where a back lit sign of polished metal lettering stood off a black painted wall, saying 'Heli' in some sort of cosmic script glowing above the heads of a catalogue couple. A man and woman, wearing smart black matching suits, smiled as we approached.

"Welcome to the Heli Lounge. This way please," the man pointed from behind the workstation.

"Please follow me," his colleague requested.

It was still far too early to be busy as she led us across the empty black and white chequerboard dancefloor to the bar.

"Our waiter will be happy to help you. We hope you enjoy your evening. The entrance to the rooftop is there," pointing to an opening otherwise resembling a non-descript passageway.

"If there is anything else you require, please ask."

"Thank you."

A gleaming chrome Boeing 747 turbine engine casing, converted into the DJ booth, was a centrepiece impossible to miss and the words 'KL's best kept secret' in black lettering on the wall behind it couldn't be argued with. Building on the helipad idea, there is no doubting the interior designer's brief, as the seating booth created from a recycled Boeing 737 side panel and polished aluminium propeller hanging from the ceiling all followed the aeronautical theme. Although not empty, it was pretty quiet inside as I paid for my overpriced beer and headed for the reason everyone came here. Had this place been designed specifically as a nightclub, the stairs leading up the roof would have most definitely been a little less basic and easier to spot. Through a doorway past the entrance to the toilets led to a narrow flight of stairs up to the summit, originally used as a tradesman's access.

Outside red warning beacons flashed like cosmic fireflies across the city skyline and a gentle breeze whispered in my ear. A two-metre cordon around the perimeter made up of interconnecting spring-loaded belts slotted into stainless steel posts, like you find in front of the counter at the bank, was all that stopped an unthinkable accident. Almost absent clouds allowed the moon to bathe its delicate hue between tables and spherical rattan booths found dotted around the tarmac pad, adding to the ambient, high-altitude atmosphere created by soft-piped music, solitary location and respectful punters. The only things attempting to obscure an otherwise perfect vista were a pair of solitary sibling clouds, sitting quietly on a neighbouring high rise in an otherwise clear sky.

The ideal opportunity to witness a sprawling nocturnal city skyline that includes both of the top two famous structures in the city. Like a giant turquoise

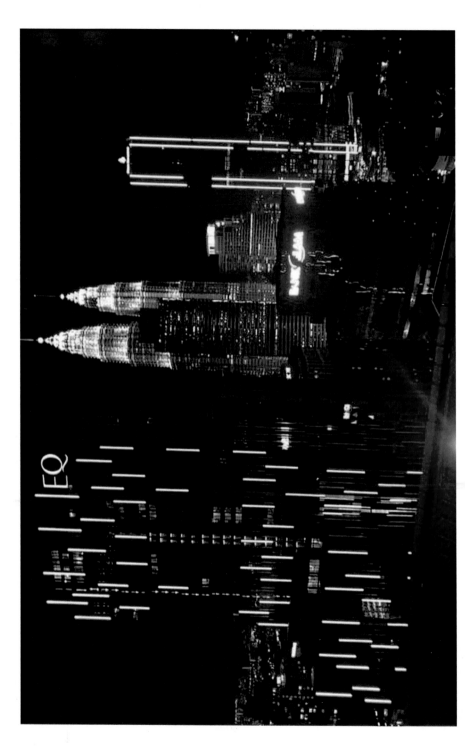

fishing float, the KL tower, awash with pale blue light in a sea of twinkling shadows, and the glistening twin metallic spires of the Petronas Towers were both in clear view. This wasn't the place for loud drunken conversations or attention seeking laughter. It was more conducive to quiet conversations, like the ones continuing around me. Soon the beer in my glass was gone, then me too, back down across the dancefloor past Union Jack mannequins and mirrors, to the elevator and eventually bed.

Laid awake, motionless and corpse-like, transfixed to the point of paralysis, my eyes drifted off, glazed and alone, through a speckled ceiling tile sky, full of random watermark clouds, pondering today's options, until at some unknown point, time stood still once more. However long it was till I woke again didn't matter; I had a plan now and this time I got up before the hangover pulled at my eye lids once again. I gave my hair a quick rub backwards and forwards a couple of times, ran my hands back over my head slowly with increasing pressure to the back of my neck, flexed my elbow wings, while giving out a long deep squeak, followed by a straight-fingered crucifix stretch and finished with a slow clench of the fists. 'I must buy another little suitcase,' I thought to myself while shuffling drowsily into the bathroom, one hand down my pants.

From what I could remember, the Batu caves didnt sound as exciting as they eventually turned out to be so I decided on the National Mosque and KL Minara tower to fill today's increasingly precious time. The thought of seeing my kids after being apart for longer than ever before was beginning to fill me with excitement. I brushed my teeth, which wasn't something I did every day, sprayed some deodorant, rubbed some gel through my damp hair and set off out wearing shorts, sandals and a T-shirt. I could feel the anticipation growing as my marathon journey home approached.

Although I'd visited Lake Gardens when I arrived in KL last month, I'd missed the Botanical Gardens the first time round so I decided to have another wander. It would kill two birds with one stone again, being pretty close to the National Mosque.

There was a misunderstanding with the Grab car I had ordered for the journey. I thought I'd prepaid online at the time of booking so when the young guy driving pulled up outside, I got out and walked away. "Hello?" a concerned voice called from the open window of the car. I turned to see the driver leaning over towards the passenger window. "It say you need to pay on my system," he continued.

"Oh okay. I thought I had paid online," I explained.

"No, look here. It say you do not pay," he explained while holding up his smartphone screen in my direction. This could easily have been a scam but the driver did not seem like the sort and I couldn't be sure if I'd paid or not so I handed over the cash.

It was still quite early in the morning for visitors, hence very quiet. Bird song and the noise of sprinklers watering the carefully manicured lawns, drowned out by the occasional car, was all that broke the silence as I walked down the hill towards the now familiar lake. This time I was going to explore the far end of the park so I followed the path in that direction. There's said to be an amphitheatre and numerous gardens that I had yet to discover, like the hibiscus and edible gardens. There's no doubting this is a special place, a huge oasis slap bang in the middle of a sprawling metropolis, but, having already experienced the waterfalls, ornamental bridges and well-nurtured shrubberies, it wasn't holding my interest. After attempting to capture the scale of a massive tree covered in vines near the herb garden as a camera image, I headed for the exit, past another Chinese jogger stood stretching out his calves against a bench. I took the same path as before up in the direction of the mosque. By the time I'd reached the gate up the hill out to the street, perspiration had worked its way through the front of my T-shirt, revealing a widening dark line. It was another typically humid day.

I took the road downhill, past the Kuala Lumpur Bird Park, claiming to be the world's largest walk-in aviary and sat on a bench outside the entrance considering spending the 50 ringgit admission fee. It wasn't till I reached the opposite hillside, after deciding not to bother, that I noticed an impressive sea of green netting like a translucent floating astroturf pitch stretched over trees on the distant hillside but it was too late to turn back now because, once again, on a wing and a prayer, I hoped to be allowed to enter the illusive nearby religious complex and the last thing I wanted to see when I turned the corner at the bottom of the hill, was people flocking in, like the last the last time.

I found out the hard way when I trod this path previously, non-Muslims are only allowed entrance to the National Mosque while it's not being used for its primary purpose. Reassuringly, things felt much different this time. No motorcycle maze to negotiate or hum of chatting crowds milling around a hamlet of food stalls across the sprawling pedestrian fringe adjacent to the 15,000 capacity complex, known as Masjid Negara. This time I wasn't so unlucky, or stupid, to have turned up on the one day guaranteed to be full of Friday worshippers.

I could see tourists were being allowed in the building, as long as they were suitably dressed that is. A row of shoe racks two metres high next to clothes rails with dozens of ankle length black cotton fabric gowns incorporating long floppy cone hoods on hangers, situated at the bottom of the steps leading to a raised deck, are provided so tourists can dress respectfully for the visit. I made my way across to a small group of American tourists, removing their footwear and poking their heads through gowns reminiscent of a garment you might see being worn by Obi-Wan Kenobi while marching through a dusty alien outpost. There was a miserable guard, a giant of a man, but not so gentle or fat. He sat behind a desk, struggling to use the pen between his sausage fingers, making notes next to the racks. He gave me and the other steady trickle of visitors the talk. "Shoes here! Please. Put on gown," he instructed. With visions of the scene in the film where Jamal and his brother Salim steal shoes from tourists outside the Taj Mahal in Slumdog Millionaire, I stashed my posh flip flops far back on the wide shelf to lessen my chances of becoming a copycat crime victim and, after dropping the gown over my head, covering all but my feet, I climbed the steps to the raised terrace.

In part, this building was based on a traditional Malaysian home, particularly the raised veranda allowing air flow and providing shade to help to keep it cool from underneath, and to keep it above potential flood waters. Up here, the elevated white marble veranda floor with its black rectangular grid inlay detailing led me towards the entrance to the main prayer hall at the centre of the building. I passed a long rectangular pond with water jets projecting from its edges on both longest sides aimed towards a row of vertical fountains running along the centre. Although highly decorative and symbolic, it had a

243

practical purpose. It was another technique to help keep the building cool. Usually mosques use something similar for ablutions in Asian countries but here washing is done using sinks and taps downstairs. The water jets help to cool the air and decorative concrete screens along the whole of the outer edge of the walkway with their white, stylised, repeating triangular, flower-patterned openings help to preserve the cool air by providing shade.

As I neared the entrance to the prayer hall along the walkway, glimpses of a line of circular raised goblet fonts outside, each with a fountain and on star-shaped plinths, passed by the angular patterns in the screened wall. An old, tall, skinny, placid gentleman wearing a well-worn and slightly oversized brown pin-striped suit, tie and over-polished black shoes, softened with time like the look in his eye, approached holding a tablet device.

"Hello, my name is Adam and I am here to answer any questions you may have regarding the National Mosque," he explained with a speedy, slightly posh vocabulary.

"Okay that's good to know. Thank you." I could see the pale brown carpet and cylindrical pillars circling the outer diameter of the main prayer hall through the open doorway. "I'm I allowed inside?" I asked.

"Yes, of course. I will show you," he explained. He looked more like an Ahmed than an Adam to me, as I followed him into a room the size of a circus ring, littered with pedestal fans and dotted with small groups of inquisitive tourists. "As you can see the prayer hall has... 14 I think... yes, chandeliers hanging around the outside of the ceiling." He explained while looking down and sliding his finger over the screen of his new toy.

The outer eaves of the multi-ridged roof, emanating from a central fulcrum at its highest point, created a recurring 360-degree pattern of triangular windows around the outer edge of the room, almost touching along their bottom edge, glazed in green and blue translucent tiles in a pattern of three further triangles within each window and allowing a glow of colour to spread evenly around the room.

"Let's see... Ahhh yes. Also each triangular window that you can see here has an inscription from the Koran."

I started to lose interest as he kept asking me to wait so he could find further information about each inscription. I stood patiently not wanting to be rude, itching to photograph the gold-embossed inscriptions around the walls and Islamic arches. The pillars finished halfway up the outer wall, at the underside of a thin gallery, following the circular chamber, with a patterned full glass panel between the gallery and roof, which allowed further blue and yellow light through repeating Islamic shapes. There were, as he pointed out, 14 chandeliers hanging around the perimeter of the room. All identical, around the size of a bright red beach ball, ruby encrusted and oozing opulence. They are said to represent each of the fourteen states.

"... and so the king ordered it to be done. If you have any questions, please feel free to ask me." He said, as I zoned back into the conversation.

"Yes, thank you, I will," I replied with relief. Peace at last. I turned away and opened my camera bag.

"Oh, and did you know the National Mosque was built in 1965? It was designed by a team of three architects, one from the UK and two Malaysians. The name of the architect from UK was... erm... but the iconic design of the roof was the work of Dutuk.... no! Datuk Baharuddin Abu Kassim," he annoyingly continued.

"FOR FUCK SAKE!" I shouted silently to my other self behind a polite smile. "That's really interesting," I lied.

This guy was one of those people we have all come across that give you constant ammunition to gossip about while their back is turned even if you don't normally gossip. You can bet someone who knows him was having a little giggle at my plight, while watching on from the periphery.

"... because, you see, it is very unusual because it has no dome, instead the roof is like a half-opened parasol. Can you see?"

I wasn't too sure of the question so I answered, "Very interesting yes. Thank you." I answered while looking into my bag.

"I am here for one more hour so, please, if you need any more assistance, I am happy to help you, okay?"

"Thank you very much for your time today. That is very kind of you, thank you. That's great, ok," I reiterated with a silent cheer.

He turned away and, as if to be going for the Guinness World Record of most people to bore senseless in one day, immediately homed in on his next victim.

He had a special gift: the ability to make interesting information sound really boring. One fact he hadn't mentioned though that people might find interesting was that the minaret where the balcony is located, where the call to prayer is relayed to us what's known as the spire, was the tallest structure in Kuala Lumpur before the days of the Petronas Twin Towers and the building I was just about to visit next: the Menara Tower.

The Menara Tower was visible from the steps of the National Mosque and it didn't look that far away but, like most things at distance, it's not until you get halfway there, you realize just how much further away they actually are, as I was about to find out. After taking off the Star Wars outfit, I set off walking. KL has a great public transport system but it's not so good for pedestrians round this area. Many footpaths near the main roads tend to just run out, leaving a bit of a task to get safely from A to B, especially when you need to cross the dual carriageways like the ones across my path. It made for a convoluted route but eventually it did randomly take me to an unsuspected free attraction in a woodland park near to where I needed to be.

The KL Forest Eco Park is a series of wooden-framed towers connected by rope bridges that float their way through the canopy of a patch of inner-city forest on a sloping hillside with the odd impressive glimpse of the city skyline. After climbing the internal winding staircase up through the timber frame of the first, tallest tower at the lowest section of the hill, the feeling of walking the deck of a listing yacht at sea dares you not to grab the handrail as you follow the swaying path past a combination of giant vines and views through a leafy canopy pitted with visions of nearby skyscrapers.

If you are luckier than me, you might not bump into the gang of inner-city bad boys hanging around intimidating any unsuspecting easy target on the lookout to forcibly relieve you of your goods within the woodland cover. Back on firm ground I followed a winding path while scoffing a family pack of crisps towards the exit through the woodland fringe. Around the next corner a big adolescent scum bag and his two mates spotted me and my goodies while rummaging in the bin. I ignored them and their antisocial behaviour, continuing past but they went quiet behind my back, until the sound of scurrying steps approaching at speed forced me to defend myself. I turned just in time to pull my bag from an angry clawing hand. He drew back just out of arm's reach showing his weapons with a menacing wide-mouthed glare, while his crew flanked left and right and, in a perfect example of attack is the best from of defence, I lunged at the ringleader with enough noise and determination to send him and his crew scurrying back into the canopy empty handed. It's obviously a hard life for these inner-city marauding macaques, having to stoop to the same level of desperate humans. Luckily the trauma was over just as quickly as it had begun.

I could see a gap in the trees: an exit. It was in the general direction of the tower, so I followed the path. It led up steps and out onto a road whose crescent, curved around towards the tower. I followed the gradual incline and noticed animal enclosures below to my left, under a natural shelf in the geology on a lower section of the woodland. It turned out to be a zoo. A steady stream of traffic was heading in my direction, coaches, taxis and cars all with the same agenda: to go up arguably the best tower experience in KL. The traffic backed up slightly, as I closed in on the entrance to the tower. The entrance to the zoo was strategically placed within view of the entrance to the tower, as were two large macaws with bright red, yellow, green and blue plumage, perched on a branch to draw in the punters.

Chino shorts with leather belts, long socks pulled up over sandals and sun hats with cameras hung diagonally over one shoulder was the combined look of the privileged few, here on organised excursions while their cruise ship waited in port. They were alighting a fleet of coaches, along with a smattering of minibus loads of tourists of a similar ilk. We filed in together, mingling into one convoluted herd. I joined a queue behind a ticket machine upstairs and waited my turn. As the line of retired western professionals shortened, I overheard an American gent ask a smartly dressed attendant, "How do we get the group discount here, sunny?" They leaned in to the machine blocking my view, then moments later the machine was mine.

"Excuse me," I said to the attendant as he walked away. "How do I get the group discount?"

"Okay, I need to authorise for you, sir," he explained. "Would you like to include the Sky Deck also?" he quizzed.

"How much is it including the sky deck?"

"80 ringgit."

"Okay, yes include the sky deck."

After tapping a couple of buttons, he left me to insert my card, without quizzing my eligibility to get the discount. Ticket in hand, I shuffled into the next queue – this time for the lift and pondered the 80-ringgit expense. Having spent a month away from home, I'd become familiar with the local economy. In comparison with the cost of living, it seemed expensive. In reality it was £15 and, if I'd have paid that for the London Eye for example, I would have told my friends and family about the bargain. The queue for the lift was the longest but five minutes of people watching later, we walked out to a memorable sight.

Trepidation clenched at my gut, taking my first steps onto the breezy 360-degree open circular platform, a sight to deter all but the most desperate mind against taking the quick way down. I grabbed the rail instinctively, gawping in awe at the seemingly infinite sprawling model city down below where reality was reduced to match box buildings and line drawing streets. As endless as a magician's ribbon, the view outdistanced my ability to fit it into my field of vision. Other than the odd lonely cloud and an opaque hue masking distant hills, it was perfect weather to experience life through the eyes of an albatross at an altitude usually reserved for rain clouds and flight paths. Unlike the Petronas Twin Towers, time is not restricted here; neither is the view. A clear glass barrier, just over a metre high and a couple of metres from the edge, allows some amazing images. The most surprising thing looking down over an area easily in excess of a hundred square miles was its pond-like topography, flatter than my singing voice, apart from one giant mountainous lump, like a boil on an athlete's belly, stuck there all alone on the outskirts of the city,

'Batu', meaning 'rock' in Malay, was the name given to the Hindu cave complex, brought to my attention recently. Since being told about the caves, I'd done some further research and seen images that looked a lot like the lump down below in the distance.

"Excuse me," I said to a busy staff member scurrying by. He stopped suddenly and turned. "Is that the Batu caves?" I enquired while pointing.

On hearing my question, he continued on his way then replied over his shoulder, "Yes." It was too far away to make out any detail but a worthwhile glimpse into the scale of the terrain that now I had to visit.

As far as I'm aware, there is no pay per view TV up here, and to me what I was about to experience was much more terrifying, so when I mention the fact that there are two sky boxes, you are under no illusion I might be laid asleep on a sofa surrounded by empty crisp packets after watching five back-to-back seasons of time travelling telepathic cannibal teachers. Sky boxes here are clear glass bottomed platforms that protrude out from the sky deck suspended by cables.

A Malaysian couple were sat on the three-metre square invisible floor, arms up and mouths wide, posing for a photo. I walked over and joined a small queue. Photographers employed to sell images will quickly put together a personal portfolio to peruse at your leisure on screens in the shop in the hope you will purchase a memento of the day before you leave. I watched the next couple as they laid, sat and stood, pretending to look afraid.

The guy with a camera round his neck turned to me, "Take off your shoes please."

Now for a guy who, in the past, has been involved in high-speed police chases, sparring with world champion Thai boxers, or worked steel erecting with a ton of RSJ swinging above my head at the top of a ten storey building, you'd think this would not be such a big deal. That's what I thought but there's something profoundly unnatural about defying the human instinct and, no matter how much I tried to convince myself it was completely safe, something compelled me to want to tip-toe across to the safety of the handrail at the far end of the box where I'd been asked to stand. 'Just think how many people have done the same thing today,' I thought to myself, as I slowly released my grip and turned around to the camera.

"Okay lay down with your hands behind your head," the snapper instructed. It didn't take long to convince my head to stop being a baby and, after a few more poses, I almost managed to walk back across the Invisible floor without looking like a burglar who'd just woke up his victim.

Aesthetically, the Petronas Twin Towers have the edge but otherwise I prefer this tower to its younger bigger twins in every other way. The unrestricted view from up here is amazing and you can stay all day if you wish. Add in the sky box attraction that is at no extra cost and you might agree, especially when you take into account the minor difference in height between the two – just 31 metres difference in the overall height. The Petronas Twin Towers do, however, boast an extra 60 metres off the ground from its observation deck, than the sky deck here but how would you notice that? Either way, you wouldn't want to slip and fall, even if it was the quickest way down. I plumped for the lift.

Chapter 11
Batu Caves

"Better late than never," I told my lonely naked self, clearing last night's empty cans, shopping bags and damp towel from the dulled vinyl floor. After days of chaos came five minutes of order. I laid out my goodies on the bed and conducted a verbal inventory. "Two pairs of kid's trainers, one pair of adult trainers, two bottles of perfume, two clip-on wide-angle cell phone lenses, an umbrella, two watches, eight T-shirts, three rucksacks, a vest and two baseball caps. We're gonna need a bigger bag."

The morning was wet. I popped up my brolly and nipped round the corner to the cafe for breakfast again. I was a bit later today and the place was almost full. I had to share a table with a local guy sitting opposite eating roti.

"Two roti and a chai," I told the waiter.

"Roti finish," he explained.

"Biryani and chai," I replied abruptly. I'm not normally arrogant but that's the way they do things around here and I was fitting in quite nicely.

My temporary neighbour didn't look up as I placed my foot through the shoulder strap of my camera case, pulled out my smartphone and put on my glasses. I'd already decided I would visit the Batu caves while on this morning's well overdue five-minute marathon tidy on what was my last full day. The tourists I'd bumped into told me to allow half a day, which meant I should go pretty much straight after breakfast, leaving time for some last-minute suitcase shopping and a few beers later on. By the time my food arrived, I'd worked out a plan to get to the caves. Froth sloshed over onto the table as he placed my tea down clumsily next to the pale blue plastic plate of rice that had appeared in front of me while glued to my phone looking for directions. The journey couldn't have been much simpler. All I had to do was get off at the last stop on the MRT. On finishing my restaurant quality food at cafeteria prices, I paid at the counter and headed back past the digs to the underground station.

At the end of the line, back up above ground, the rain clouds had disappeared. I walked past an improvised car park, eyes fixed to the flailing arms of an animated unofficial attendant directing cars into muddy puddle ruts under a flyover, until a glimpse of a towering gold figure across the road shouted at my eyes. The area was smattered with people, some with baskets and blankets, walking in and out of the main outer gates, filtering around a bottleneck of backed up taxis trying to avoid driving deeper into a jam that was spilling out from inside the gates. Once my feet touched the tarmac, I got my first unrestricted view of the youthful golden giant: Lord Murugan, staff in hand, standing tall at the foot of an even taller flight of multi-coloured steps leading up the middle of a prehistoric limestone outcrop, that in turn towered above everything.

Stalls and a smattering of ramshackle shops running along the back edge of the car park selling food, gifts, coconuts and souvenirs had attracted a healthy crowd, both human and monkey but it was no competition to the draw of the main attraction. I carried on and, like in a scene in 'Alice in Wonderland', I seemed to shrink more each step closer to the 43-metre figure whose delicate 24 carrot fingers matched my legs for size, until I slipped unnoticed under the fourth floor gaze on his boyishly handsome round face.

Cloud was wilting fast, parched by the glare of a rising ball of fire, heating the vast hard charcoal field of painted bays. I'd almost reached the foot of the giant feature staircase amongst a rising swell of worshippers and curious travellers flowing under a bay of ornamental archways, marking the beginning of a monumental ascent, but the playfully infantile pallet of the building to its left proved too much of an intriguing prospect to pass by. The vision through a row of pointed arched openings along its longest side, of incense snaking a smoky path around golden alters and surreal coloured statues, was a scene I was compelled to investigate further.

A footpath leading in from the left of the complex with further stalls lining the route, busy with a further stream of pedestrian traffic coming in from a side entrance, passed by this playfully pastel blue, orange, pink and white rectangular place of worship. Its flat roof and open windowsills, favoured by scavenging macaques, became their arena where confrontations between competing males played out with nothing more than short chases after overly dramatic noisy outbursts.

In front of the entrance was a modestly sized tiled patio within a dwarf wall where people sat on the ground, heads daubed in talcum paste, clutching garlands of flowers, in contemplation of an experience continuing to emanate from the open doorway. Inside, people young and old milled around shrines adorned with garlands of saffron blooms, roped-off alters and family groups sitting in celebration with party food and newly christened babies in clusters on the floor. The sight of bald-headed infants daubed in white chalky powder, proudly on display, were images I was dying to record but it felt too intrusive. A white guy sat alone outside, himself with white finger marks smeared on his forehead, got up and came over. He'd noticed my hesitation.

"You are allowed in, you know. The priests will bless you if you stand at the railings. Just find a spot," he explained in an unmistakably English accent.

"I wasn't sure if I was allowed. Thanks," I replied.

"Oh yeah it's fine. Here," he held out a single marigold.

"Thank you."

I took it and walked towards the door, just as an altercation on a stone archway directly above my head kicked off. An adult male was attempting to relieve a youngster of a garland of flowers. It was just a matter of how much intimidation it would take to make him drop the contraband before someone's eardrums burst. Eventually the screaming youth bolted empty handed, having abandoned his fresh blossom snack. The bully dropped down to the floor at the side of the string of tiny white pearl like blossoms, looked around slowly with a gloat, picked up his snack and sauntered off. These monkeys love to eat the flower garlands sold to tourists from nearby stallholders. Unsuspecting tourists that tie the blooms into their hair or hang them around their necks, will undoubtedly be relieved of them by the time they reach the top of the 272 steps to the cave entrance, if not before.

Inside people flocked around a number of different alters. Behind a barrier at each one was a priest wearing nothing but forehead paint, flower garland and white sarong tucked under a muffin top torso, carrying a tray with flowers, a dish of white paste, a dish of pink paste and occasionally some slices of fruit. Places were sparse against the barriers but, squeezed in alongside other individuals, I waited for the attention to come around to me. Down the line, the priest anointed each person in turn. As he approached, like everyone else, I leaned in over the barrier. He smeared paste onto the centre of my forehead with his finger, before moving on to the next person. I dropped back to allow others the opportunity to be included in the ceremony.

Although mostly Indian, there were other nationalities around. A Chinese guy with a camera round his neck for instance giving me the green light. The problem in a situation like this for me is knowing when to stop but, thanks to a memory card bigger than the priest's appetite, I didn't have to worry about that until later.

Another ubiquitous primate sat on a windowsill casing the joint for blooms. The brightness from outside created a natural frame for a photo but I was too slow in capturing the moment. He'd gone before I had a chance to press the shutter but, unlike the hairy tea leaf, the statue of Genesha to my left wasn't going anywhere. Here was a shrine to the son of Shiva and Parvati, a man with the head of an elephant, said to be the god of wisdom, success and good luck, so it's no surprise he's one of the most worshipped of the Hindu gods. Stood on a plinth made of a giant lotus leaf, with man boobs and pot belly hanging over a pink silk sarong, it's pretty clear he's had his picture taken many times before. I snapped a few shots, safe in the knowledge I could look back to remind myself of the details I might not otherwise remember. His golden-domed helmet for instance, with its decreasing tiers and pointed tip, or the garland of bright orange fresh marigolds hanging around his neck that had not yet been stolen. Maybe the macaques know the line they should not cross.

Half a day now seemed slightly limiting. I made my way back outside, through a line of elaborate archways, under figures wearing gold helmets, golden-hemmed blue and saffron robes and garlands around their necks, standing on the roof between coloured pillars in shelters crowned with pink and blue scalloped blooms, looking down over the entrance to the grand staircase. It marked the beginning of the steps to the cave complex, at the heels of the golden giant. A repeating sequence of colours, painted in sections, around 20

254

steps at a time, pointed the way. Blue then red, green and yellow, all the way to the top, with concrete handrails and newel posts dividing the steps into four lanes, each around three metres wide.

By now, parasols rather than umbrellas would be beneficial. The heat was no help to any asthma-suffering grannies contemplating the climb to the summit, especially those with food, water bottles or flowers on show. Dozens of monkeys lined the route, perched on high railings, rocky outcrops and lighting poles, on the lookout for loot and these guys had all the tricks. A few metres up the hill, a woman gave out a scream. I didn't see the incident, masked by the crowd, but it didn't take much working it out as I passed a monkey licking up a spillage of milkshake from the floor next to an upturned paper cup. Infants watch and learn as adults practice the art of ripping out flower garlands from people's hair, or knocking food, water bottles, or in this case milkshakes from your hand, grabbing the item from the floor and scurrying off to higher ground to devour quickly, before big brother bumps it. No one runs the gauntlet to the top without being either a victim or a witness.

The effort was just about to become worthwhile as I counted down the last few steps, joining a clutch of spectators stood against a railing on the plateau to catch my breath, only to have it taken away again by the scene laid out back down below. From here the true size of the space allocated for stallholders and parking was apparent, covering the size of three football pitches, with a sprinkling of bodies congregated around its edges, people and monkeys alike, overshadowed partly by the back of the towering figure stood guard over the cave entrance, looking out at the distant wheels of daily life rumbling on, beyond a fleet of parked vehicles and past the outer gates.

A view of such magnitude would hold my attention much longer under normal circumstances but the jagged aperture inside, beyond a little souvenir shop set into a crevice on the right with a heavy gauge steel mesh safety barrier over its roof, complete with a boulder-shaped crater from a previous rock fall, flashed colourful glimpses of the vastness of the chamber beyond.

A relatively small flight of steps now led back down into a cavern easily large enough to accommodate not only the shrines already there but a small village. This is the temple cave, or the cathedral cave as it's otherwise known, possibly due, in part, to its 100-metre-high cavern ceiling. Light from an opening at its opposite side illuminated around 40 more concrete steps leading up once more but a cluster of buildings were in need of further investigation before I reached that point.

Blue peacocks with fanned green tail feathers flanked the entrance to a multi-coloured shrine. An over-extended tiered roof, standing alone and bold as an intentionally overstated feature, with three window openings, in line one above the other, each smaller than the last as they reached up towards pointing limestone fingers. Each back lit, one illuminated red, then green and blue at the top. A pair of multi-coloured fabric pompom garlands either side of the entrance, each hanging over three metres long, dangled down in front of a pair of disproportionately large, six-metre high wooden doors covered in ornately carved square panelling, hiding whatever precious contents lay behind its locked bolts.

Dulcet melodies from warbling Bansuri flutes accompanied by tiny intermittent bell chimes levitated around the chamber amongst spirts, spiralling mists of incense and cool moist air, heightening the meditative aura. Deeper inside, another pot-bellied priest daubed devotees' heads over a golden fence surrounding another temple on the far left of the auditorium, where soft strokes of concealed light spread a gentle glow over green pillars, red stylised roofs and sand filled pedestals crammed with once smouldering stubs, amongst freshly lit clumps of smoking sandalwood skewers.

Leading up to a source of daylight, the final 40 stairs cut through an opening in the rocks, to the highest point of the temple complex, at the bottom of a deep moist open cavern, where a further vibrantly coloured shrine sat proud, under a golden roof. Behind it, small cavernous mouths with statues of further Hindu gods bathed in warm light, semi-hidden behind a jawline of giant stalactite and stalagmite teeth, was a mesmerizing sight worthy of the epic hike, had it been the only thing to see up here.

The souvenir shop on the way back was a bit disappointing. The best of a bad bunch, which I wasn't about to buy, was a fat sitting Buddha with mechanical arm that pivoted at the shoulder, moving up and down in a perpetual waving motion, like the Chinese cats you find on the counter of our Sheffield takeaways.

Not wanting to leave without a memento of the day, I bought a car sticker for my camper van with a phrase saying something like 'always be happy and do good for others'.

Back down in the shadow of the rock, I gave the stalls a closer look, quickly finding a performance of squeamish precision with more than a hint of danger that left no room for error or spectators. I squeezed in amongst the three deep crescent of open-mouthed onlookers, as a tall thick-set Indian guy, with a sweat-stained pale blue dress shirt, bloodshot eyes, short black hair, dark tan and cleaver, stood beside a upturned log around half a metre tall and enough green coconuts to fill a pick-up truck tipped on the floor. He was entertaining mesmerised customers while they waited in line to be served. His colleague collected money and took the orders. They were coming in thick and fast like the coconut ninja's slashing lump of sharpened steel.

With one chop and a bit of after force to see it through, he made a flat base by removing the bottom edge, then placed the locked in beverage down on the log plinth. Next with a quick swish, the stork is gone, replaced by his finger ends on the top centre, pressing down as he chopped through the top third with a diagonal swipe towards the outer edge, swivelling and repeating at lightning speed, each time squeamishly close to an unwelcome manicure, until like a knife-sharpened pencil, he made it all the way round. The last swipe was horizontal and left the blade in the flesh while he grabbed a straw, then as if to remove the top of a boiled egg, he prized the top off, stuck in a straw and thrust it into the hands of a somewhat relieved, yet happy lady and, within a long breath, off he went again. The whole process took an impressive six seconds from start to finish. At that rate, ten in a minute would be the certified record to beat, while the adjudicator looked on, clipboard and stopwatch in hand.

Over on the car park side, in front of stalls selling dried fruit and nuts, a splinter troupe of adolescent macaques were loitering, making a nuisance of themselves on a red hexagonal block paved pathway. With half an eye on unattended food or leftovers and half an eye on playing tig, they sprinted backwards and forwards between prams, foreigners, discarded coconuts and the elderly, with boisterous vigour. Then one of the little rouges, on spotting a discarded vessel, ran over and stuck his head fully inside a coconut shell cavity, using his long sabre-like fangs to scrape out the remaining flesh. Luckily my camera was at hand to record a comical image of the moment a monkey seemed to be bent over wearing a green organic crash helmet, head down, about to kick up into a freestyle monkey breakdance head spin.

I felt like I just scratched the surface of this amazing vast natural wonder this morning, said to be around 400 million years old, spiced up by the last hundred years, blink of the eye, by an equally amazing occupation of vibrant Hindu temples, whose occupants are outnumbered ten to one, living alongside a simian settlement of outlaws but, although they are responsible for break-ins, burglary, muggings, extortion, public indecency and intimidation on an hourly basis, the marauding macaques are a major part of the attraction here on the outskirts of the city, in the Gombak district.

Time was running out; my feet were throbbing and my belly empty. I headed back to the digs to recharge my batteries via the Central Market again, where I hoped to pick up a cheap case in readiness for the big return journey.

The Central Market is a two-storey indoor market built nearly 100 years ago, with almost as many stallholders outside on the approach, as indoors these days. A young guy at one these outdoor stalls approached me on noticing my interest in his suitcases.

"You want? I do good price for you – 45," he explained.

It went in one ear and out of the other as I inspected the goods but, rather than ask again I just replied, "Okay I will think about it." He was a little too pushy for my liking and I walked off.

Up to the eighties, it was known for fresh produce and wet goods here. Then a makeover that contributed to it being awarded national heritage site status helped it to evolve into a more cultural experience, where art and handicrafts began to find a home. After filling up on yet another Chinese buffet at a large place across from the mobile phone stall, I set off to sniff out a luggage bargain, passing all number of stalls selling Chinese cultural trinkets and lanterns, personalised calligraphy, jewellery and the like. Inside the stalls are set out in a grid system, row upon row.

It's the sort of place you can easily get lost, which I was soon to find out when I decided to go back to the stall that I'd seen on entering through the side door a few minutes prior. A hand-luggage sized electric blue hard shell, with wheels and telescopic handle for 50 ringgit. I'd not been able to find another stall to get a price comparison inside and, in one of my increasingly common senior moments, completely forgotten about the pushy guy's stall outside. Backward and forwards, up and down, twice, three times. 'It surely can't be that hard to find, dickhead!' I thought, chastising myself, as I missed it for a fourth time.

I was stood outside an empty fish pedicure stall, with clear glass tanks teeming with skin-loving sprats. I decided to break off the search for a few minutes and enquired as to the cost of allowing a shoal of ravenous sticklebacks to eat me alive. Whatever the price was, I deemed it worthwhile, parked my bum on one of the padded leatherette benches and dipped my toe in, then straight back out again, afraid by the sight of a frantic swarm on the attack. Next a little further, up to the ankle, but only for a second or two, the attention was too intense. The sensation of an army of toothless baby piranhas trying to bite off your feet simultaneously from every angle with mouths too small to do too much damage felt too weird but, after sitting in front of a modest audience of amused shoppers for a couple of minutes, I managed to keep both legs under the water for long enough to perform the dual task of providing their lunch and exfoliating my lower limbs. Five minutes in and I actually started enjoying the experience, even with the odd painful nip.

Foot flake free and rejuvenated, I found the elusive luggage stall straightaway this time and made my purchase. Back outside the pushy stallholder noticed me pulling my new blue case heading towards him.

"How much you pay?" he asked with a sharp tone.

"50," I replied.

"50? Why? I told you 45. This is much better case." I shrugged my shoulders and turned up my palms. Then he started to shout. "I tell you! Why you not buy? I gave you good price and you buy this shit," he continued, becoming angrier by the second.

I glared into his eyes and shouted, "Fuck off, dickhead. I can do what I want," in a slightly less polite tone than he might have expected. It did the trick.

Back at my shitty little crash pad, I opened the fridge, cracked open an Anchor then packed my new case before one last moon-lit wander down Food Street in search of a food stall at the bottom end selling beers from a large cool box on wheels outside. They were the cheapest around.

As I reached the top corner of Food Street, the unmistakable aroma of the spiky, melon-sized sickly fruit that intrigued me when I first arrived in the country was floating around in the air like a festering kebab amongst a field of strawberries. Durian first became known to me when I spotted signs displayed in places that prohibited the sickly, savoury, sweet, combined odour from tainting their public space. Imagine a sign with the black silhouette of a spiky melon sized conker inside a red circle with a line diagonal through it, reminiscent of a British 'No entry' road sign, on buses and in hotel lobbies.

Animals are said to be able to detect the so-called king of fruits from half a mile away while foraging in the forest, which is easy to believe when your retch reflex contracts repeatedly after one whiff. There are worse smells, like a rotting carcass or blocked drain for instance, but it's the combination of sweet and savoury that some people detest. Described by some as garlic-tainted caramel or a chorizo peach, it's like no smell I can liken it to to help describe this true divider of opinions. Two Chinese guys were sat at the outer tables at the top corner restaurant, pulling out the pale cream, moist, fibrous segments from under its spiky green armoured shell, wearing protective clear plastic 'fuel pump' gloves to prevent the stench tainting their skin. I'd tried it earlier in the trip and, although it tasted slightly better than it smelt, I still gave most of it away to a gang of amused kids, who found the look of disgust on my face highly amusing.

Next door to the two giant metal steamers of the dim sum stall, holding arrays of coloured dumplings representing different combinations of Asian fillings, its neighbour qualified for a photo under the category 'being almost as unlikely to be eaten by an Englishman, than his own testicles'. A stainless-steel box trolley with a yellow illuminated sign attached on poles just above head height read 'FROG PORRIDGE' in large red letters, along with some Mandarin wording above it, which I can only guess repeats the offer of an amphibian-based gruel. I captured the image on my smartphone and continued down to the

260

滋润养颜雪耳 FUNGUS RM 3.50   菊花 CHRYSANTHEMUM   RM 3.00

清心肝火茶 GINSING TEA RM 4.50   王老吉 WANG LAO JI   RM 3.00

海底椰 SEA COCONUT   RM 3.50   夏枯草 XIA KU CHAO   RM 3.00

龟苓膏 GUI LING GAO   RM 3.50   冬瓜凉茶 WINTER MELON   RM 3.00

芦荟 ALOE VERA   RM 3.50   冰冻罗汉果 LUO HAN GUO RM 3.00

加药 SPECIAL ADDING RM 6.00

bottom end of the street in search of the beer man. He wasn't around tonight so I took the shortcut to the 7-Eleven on the main road, through the sort of dimly lit alley where the silence is broken by the sound of bins falling over, followed by a cat squealing, before getting cornered by two knife-wielding vagrants in American films.

Carrying two cans swinging in a bag, I made it back, laid on the bed and browsed my photos between feeding my habit, one gulp at a time. The frog porridge image made it onto Facebook, along with an image of a skewer of deep-fried crispy squid and the caption: 'I've never been that keen on porridge so I opted for something a bit more adventurous Lol'. My old friend Judas replied from the UK: 'Nice. I had deep fried crispy frog skins on the Thai/Laos border a few years back they were lovely. Give the frog porridge a go (smiley face) x'. I replied: '(thinking emoji) Breakfast maybe x'. Another ten minutes social networking saw me turn out the light for the final time on Malaysian soil and drift off thinking of how much my kids were going to love the gifts I was about to bring home.

I woke up late the last morning but it didn't matter and, after a quick scratch and a stretch, I nipped around the corridor to the reception. The Indian woman was on duty as always, giving me a smile as she dealt with a young white guy checking in alone. He dragged his bag to one side and sat down.

"Hi, what time do I need to be out of my room today?" I enquired.

"You need go at eleven, but you can leave your bag here," she replied.

"Okay that's great. I leave for the airport at one. Is that okay?" I asked. She replied with a bobble of the head. "Great," I said with a smile.

This is not the place for drive thru intercoms or exhausted fast-food menus. To me it's about a four-meal drive, off the well beaten track, egged on into extreme adventures, in a culinary direction that snakes an exotic three course path and an unknown root likely to turn stomachs, rather than corners, of those that might consider me a strange vegetable for loving such diverse journeys into the consumption of what I consider to be one of the main directions of exotic travel experiences. Here welcome diversions at junctions of bland normality is the way I normally travel so not considering the frog porridge route until after JD set the seed was an oversight. Overnight the

261

idea had blossomed into a definite plan so, with time for one last experience, washed down with one or two last Anchors, I dropped my bags at reception and skipped around the bumper of a taxi, through a steady stream of traffic, back across to the street more famous for its food than its early starts. I'd forgotten that by day it was an actual street, used for its primary purpose during daylight hours. Things don't get warmed up around here till early evening and it was barely lunchtime.

After an uneventful stroll in hope of finding the stall that originally peaked my interest, or any alternative that wasn't closed, I retraced my steps back to the top right corner of the street, to the restaurant where the guys had been eating durian the previous day. In my blinkered mission centred around the stall on food street, I hadn't noticed this place was open. I parked my arse down at a table outside on the path, against a low banister, stretching across the front of a pair of open shutter doors. Sat opposite at the other side of the barrier, two Chinese men were having a business lunch and I could hear every breath. It brought back memories of the meeting between the group of businessmen at the seafood restaurant in Singapore earlier in the trip.

I caught the waitress's attention as she passed. "Do you have frog porridge?" I asked.

"One?" she asked.

"Yes and one Anchor please."

Negativity began to permeate out over my table like a bad smell as things went quiet inside. The awkward silence grew until someone was forced into speaking up.

"I have good contacts who I can call, they can help make things run smoothly. I know the right people in this area, for many years, I know how things operate around here." His gaze gradually slipped the longer there was no reply. A few moments later he straightened his head and tried again. "You have children, how are they doing at school?" he enquired.

"My daughter is doing well and is hoping to finish her masters with top marks next year, but I would like to know what you can you bring by way of contracts?" he quizzed.

"Well, erm, like I said, I have many contacts in this field who respect me. I can use my influence to help gain contracts as required, that should be no problem. My brother-in-law is held in high regard in the company and will help in any way he can," he grovelled. Other than talking shop while eating food, I now realised there was no resemblance to the Singapore meeting. The guy wanting something in that instance was confident and impressive with answers to questions that had the group won over with a slick professionalism vastly lacking in this instance. I was starting to feel embarrassed for the poor guy as my bowl of food arrived.

A large white melamine bowl filled to the brim with a semi-translucent white porridge was placed down with a two-handed bow by a Chinese granny, shuffling back before turning. There was a dollop of red, fiery looking sauce sat on top, alongside an unbreakable slurp spoon floating next to a weird looking, pale, wavy-edged morsel breaking the surface. It looked more like a baby dinosaur's forelock than amphibian body part; nevertheless I dipped my spoon, stirred and tasted the gluey brine. It lacked seasoning, so after a quick sprinkle, I dredged up a morsel and set to work removing the flesh from the bones using the 'chicken wing' technique. I'd love to say it didn't actually taste like chicken but, as with many other obscure delicacies, it did. As it's prepared, a robust pair of scissors make easy work of removing the feet usually, along with the green, Jurassic, wart-infested outer layer, or skin as it's commonly known, leaving a white muscular flesh that's divided, while still on the bone, into manageable morsels, each contrasting weirdly against the darkness of its auburn, almost black, fractured skeleton. Plenty of severed limbs, large ones at that, perhaps enough for two, had seen the cleaver to produce this lunchtime feast, with a soft, almost fish-like texture. There's a reason its way cheaper than crab, although I have had much worse. I finished my beer, which is more that I can say about the food. Feeling almost full was a good excuse to leave half a bowl that, had it been king prawn, would almost certainly be empty.

Sat in reception back at the digs, my mind set off home alone. I pulled my bags close and I waited for the call back. The unwanted breakdown of my marriage and the dark hole it left in my mind was the driving force behind putting six and a half thousand miles between my broken heart and my estranged family. Cultural diversity and the time to concentrate on activities I didn't normally have the time to enjoy helped to fill the hole but the reality of the homeward journey made me realise I was bringing back more than dodgy designer labels and counterfeit trainers.

Not wanting to leave any bags unattended, I waddled down the stairs with growing impatience as the unreliability of taxis was once again brought into question. The escapism this trip provided undoubtedly helped me rebuild much of the mental strength that had drained to a point I could justify temporally abandoning my kids but the thought of life back home could no longer be substituted with booze and beansprouts. I received a text: 'Your car has arrived'.

For as long as my mental health would allow, I'd made increasingly desperate attempts to make amends for my part in the breakup of my marriage to Kay, once I saw her drifting faster through stormy waters towards to the Falls of No Return. Our kids, Bailey and Isabella, were becoming victims of a breakdown that was all too familiar to me. This was to be my second divorce involving kids. The first one was bad enough and, even though it was now decades ago, I remember the torment that was only just beginning this time round. I opened the boot and dropped in my bags.

The prospect of new partners and the baggage a convoluted past creates were pretty much a given to create issues for our kids at some point on my return but at least now I was better equipped mentally to take on the next forced step, pushed the wrong way through a dark tunnel towards a unknown light.

I climbed in the opened the door. "The airport please, driver."